FAMILY WEALTH
COUNSELORS LLC

David F. Hokanson
Family Wealth Counselors
4434 W. 90th Terr.
Prairie Village, KS 66207
816-392-1502 (cell)

GIVING

PHILANTHROPY FOR EVERYONE

THE ESPERTI PETERSON INSTITUTE CONTRIBUTORY SERIES

Eileen Sacco, Publisher

Generations: Planning Your Legacy
Giving: Philanthropy for Everyone
Legacy: Plan, Protect, and Preserve Your Estate
Strictly Business: Planning Strategies for Privately Owned Businesses
21st Century Wealth: Essential Financial Planning Principles
Ways and Means: Maximize the Value of Your Retirement Savings
Wealth Enhancement and Preservation, 2d ed.

GIVING

PHILANTHROPY FOR EVERYONE

*Practical Answers
from America's Foremost
Charitable Planning Authorities*

— *A Special Edition* —

Robert A. Esperti   Renno L. Peterson

David F. Hokanson

8060

CFP™ and Certified Financial Planner™ are certification marks owned by the Certified Financial Planner Board of Standards, Inc.
LEAVE A LEGACY™ is a registered trademark owned by the National Committee on Planned Giving.
LifeSpan™ and LifeSpan Legal Services™ are registered trademarks owned by Quantum Alliance.

ISBN 0-9674714-5-1
Library of Congress Control Number: 2002103310

Publisher: Eileen Sacco
Senior technical editor: Richard Gumm
Project editors: Ann Rowe, Connie Brands
Project manager: Christy Allbee
Marketing services: Lydia Monchak
Jacket design: Richard Adelson, china60@aol.com
Composition, design, & editing services: Glacier Publishing Services
Printed and bound in Canada by Quebecor World Printing

An Esperti Peterson Institute Book
by Quantum Press LLC
Quantum Alliance³ Companies
621 17th Street, Suite 2250
Denver, CO 80293
303.893.2663

Contents

Preface

The United States is the most generous nation on earth. People who live here, citizens and non-citizens alike, give to myriad causes. Some give small amounts, some give huge amounts, and others give of their time, but all share a strong desire to help charitable causes, which, in turn, helps others.

We in the United States can be relied upon to help each other out in disasters and in good times. This can be seen in the heartfelt response to the terrorist attacks in New York and Washington, D.C., on September 11, 2001. We witnessed, as a nation, something that shocked us to the core. Beyond the outrage and anguish that we felt, we recognized that we have become vulnerable to new kinds of disasters. We responded immediately to the need—with blood, sweat, tears, and financial aid. We gave freely to assist the victims of those tragic events. According to *Giving USA's* annual report for 2001, charities raised a total of $1.88 billion. Incredibly, we managed this in the midst of what economists called a serious economic downturn!

Giving: Philanthropy for Everyone is a product of those charitable inclinations that are deeply rooted in our social fabric. Through caring about the needs and lives of others, we build better communities. Sharing our good fortune with others who are less fortunate is a means by which we acknowledge our societal interdependence. Philanthropy addresses issues that government is often unable or unwilling to deal with adequately. Through our charity, we address needs that have not been met, rectify wrongs that have been too long ignored, and fill gaps in social services that have gone unfilled. We cannot overstate how charity can enrich your life and the lives of others in a lasting, profound way.

After achieving financial security for ourselves and our families, our culture teaches us that there is an inherent obligation connected with success, whether that obligation arises from a sense of civic responsibility, religious conviction, or the kind of self-interest that was called "enlightened" in the heyday of Andrew Carnegie and John D. Rockefeller Sr. We believe, as a society, that we should share the bounty of our successes with our less fortunate fellows.

Charity is part of the American dream. Our goals in writing *Giving* are to help readers understand the charitable planning options that are available to everyone of every economic means, and to show how individuals and families who make philanthropy a part of their financial and estate planning will enhance their lives while preserving assets. If that seems a complete contradiction—that giving away assets will preserve them—we encourage readers to use *Giving* as a seminal point for discussions with their advisors on charitable giving.

Giving is the product of a national research project that involved the planning knowledge, ideas, and expertise of the most talented charitable planning attorneys, accountants, and financial advisors in the United States. It is not an annotated reference on charitable giving. Our contributing authors were given the following task: provide readers with the best answers to the questions that their clients most frequently ask them. Because of the question-and-answer format that we use, you can make sense out of the bewildering complexity that surrounds charitable, estate, and financial planning.

We offer insights into the decisions you must make to determine the appropriate charitable techniques for you. You should use the information contained in *Giving* to formulate questions for your advisors as you develop your own giving program.

The consistent nature of the questions submitted by our contributing authors has upheld our belief that most people have similar concerns regarding charitable giving, and that holds true no matter the differences in culture, economics, or locales. This rather startling consistency has been the highlight of every book in the Esperti Peterson Institute Contributory Series.

The responses of our contributors reflect their differing viewpoints, professionally and personally, as to the best means to the charitable ends of their clients. As editors, we have attempted to blend these differences into an overall perspective that will provide readers with the best understanding possible. At times, similar questions with differing responses have been included in order to present a variety of good approaches. While addressing similarities in concerns expressed by their clients, our contributors have attempted to give readers a clear idea of how many options are available for charitable planned giving. These options are what make every charitable planned giving program as unique as the individual implementing it.

There is some repetitiveness throughout the text. We know that a certain amount of repetition can act as a guide to help readers connect ideas within a book. Our goal is to allow readers to turn to almost any section and find it useful, even if they read no other section of the book. If you read *Giving* from start to finish, you will encounter some repetition. If you skip around as you read, you will still be able to understand each topic and its background.

Giving has five parts. Part One has four chapters. In chapters 1 and 2, our contributors introduce readers to the concepts of directing their *social capital* to charitable causes and developing a family philosophy for charitable giving. Chapter 3 discusses what a charity is and how to determine if a charitable organization is qualified with the Internal Revenue Service (IRS). The fourth chapter discusses the elements of a gift: the various ways to make gifts and the forms they can take, the importance of intent, and the differences between a future and a present gift. In Part One, our contributors show readers how understanding the proper approach to giving can make a gift to charity all that more meaningful and effective.

Part Two offers an overview of the income, gift, and estate tax deductions that are allowed for charitable gifts. Even though our contributors make it clear that tax reduction is not the primary reason that their clients make charitable gifts, there are, nevertheless, tax advantages that donors should not overlook. Charitable tax deductions are the icing on a very satisfying cake and because they create an economic incentive to make charitable gifts, donors should take advantage of these tax benefits in structuring charitable gifts. Chapter 5 discusses the federal charitable income tax deduction, which is an immediate and important aspect of charitable giving. Chapter 6 explains federal gift and estate tax deductions in the context of the Economic Growth and Tax Relief Reconciliation Act of 2001. Last, but not least, donors must understand how the IRS requires donors to value and substantiate charitable contributions. These rules are covered in chapter 7.

Beginning with Part Three, and throughout the balance of *Giving,* our contributors explain various strategies available for implementing a charitable giving program. Within these strategies, our contributors discuss how donors can make charitable gifts, the advantages and disadvantages of the many charitable giving strategies, and why particular donors use particular strategies. Chapter 8 explains the charitable remainder trust (CRT). Based on the research that our contributors submitted, CRTs are the most popular charitable giving strategy among their clients because they can achieve a multitude of planning goals. Chapter 9 examines the charitable lead trust (CLT), which is the obverse of a CRT. A CRT and a CLT each help families achieve different objectives. Both of these types of trusts are irrevocable and are governed by very specific rules under the Internal Revenue Code. Chapter 10 rounds out Part Three by presenting the issues that are common to both trust types, including the best property to transfer to the trusts, and transactions that are specifically prohibited in establishing and operating a CRT or a CLT.

Part Four explains how individuals and families can use charitable giving strategies to achieve other goals within the context of their financial and estate planning. Chapter 11 describes how charitable giving can reduce income taxes, defer capital gain taxes, increase income, and diversify an investment portfolio. In chapter 12, our contributors discuss the uses of charitable giving within the framework of the estate plan. Making charitable gifts during a donor's lifetime versus making those gifts through testamentary arrangements in a will or living trust will produce different tax results. In addition, charitable giving creates some special uses for life insurance and requires special consideration for retirement accounts. Chapter 13 covers the important topic of how small-business owners can use charitable giving to integrate business succession planning with family needs. Charitable strategies present wonderful ways to create retirement plans that can be used in addition to or instead of a qualified retirement plan or an individual retirement account. These charitable strategies offer the flexibility of allowing donors to receive distributions without penalty, even if they are taken out before a donor reaches the age of 59½. We discuss these plans in chapter 14. Part Four concludes with a discussion of how to make gifts of real estate directly to a charity or through other vehicles such as bargain-sale transactions and conservation easements. There are several important issues involved in donating real property to charities. Donors must consider these issues and address them as part of their charitable planning.

Part Five is concerned with how much control a donor may retain over a charitable gift. Chapter 16 explains, in easy-to-understand language, the complex requirements for establishing and maintaining a private foundation. The unique character of supporting organizations, how they function, what their limitations and advantages are, and the requirements that must be met in order to operate a supporting organization are presented in chapter 17. Endowment funds and donor-advised funds are explained in chapter 18. Donor-advised funds provide a simple alternative to the foundation for individuals and families to carry on a philosophy of giving at a reasonable cost to establish and maintain. In chapter 18, we also compare the benefits and disadvantages of the donor-advised fund, the supporting organization, and the foundation. Chapter 19 brings *Giving* to a conclusion with an overview of investing charitable donations, which is particularly relevant to CRTs, CLTs, foundations, supporting organizations, and donor-advised funds.

Giving has six appendixes. Appendix A consists of a special set of questions and answers on working with advisors and charities when planning a charitable giving program. Appendix B provides a list of resources for finding qualified charities, starting foundations, and finding special causes to support. Appendix C lists the designations and accreditations of prospective advisors and the agencies that govern and regulate such professionals. Lists of referral organizations and professional organizations are also included. Appendix D describes the stringent application process that the contributors to *Giving* underwent prior to their acceptance into the project. Alphabetical and geographic lists of all contributors to the book are presented in appendixes E and F, respectively.

As with all general reference books, readers should be careful not to treat the information in *Giving* as a recommendation for any particular course of action in individual circumstances. No other concept came through to us more clearly as editors than the diversity of successful strategies available to individuals, as well as the damage that can result from using the wrong strategy. We specifically recommend that in planning for your financial well-being—including charitable giving—you seek advice from competent professionals in each relevant discipline.

Giving is a collaborative effort of many planning professionals. We are proud of the efforts our contributing authors made to bring you such practical information and strategies for effectively implementing charitable planning. We hope that the information in this book helps you, the reader, attain a better understanding of charitable giving techniques.

We especially wish to thank David F. Hokanson for his contributions to *Giving* and are honored to dedicate this special edition to him.

Robert A. Esperti
Renno L. Peterson
August 2002

Introduction

David F. Hokanson

The publication of *Giving: Philanthropy for Everyone* is perfectly timed to address the needs of a new generation of people who have the good fortune to have accumulated wealth. More people than ever before have wealth today, but they are not necessarily enjoying it. Traditionally, advisors have done a great job of number crunching and legal documentation, but they have not always done a good job of opening the eyes of their clients to all available options. Too many advisors support the myth that the only choice is to support the general welfare of the nation in the form of taxes. It is time to dispel this misconception.

In this great nation, it is true that with wealth comes the responsibility to support the country's general welfare. However, the notion that we are forced to do this in the form of taxes is not true. We have the choice: Give by paying taxes, or give of our own volition to the causes we choose. And, the government supports our choice to be philanthropic with tax incentives for charitable giving.

For much of my 33-year career, even I ascribed to the perception that the government would get 50 percent or more of an estate and the family would get the balance. I thought that providing benefits for charitable causes would reduce what children received. In the past few years, I have learned otherwise.

The good news, which we explain in *Giving*, is that you can use planning techniques to provide a lifetime of financial security for yourself *and* be a philanthropist; and still pass on the full value of your wealth to your children—if that is your vision. This knowledge changes attitudes. It rejuvenates. It energizes. It motivates rethinking the positive impact and lasting significance you can have as a result of your financial success.

I stress the importance of good planning, which often includes a retreat to allow you to take time to focus on the values and issues that are important to you. The counseling retreat has nothing to do with money, taxes, or legal arrangements. It is a time to reflect on what is important to you and why you want to pass on those important things to succeeding generations.

You and your advisors will develop a vision and a mission statement for your plan. This document will guide you, your children, and all of your trusted advisors. You will clearly define what must happen to help you strike a balance between achieving financial security for yourself and your family and making contributions to the local, national, or global charities that you consider meaningful. This process gives new meaning to the phrase "make a life, not just a living." The document puts you in control of your team of advisors.

This brings us to another key element in the family wealth counseling process: It clearly requires a team of advisors. No professional should try either to be the only advisor in a client's life or to dominate the client's team of advisors. When advisors are not working together, they can often offer differing advice, and then the clients become confused and can make wrong decisions—or no decisions at all. At best, this places the professional advisor in a defensive position; at worst, it shakes client confidence.

The counseling process enables each client to provide clear direction to his or her advisors. All of the things that make the client unique move to the forefront, so the professionals who do the analysis may share a common goal: to develop a single comprehensive plan that serves the client's best interest. During the last 30 years, I have had the good fortune to develop strong working relationships with attorneys, accountants, trust officers, and peers in the insurance and investment business. What exciting synergy is created when minds from various disciplines come together!

When my retired business partner, Jim Stevens, learned that I was contributing to *Giving*, he asked me if he could write a few words to you, the reader. With deep gratitude, I share his words with you:

Dave Hokanson is the most determined person I know. He is driven to succeed and is willing to pay the price to make it happen. He started his career with nothing. It can truly be said that what Dave and his wife, Jeanne, have accumulated in their lives together has been earned the old-fashioned way.

These traits, evident when I met Dave in 1970, are what distinguish his business career. He is hardworking, almost to a fault. He can look at almost any problem and, rather than seeing the problem, he sees the solution. When Dave writes about commitment to voluntary philanthropy, hard work, and careful management of one's wealth, he is relating the way in which he lives his life. He has achieved some enviable measure of success, but he remembers from whence he came and lives his life accordingly. He is committed to family, friends, his community, and more charitable and professional causes than I can even remember. It has always been his way, and that gives his advice a certain edge of authenticity that deserves respect.

Acknowledgments

I want to thank Jeanne, my wife of more than 33 years, for her love and constant support and for maintaining a wonderful balancing act. Living with an entrepreneur is tough. She has done a wonderful job of helping me manage my thousands of thoughts and keeping me focused on what is important. She beautifully plays the roles of friend, lover, mother, and devil's advocate when necessary.

My daughter, Kelly Voitenko, and my son, Duffy, allow me to distract myself from the crazy business world by immersing myself in their personal activities, many times to their embarrassment. I hope they find the same joy in their careers that I am fortunate to enjoy in mine. A father could not be more proud and pleased with the final product (obviously, a direct result of selecting a good lifetime partner).

Without the support, friendship, mentoring, counsel, and advice of Jim Stevens, my partner of 17 years, my business career would not have developed in such a wonderful way. Jim, in retirement in his early 50s, is a great example of what you can achieve by giving back to a community a piece of what you received during your career.

Paul Priefert deserves special mention. He is my soul mate and a perfect complement as I continue to enjoy my career. We seem to start with different points of view but end up with the same viewpoint. I am always comfortable with the output.

I am grateful for my dedicated staff, who supports the ongoing operations of a 33-year career so that, as I work with clients, I can focus solely on their objectives.

Finally, to wonderful friends and peers, who always seem to be available with support and input whenever I need them, thank you all.

David F. Hokanson, CFP, MSFS, ChFC, CFWC, is president and member of Family Wealth Counselors LLC. He is a member of the National Association of Charitable Estate Counselors, founder and immediate past president of the National Association of Family Wealth Counselors, and a participant in the Esperti Peterson Institute Masters Program.

Mr. Hokanson conducts seminars in tax reduction and estate planning for accountants, attorneys, and CEOs. He is an adjunct professor of The Academy of Multidisciplinary Practice and senior fellow of The Estate and Wealth Strategies Institute at Michigan State University.

Mr. Hokanson was selected to comment at a hearing before the IRS concerning charitable remainder trusts. He is coauthor of *Family Wealth Counseling: Getting to the Heart of the Matter.*

PART ONE

Understanding Charitable Giving

You may be at the point in your life where it is no longer enough—emotionally, spiritually, or intellectually—to simply continue to accrue material wealth. You have likely stopped focusing exclusively on your family and are noticing the people and places in your community more than in the past. In doing so, you have probably uncovered many of the problems in our society that need resolution. You may be ready to become a part of the solution to these problems.

This is what charitable giving is all about. Simply put, charitable giving is the process of identifying a problem and then figuring out a way to solve it. In more complex terms, charitable giving is about creating a better world for all of us by eliminating, in some way, no matter how limited or expansive, the causes of disparity and suffering in our world. Charitable giving is doing something simply because it is the right thing to do. As you read *Giving*, you will also discover that you and your family will benefit in tangible ways from your charitable contributions while enjoying the intangible rewards of performing worthy endeavors.

People give to charity for a variety of reasons. The contributors to *Giving* hear most of these reasons from their clients. The reason with the least amount of significance for their clients is to reduce their taxes. Our contributors present several surveys that also attest to this fact. You may ask, Why do people give if they are not principally motivated by a financial benefit? Our contributors answer this question in chapter 1 with a discussion of the motivating factors that stimulate charitable giving.

Many people give out of a desire to give something back to communities or organizations that have helped them in the past. As a sign of appreciation, these people often give more than the original gift they received. Some individuals give as a result of their personally held values or principles. People who tithe to religious organizations usually do so as a result of their values or principles. Some individuals and families give to charity to create legacies that will last into the future in the hope of preserving the tenets or providing the assistance that they believe will be of value to future generations. All hope to directly or indirectly affect society.

In addition, more Americans are becoming aware of the fact that their income and assets consist of two types of capital—personal capital and social capital. *Personal capital* is that portion of income and assets over which an individual has complete control. *Social capital* is the portion of income and assets that is allotted by law for public use. Paying taxes is often referred to as "involuntary philanthropy" because governments spend a large percentage of each of our tax dollars on social programs. The good news is that you can direct your social capital away from government coffers and into charitable programs that may better fulfill your dreams. To effectively redirect your social capital from the U.S. Treasury and into charitable programs, you must properly plan your charitable giving. Chapter 1 explains both types of capital and how you use charitable giving strategies to direct your social capital.

Planned giving is a new concept to many people. Chapter 2 discusses the process and advantages of planning your charitable giving. The process begins with defining your goals, which you do by answering questions such as, What do I hope to achieve by giving to charity? If you choose to involve your family in your planned giving program, they should be included in this process. In keeping with the subtitle of this book, *Philanthropy for Everyone*, the contributors suggest many ways that parents can make philanthropy a family affair, ranging from getting the children involved in volunteer work—perhaps serving meals at a homeless shelter on Thanksgiving—to family meetings, to managing a family foundation. In chapter 2, we introduce and suggest the strategies that are available to achieve these goals so that you can go right to the other chapters in *Giving* where we explain the specific strategies.

We discuss types of charities in chapter 3. Probably no other book for the general public explains more clearly what the Internal Revenue Service means when it says "charity." There is an assumption that the word *charity* has universal meaning. Most of us think that charities are well-intentioned organizations, set up and run by good people doing good deeds. We also assume that all donations that we make to charities are tax-deductible and that the charities have been blessed with certain tax benefits. For the most part, these perceptions and assumptions are true, but not always. There are several types of charities, each with its own characteristics and purposes.

Recognizing the difficulties in understanding charities as defined in the tax laws, our contributing authors have addressed the fundamental questions that you should ask about charities. While some answers may border on the technical, they all reduce a very complex subject matter to its essence. These answers clearly convey just what it takes to become a tax-exempt charitable organization that offers income, gift, and estate tax advantages to donors.

You should not underestimate the importance of chapter 3. Too many casual philanthropists assume that the charities will use their donations for the purposes they intended. Without understanding the principles on which a charity is based, the protocols under which it operates, and the managers who manage its money, it is difficult to know how charities actually use donations. If one cares enough to make a gift, one should care enough to research the charity that will receive the gift. With an understanding of the concepts in chapter 3, you should know how to perform research about charities and can be more confident that you know what a charity should be. This understanding will help to ensure that the charitable gifts you make will be used by legitimate charities for the purposes or goals that you intend.

Many people assume that a charitable gift is simply writing a check or giving property directly to a charity. In chapter 4, our contributors explain that charitable giving can be more than that. First, there are many different kinds of property that we can give to charity.

Second, there are many different ways to "deliver" that property to charity. And third, even though tax savings are not the driving force behind most gifts to charity, people who make gifts still want to take advantage of the available charitable tax deductions. Our contributing authors have submitted numerous questions and answers that successfully define the parameters of what charitable gifts are all about and how they can and should be made. The questions and answers in chapter 4 run the gamut—from the specific rules for making gifts to the many forms that gifts can take. If you want grounding in what it means to make a charitable gift that is income tax–deductible, chapter 4 creates a strong foundation. Once you understand the material in this chapter, the more complex gift-giving techniques will start to make a great deal of sense.

chapter 1

Reasons to Give

WHAT IS PHILANTHROPY?

ᛢ Isn't philanthropy just giving money to charity?

It can be. Philanthropy can also be donating time, talents, and property. But it's even more than that. *Webster's New World Dictionary* defines *philanthropy* as:

1. A desire to help mankind, especially as shown by gifts to charitable or humanitarian institutions; benevolence.
2. Altruistic concern for human welfare and advancement, usually manifested by donations of money, property, or work to needy persons, by endowment of institutions of learning and hospitals, and by generosity to other socially useful purposes.

In general, philanthropy deals with emotional issues long before the wallet is opened. Many people just wish to do good deeds, others want to be remembered by leaving behind a financial legacy. Philanthropy is personal and is what each of us chooses to make it.

WHY PEOPLE GIVE
TO CHARITY

CR *Why do people give to charity?*

Celebrities or prominent citizens often say: "I wanted to give something back to the community." Where does this sense of giving come from? Is it derived only from the deep-rooted religious principle of tithing? Is it derived from a sense of obligation—that our overabundant or inherited privilege dictates that we give back?

The genesis of philanthropy can be found in any or all religious, philosophical, ideological, and social perspectives. Each of us gives for different reasons: social reasons that satisfy our desire to help and to connect with other people; philosophical reasons that fulfill our desire to become significant—to know that we made a positive impact on this world and the lives of the people we touched; and also for spiritual reasons that fulfill our desire to find immortality. Many people focus on the ideological desire to teach values and goals to their children: They want to teach family members the importance of philanthropy as it relates to their communities, their country, and their world. They want to create partnerships with charities, create and manage changes in society, and integrate giving into their personal lives and financial and estate planning needs. In short, philanthropy fulfills a basic need to attach meaning to life—to know that our lives matter and that we made a difference in the world while we were here.

CR *Do many people give to charity?*

As a matter of fact, *why* we give may not be as important as the fact that so many Americans *do* give—to churches, synagogues, shelters for the homeless and battered, and to thousands of other large and small charities. According to a survey by Johns Hopkins Comparative Nonprofit Sector Project, 73 percent of Americans gave money to charity in 1999. And not all of these donors were wealthy. Independent Sector notes that Americans with household incomes less than $10,000 gave 5.2 percent of that income to charity versus 2.2 percent for individuals with household incomes of $100,000 or more. And 49 percent of Americans said they volunteered their time to charitable causes and civic activities during 1999.

The aggregate amount that Americans give is staggering.

According to *Giving USA* (American Association of Fundraising Counsel), we gave $190 billion in 1999; $210.89 billion in 2000; and, $212 billion in 2001.

○_R *Why do Americans give so much time and money to charity?*

There are probably as many reasons as there are donors. The July 24, 2000, issue of *Time* and a multitude of reports and surveys sponsored by universities and planned giving councils discuss this exact question. One sponsoring organization, U.S. Trust, surveyed 200 affluent Americans (reported in *U.S. Trust Survey of Affluent Americans,* November 1998, Financial Market Research, Inc., New York, N.Y.). The criteria for "affluent" were a person with an adjusted gross income of at least $250,000 and/or an estate of at least $3 million. The results support the belief that Americans give out of a sense of wanting to make a difference. Each respondent indicated more than one of the following as a reason why he or she gives to charity (percentage of those respondents stating each reason is given in parenthesis):

- A desire to support worthwhile causes (79 percent)
- A belief that those who have been financially successful have a responsibility to share their good fortune (69 percent)
- A desire to help meet critical needs in their communities (63 percent)
- A desire to help organizations that have benefited them (50 percent)
- A desire to set an example for their children (46 percent)
- A desire to fill in the gaps left by government cutbacks (29 percent)

○_R *What does the study say about nonphilanthropic motivations?*

Amazingly, the study indicates that only three nonphilanthropic factors significantly influenced the respondents:

- 11 percent of the respondents give out of a desire to take advantage of the tax benefits resulting from charitable gifts
- 4 percent of the respondents give out of a desire to earn respect and recognition from friends and business associates or within their communities
- 2 percent give because of pressure from social acquaintances

We advise many elderly clients and have discovered that the older generation is very motivated by the more nonphilanthropic desires to connect with other people and to make an impact on the people around them. In this day and age of increased technology and transitory families, the elderly often feel lost. They are sometimes grandparents in name only because their grandchildren may live 500 miles or more away and they cannot easily pass on their life's lessons. By making charitable gifts while they are alive, elderly individuals not only see their bequests at work but also generate recognition, appreciation, and respect from the charitable organizations they support.

ℂℝ *Are there other reasons why people give to charity?*

According to charitable giving expert Russ Alan Prince and his coauthors, there are "seven faces of philanthropy." Each philanthropic donor type is motivated by different reasons. While the reasons differ among donor types, the conclusions regarding motivations are similar to those found in the U.S. Trust study. Table 1-1 contains descriptions of the seven donor types.

TABLE 1-1 Seven Donor Types

Donor type and motivation	Vocabulary used
Communitarian (26% of donors)	
▪ Doing good makes sense. ▪ My business has profited from the community and I want to help the community prosper in return. ▪ Supporting local charities helps my community prosper.	Service to community and society, leadership, influence, recognition
Devout (21% of donors)	
▪ Doing good is doing God's will—it gives me a sense of purpose and mission. ▪ My community is my church. ▪ The Lord has blessed me with the ability to make money.	Supporting each other, doing good, duty, God, pay back, values, love, commitment, spirituality
Investor (15% of donors)	
▪ Doing good is good business. ▪ I can benefit others while helping myself. ▪ I am looking for the best way to give.	Accountability, effectiveness, opportunity, results, well-managed, professional, avoid taxes, financial

TABLE 1-1 Seven Donor Types, *continued*

Donor type and motivation	Vocabulary used
Socialite (11% of donors)	
▪ Doing good is fun. ▪ Charitable functions are networking opportunities. ▪ I am a community leader.	Supporting each other, serving community, leadership, charity functions, recognition, socialize, enjoyment
Repayer (10% of donors)	
▪ Doing good in return. ▪ I repay my community or individuals from a sense of obligation or feelings of loyalty.	Service, socially responsible, doing good, opportunity, pay back, grateful, difference in life, obligated, community
Altruist (9% of donors)	
▪ Doing good feels right. ▪ I give out of generosity and empathy to urgent causes. ▪ I feel I am doing something important when I give and it makes my life more meaningful.	Socially responsible, doing good, self-fulfillment, sense of purpose, mission, gratification
Dynast (8% of donors)	
▪ Doing good is a family tradition. ▪ My family has socialized me to give and help others. ▪ Taking care of my community is part of my responsibility.	Supporting each other, socially responsible, doing good, family tradition, family history

Sources: Russ Alan Prince, William J. McBride, and Karen Maru File. 1994. *The Charitable Estate Planning Process.* Lexington, Ky.: Lexington House, pp. 33–38, and Russ Alan Prince and Karen Maru File. 1994. *The Seven Faces of Philanthropy.* San Francisco, Calif.: Jossey-Bass Publishers, Inc., pp. 13–139.

☙ *How do people choose charities?*

The U.S. Trust study indicates three factors that significantly influenced the respondents' choices of charities:

1. the reputation and integrity of the charity (81 percent),
2. the charity met an important need (79 percent), and
3. the charity used its time and/or money efficiently (75 percent).

Putting these factors into context, all of the surveys, reports, and articles that we've referred to are in agreement that the new generation of philanthropists does a lot of research before choosing a charity, wants to take a more hands-on approach to giving, and will hold charities accountable to produce results. We confirm that our younger clients' attitudes follow these same lines. The newest group of philanthropists, those who are at the upper end of the baby-boomer generation, gives differently than their parents who were more likely to contribute to causes and charities they believed in with less concern as to accountability by the charities.

In summary, people give to charity to:

- perpetuate ideological, philosophical, and religious values;
- leave a legacy;
- provide for community, nation, world, and society;
- direct social capital; and
- reduce taxes.

Perpetuating Ideological, Philosophical, and Religious Values

How does giving reflect values?

It only makes sense that we belong to and support the local, state, and national charities that share our values. Consequently, by supporting these organizations, we perpetuate and pass on our values to others today and in the future.

Leaving a Legacy

What do you mean by leaving a legacy?

By contributing time, talents, and money to charitable religious, educational, cultural, service, and health care organizations, each of us has the power to enrich the lives of others. A *legacy* is a living reminder of individuals who cared about their communities and supported causes that were important to them. A legacy is as simple as someone making a small lump-sum monetary gift to the Muscular

Dystrophy Association in the name of a father who died of Lou Gehrig's disease or leaving a library to a high school in gratitude for the education received there. A legacy can also be as complex as a foundation, such as the Bill and Melinda Gates Foundation, which finances international children's health programs.

The legacy that you leave is not just the wealth that your heirs inherit. Your legacy is the part of you that lives on in the hearts and minds of others after you are gone. It is the influence you had on your family and loved ones and the impact you had on society.

Providing for Community, Nation, World, Society

What role does philanthropy play in meeting the needs of society?

The number of philanthropic foundations more than doubled from 22,000 in 1979 to 47,000 in 1999 (*Philanthropy Network News,* March 31, 2000). We've already learned that Americans gave $210.89 billion to charity in 2000 and $212 billion in 2001. These contributions fund efforts that local, state, and federal governments are either unwilling or unable to accomplish. American philanthropy is a serious economic energy that maintains much of our society and way of life.

In October 1999, at a presidential conference on charitable giving, President Clinton asked the federal government to take steps to boost philanthropy in America. To emphasize how we can generate a more constructive philanthropy, he said, "We all begin by accepting that we no longer believe that there is a choice out there—which was never a real choice—between government meeting all of our society's needs and government walking away from them all and letting philanthropy do it. We have to have a better partnership, and it will work better if we do."

Directing Social Capital

What is social capital?

Social capital refers to money and assets that you *cannot* keep within your family. *Personal capital* refers to money and assets that you *can* keep within your family.

≪ How does the concept of social capital affect me?

Every time you receive a paycheck you are confronted with the concept of social capital because the income tax law requires that you share a portion of your gross pay with others. At your death, the estate tax law demands that you share a portion of your estate with others. Income, gift, and estate tax laws mandate that there is a certain amount of money that you and/or your estate are required to pay to the government.

Social capital is that part of your wealth over which you are simply a steward; you have temporary control of it, but eventually the government will use it to provide benefits for the general welfare of society.

≪ What is an involuntary philanthropist?

When you donate your income or estate tax as social capital, you are a philanthropist. Your charity of choice is the federal treasury and your charitable beneficiary is government largess. You are, in effect, an *involuntary philanthropist* because you have no ability to name a bridge after your mother or to put your name on a pothole or on an aircraft carrier. Congress will use its judgment in determining how to spend your social capital donations and won't even say, "Thank you."

≪ What is the alternative to having the government spend my social capital?

While you cannot keep your social capital (the amount you pay in taxes), you can control it! By using charitable income and estate tax planning techniques, you can decide to whom your funds are to be distributed and for what benefit or purpose those distributions are to be used. This planning is referred to by financial and estate planning professionals as "directing your social capital."

≪ Is the IRS or the U.S. Treasury opposed to charitable tax planning because it reduces tax revenues?

The government actually encourages charitable, tax, and estate planning. The charitable provisions of the Internal Revenue Code have been in existence for most of the twentieth century, and, in 1969, Congress passed sweeping laws to protect and promote more contributions to nonprofit organizations.

Federal and state governments understand that the tax revenues they lose through charitable deductions will be used more efficiently and effectively by local charities to support social infrastructures than if those same dollars were passed through the governments' hands. Charitable activities can be accomplished in the private sector at about one-third less than the amount it would cost the government to accomplish the same objectives. In addition, the quantity and the quality of social services are increased when volunteers and professionals who have hands-on involvement in those services provide them on a local level.

Charitable giving is part of the fabric of America and is clearly encouraged and supported by the tax code.

ᘓ *How does Congress spend involuntary social capital dollars compared with how donors choose to give away the social capital dollars they contribute voluntarily?*

Figure 1-1 illustrates how Congress spent our tax dollars in 1999 (according to the IRS). According to *Giving USA 2000 Update* (American Association of Fundraising Counsel, Inc.), charitable contributions for 1999 were as shown in Figure 1-2.

Reducing Taxes

ᘓ *What if I am not philanthropically inclined?*

Unless the existing Economic Growth and Tax Relief Reconciliation Act of 2001 (2001 tax act) is changed, every American with a taxable

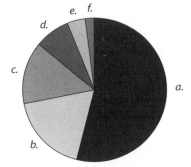

a. Entitlements (e.g., welfare, social security), 54%

b. National defense, 18%

c. Interest, 14%

d. Physical, human, and community development, 8%

e. Surplus to pay down the debt, 4%

f. Law enforcement and general government, 2%

Figure 1-1   Federal spending in 1999

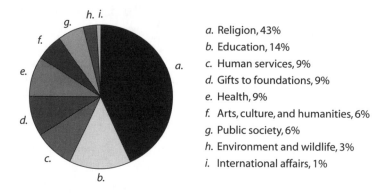

a. Religion, 43%
b. Education, 14%
c. Human services, 9%
d. Gifts to foundations, 9%
e. Health, 9%
f. Arts, culture, and humanities, 6%
g. Public society, 6%
h. Environment and wildlife, 3%
i. International affairs, 1%

Figure 1-2   Charitable contributions in 1999

estate who dies in any year other than 2010 will pay a significant portion of his or her estate to the IRS. The real question that confronts noncharitably inclined individuals is, Would you prefer that a major portion of your estate pass to the federal treasury and be spent as shown in Figure 1-1 or would you prefer to direct those same dollars to projects and initiatives of your choice?

When individuals grasp the power that they can harness by voluntarily choosing to distribute their social capital through charity, the answer to this question is usually quite obvious and generates great excitement.

◌ᴢ *Are there financial incentives for charitable giving?*

Charitable gifts can impact your taxes in two ways. You will usually receive an income tax deduction for the value of your current gift and then a reduction of estate taxes when you die.

By implementing any of the charitable giving strategies described in this book, people can often increase their after-tax personal income, diversify their holdings, and leave their heirs with a larger inheritance than they would otherwise have been able to leave.

◌ᴢ *Will charitable giving still make financial sense if the estate tax laws are repealed?*

Some planning professionals and planned giving officers believe that charities are likely to suffer financially from the 2001 tax act's phase-in of lower estate tax rates and the eventual elimination of the estate tax.

However, the surveys and statistics that have been presented here contradict this view. The personal satisfaction people gain from supporting their charities is more important to them than any tax advantages they could receive from making the gift. Tax benefits are an added attraction and will undoubtedly continue to be so as Congress continues to change the tax laws.

CR *How do the income tax laws work when I direct my social capital to a charity?*

As one example, the law allows individuals to receive a tax deduction for up to 50 percent of adjusted gross income for cash donated to public charities. Let's assume Theresa has an annual income of $150,000, that she is in the 30 percent tax bracket, and that she gives $70,000 in cash to a public charity. She can take the full $70,000 deduction because it is less than 50 percent of her adjusted gross income. She saves approximately $21,000 in income taxes (30 percent of the $70,000 deduction).

CR *My estate plan is set up so charity will receive the bulk of my wealth at my death, with the balance going to my two daughters. Because I've virtually eliminated estate taxes and taken care of my kids, what additional planning is there to do?*

Your current strategy of leaving a substantial charitable bequest is an excellent way to reduce estate taxes; however, you do not receive a current income tax deduction for your philanthropy. By using charitable strategies while you are alive, you can enjoy current income tax deductions that allow you to further leverage your philanthropy at your death.

CR *What if the only reason I might be interested in directing my social capital would be to receive the tax benefits?*

Very few of our clients use tax incentives as their *primary* motivation for charitable giving. However, if you are going to make a charitable gift, you should make it in the most tax-efficient manner possible. Generally speaking, most charitable gifts will result in an estate tax and/or income tax deduction.

CHARITY BEGINS
AT HOME

CR *Doesn't charity begin at home?*

We suggest that the concept of "home" should extend beyond your property line. If you still live in the community where you were raised or where you raised your family, it would make sense for you to give back something to improve the quality of life for others in the community.

You are in a far better position to know what your community needs than either the federal or state governments. Through your charitable gifts, you can compound the joy of improving your community by honoring and recognizing family and friends who have lived and will continue to live there.

Philanthropy is no more complicated than just wanting to share your good fortune with your community or those who have been less fortunate. For most people, this is great a joy.

CR *Wouldn't my charitable gifts deprive my children of what they are entitled to as my heirs?*

Some parents feel that children are not necessarily entitled just because they are the progeny. In other situations, this question is directly related to the size of the estate.

If your estate is large enough to incur estate taxes when you die, you will be giving to everyone's least favorite charity, the IRS, whether you want to or not. If you prefer to leave as much of the value of your assets as possible to your heirs and still have some control over who receives what you will inevitably be giving away, charitable giving will be of interest to you. In fact, it might actually allow more of your assets to pass to your heirs than if you had not made the charitable contributions at all. You will also have the benefit of knowing that your assets went to help a cause that is meaningful to you.

Balancing and sharing limited assets is a real struggle in the lives of many individuals. It requires consulting with children and involving them in charitable decisions. Their long-term well-being may be better served through their participation in philanthropic endeavors than by your supporting them.

CR Is there a way to provide for my family and give to charity?

A collaboration of legal and financial professionals can often design a plan that achieves both goals for families within a spectrum of economic means. We discuss these strategies in detail in *Giving*.

PHILANTHROPY IS FOR EVERYONE

CR As an advisor, how do you feel about giving?

I enjoy it. It makes me feel good to help others. I wouldn't be the person I am today without the efforts of others who contributed time, energy, and resources to make my life better. When I help others, I am returning the favor by passing it on.

It also makes me feel less greedy—I tell myself that I am not just working for myself, but that I am also doing good deeds for others. It makes me feel connected to the charity and its activities; it makes me care more about the charity and its activities, which makes me less self-centered and more caring about the less fortunate. I count my blessings more and see my glass as half full rather than half empty.

When I contribute, I have a sense that I am making things better, that I am part of the solution, and that I am not adding to the problem. Thus, my sense of self-worth is enhanced.

CR Don't I have to be a millionaire before I consider giving?

Some people think that they have to be millionaires to be involved in giving. However, there are various ways that every person, regardless of his or her economic station in life, can help a favorite charitable organization. Remember the statistics we cited earlier about the individuals, poor and wealthy, whose donations made up the $190 billion in 1999. For many organizations, small, regular donations collectively represent 90 percent of their operating income. You can make small cash donations, you can volunteer your time, or you can donate property and gain significant financial advantages at the same time that you are helping your church, community, or service organization.

ᗡ I'd like to direct my social capital, but what if my gift is too small to do any good?

A small gift that you make directly to the charity of your choice is significantly better for you and your community than if you let Congress make the gift. In other words, no gift is too small.

ᗡ Is it realistic to think my contribution can actually make a difference?

If your charitable giving consists of a lump-sum donation here or there, or change tossed into a donation canister, there is no assurance that your donation will make a significant difference. However, if you approach your charitable giving as a calculated investment with an expectation of accountability and effectiveness, you can be sure that your gifts will make a difference and you can also take great pleasure in the process.

Think of a small gift as a pebble being kicked over the side of a mountain. As that pebble falls, it gathers other pebbles that mobilize rocks and then boulders. Philosophically, one might say, "There is no such thing as an insignificant gift!"

chapter 2

Planned Giving

DEFINITION OF
PLANNED GIVING

◌ *I often get mailings about planned giving. What is planned giving?*

Planned giving is structuring your donations into a unified plan so you maximize the benefits of your gifts while you are alive and after your death. It involves applying some of the strategies we discuss in this book to use the social capital portion of your wealth in a manner that results in increased benefits for you, your loved ones, and the charities you choose.

◌ *Everyone is always asking for money. How can I tactfully say no without feeling guilty?*

We all receive phone and mail requests from needy and worthy causes for donations. As a result, we struggle between prioritizing our limited financial resources and having to respond with the dreaded "no."

To be sure, there are certain obligations that you simply cannot avoid. However, to make your charitable donations count, you must focus on the causes and organizations that matter most to you and your family. Explain to solicitors that you prefer to receive requests in writing so your family can evaluate them. Even better, create a coordinated giving plan. You will then have a guide to the charities and causes you are most interested in supporting.

PHILOSOPHY FOR CHARITABLE GIVING

☞ *I've heard of a charitable philosophy statement or charitable mission statement. What is it and why would I want one?*

A *charitable philosophy statement,* or *charitable mission statement,* is important for individuals or families who want to focus their donations; it is a must for anyone who is creating a charitable giving plan. A focused philosophy provides greater satisfaction than piecemeal giving because it requires that each family member participate in the charitable giving process and take responsibility for the distribution decisions.

If you are like many of our clients, you will want to create a philosophy that is uniquely yours. Your statement will be a living, breathing document, almost like a constitution that guides you and your family through the giving process. Periodically, your family may amend the philosophy to reflect changes in your collective charitable aspirations and your level of sophistication.

The process of creating the philosophy takes time, but, like so many things in life, it's the journey, or the process, that seems to count most. It can be a wonderfully positive experience that will involve you and your family for the rest of your lives.

☞ *What does a charitable philosophy statement contain?*

In its most basic form, a philosophy statement sets forth your charitable goals and might look like one of these:

■ "Our family fund is devoted to improving the environment through donations to organizations that promote clean air and water."

■ "Our family fund shall promote the health and welfare of children by contributing to those organizations that advocate children's rights and that feed, clothe, shelter, and educate needy and disadvantaged children."

ᛓ *How do I create my philosophy statement?*

First, define your goals. To do this, think about your hopes, dreams, desires, beliefs, and fears and then write them down. Writing them down will clarify your thinking and allow you to refine the philosophy. Keep refining your philosophy until it exactly reflects your charitable values, beliefs, and passions. To give you some ideas, a few of our clients' goals and suggestions for possible strategies are presented later in this chapter. Your advisors can help you, and you can use a philanthropic questionnaire to aid in the process.

ᛓ *What is a philanthropic questionnaire?*

A *philanthropic questionnaire* is a tool that

- helps you to determine how much of your wealth is ample for you to maintain your financial peace of mind and security;
- helps you to come to terms with the role money has played, currently plays, and is likely to play in your life and the lives of your family members;
- forces you to explore your greatest concerns or fears about money for yourself and for your children and grandchildren;
- helps each family member discover the roots of his or her own and each other family member's view toward money by asking questions such as, What is your first memory regarding money? How did the way your parents handled money affect you? How did your parents give to worthy causes?;
- allows you to define the results you expect from the gifts you anticipate making by asking questions such as, Is there anything you would like to change that could be changed through your participation in a charitable cause or donation?; and
- helps you to define the social legacy you wish to leave.

When you and your family answer these questions in a relaxed, comfortable atmosphere, there is enormous creative energy and the process is productive and enlightening. Many of our clients frequently comment that they never thought of asking some of these questions before.

℞ Where can I get one of these questionnaires?

Many financial advisors and planned giving officers at charitable organizations routinely use such tools and will gladly make them available to you.

℞ What happens after we complete the questionnaire?

You use the answers from the philanthropic questionnaire to create your charitable giving philosophy or family mission statement, which should include

- the types of charities to which you will give time or money to support your stated goals and causes;
- how much you will give to each charity;
- how you will give to those charities (i.e., gifts of money or time); and
- your choice of methods and strategies for implementing the mission statement and making your financial gifts so you, your family, and the charities receive the greatest benefit.

FAMILY CHARITABLE PLANNING

℞ Should we include our children in discussions about our planned giving ideas?

Yes, it is important to include your children in planned giving discussions. In our experience, if you include your children, it is very likely that they will not only be receptive to hearing about your charitable plans but will take delight in participating in them.

This type of discussion is a tremendous opportunity to initiate important family dialogue concerning individual values, to solidify the family unit, and to build each family member's self-esteem while your family develops and achieves a common goal to assist the community.

Once your children grasp how empowering charitable giving can be, they are likely to embrace the discussion and become energetic participants.

⌾ How might my wife and I introduce the concept of charitable giving to our children and grandchildren?

Over the years, many clients have asked us to help them teach their children and grandchildren about the importance of philanthropy. There are many ways families can do this. The most common method our clients use is the family meeting, where the process of developing the charitable mission statement begins. Most families continue to meet every 6 to 12 months so children and parents alike can decide which charities they would like to help during the next period and how much money to allocate to each.

⌾ Will periodic family meetings help us to mentor our children?

Helping children understand what they can accomplish through, and the enjoyment that they can derive from, philanthropic endeavors is, without a doubt, a major legacy you can pass on to your children.

By participating as a family in charitable giving, you can also teach your children how to budget limited family financial resources or handle the benefits of affluence and wealth. Over time, you have the ability to teach, mentor, and counsel children and grandchildren about such practical matters as money management, business management, and investment strategies.

The learning experience isn't always confined to the children. Family charitable planning is also a good way for parents and grandparents to discover the differences among their children and grandchildren and to learn ways to accommodate those differences.

⌾ My children are grown and live in different parts of the country. How can I involve them in family charitable planning?

Many of our clients have come to realize that family philanthropy can be a unifying force, geographically as well as philosophically. What better reason to bring the family together on a regular basis— physically, telephonically, electronically, or otherwise—than to discuss the common goals and common causes of the family's charitable plan?

How do families initiate their first meeting?

There is no one right way to start your family charitable giving program, except that it should be a creative and fun journey, one that leads to significant personal transformation for each participating family member.

Charlene, one of our clients, set her first family meeting several years ago on December 1. She told her children in advance that at the meeting, she would expect them to recommend charitable groups and causes that they felt the family should support. Her son brought extensive Internet research on charities that interested him; her two younger daughters told about a schoolmate whose family recently became homeless. Charlene's family agreed to divide their yearly gifts among five charities that they chose after several subsequent meetings that evoked laughter, tears, passionate arguments, and, finally, consensus.

My wife and I really like the idea of charitable giving but are afraid that our children will not react as positively as the children you've described. What should we do?

This is a concern that often points to some fear or unresolved issue that exists between the parents and the children.

Recently, we had the privilege of helping a family work through such issues. When Norma and Ron advised their children of their charitable intentions, the children became angry, which, in turn, made Norma and Ron feel guilty. It wasn't always pretty, but, through the planning process, we were able to discover that the real reasons for the children's anger and Norma and Ron's guilt were unresolved issues that dated back several decades. This process allowed Norma and Ron and their children to benefit charity while providing them with a platform from which to resolve issues that had disrupted the harmony of their family for decades.

The process of creating a family charitable philosophy statement can be extremely beneficial to such families. It can provide an opportunity for parents and children to sit down together and discuss undertaking positive actions in an atmosphere free of historical family disputes. Once they establish a certain degree of communication, family members may find that they are ready to address whatever has caused conflict in the past between the parents and the children.

ℓ *Do your clients let their children decide which charities will be included in the plan?*

Many of our clients specify a certain amount that each child is responsible for giving away. They do this in the hope that it will teach their children to take responsibility for sharing with others throughout their lives.

ℓ *What if we don't agree with our children's choices?*

Your children may come up with a number of worthy causes that may not be your worthy causes. In fact, your children will probably not agree among themselves about what organizations should receive your family's limited resources.

This is when you can teach your children the arts of persuasion, compromise, and consensus-building. Disagreement can be a wonderfully useful tool to teach your children—in a spirit of love and giving rather than anger—lessons that they cannot learn elsewhere.

ℓ *Will there be family discord over the choice of beneficiaries?*

Choosing the charities and the amounts to give to each and determining the right strategies for maximizing the benefits of your gifts represent the work implicit in planned giving; but it is work that's also fun and satisfying.

In our family's experience, we were able to start a conversation that brought all of us together in greater intimacy. My wife and I sat down with our two children—Nance, a college freshman, and Michael, an eighth grader—to determine who the beneficiaries of our family foundation should be.

Instead of talking about specific charities and how much we would give them, my wife and I found ourselves discovering our children's social and charitable passions. We had never before considered that our children had their own ideas, feelings, hopes, and fears about anything outside of their own needs for immediate gratification, let alone that they were concerned about global issues.

As parents, we were humbled and proud at the same time. The kids were excited about and empowered by the prospect of participating in something that could touch the lives of others. The process took us from the cover of the *J. Crew* catalogue to AIDS research, to world hunger, to space exploration, to wildlife management. As a family, we discovered that we shared feelings and passions.

The choices we made, we made together. We formed a family bond and mission that I believe will live as a legacy for generations to come. Each of us will cherish and long remember the intimacy of this experience.

INTRODUCTION TO STRATEGIES IN *GIVING*

Initial Considerations

ଜ *Are there general factors to consider as I create my charitable plan?*

Yes, you should consider these factors as you create your charitable plan:

- A well-conceived charitable plan should provide flexibility for you to change your mind and change the plan if you wish.
- Your personal, professional, and financial commitments today may not be the status quo tomorrow, and your favorite causes will no doubt change over the years.
- Start small, with a narrow focus and a short time frame. This will provide the flexibility you need to change your plan as your giving patterns and financial resources change and evolve during the stages of your life.

ଜ *Should my charitable giving plan have definite time frames?*

Yes, it should. Not-for-profits need different types of pledges or gifts. You can make a one-time gift today to help with the charity's operating expenses or you can make a grant to an endowment fund, which is a long-term commitment to support a charity.

Unquestionably, coordinating your personal goals, the needs of the charities, and your financial resources within a specific time frame are part of a giving plan.

ଜ *Should I give while I'm alive or should I defer my gifts until after my death?*

The easy answer to this is, yes, but the choice of making gifts during life or at death (testamentary gifts) is a function of tax planning and timing in conjunction with your personal desires and financial realities.

From the tax planning point of view, it is typically more beneficial to make charitable gifts during your life rather than upon death because you receive income tax deductions if you make lifetime gifts that are not available if you make testamentary gifts. Depending on your particular circumstances, a combination of lifetime and testamentary giving strategies may be particularly beneficial to you and your family.

The personal component to giving suggests that giving during your lifetime is preferable to testamentary giving because you can set an example for your heirs to follow, you are around to personally enjoy making the gift, you can monitor the charity's use of the gift, and you can see the results of the gift.

◌ *Do I have to give away my money all at one time or can I give it out over time?*

You can do either or both. Because there are so many ways to make charitable gifts and because every family situation is different, it is important that you consider implementing an integrated and coordinated charitable plan that will allow you to make the right decisions about your giving program.

◌ *At what point in my life should I consider a giving program?*

There is no wrong period in your life to begin a giving program, providing you do the appropriate planning to make certain that you maintain your financial status.

Historically, and in our experience, most people seriously begin their charitable programs when they are in their fifties and sixties. By this time, they have raised their children and are more financially comfortable to begin thinking about the needs of society and giving back through meaningful causes.

The important thing to remember is that you can become a philanthropist at any age and at any time and receive the benefits from your donations, as long as they are within your financial means.

◌ *Is it in poor taste to give a charitable gift and to want acknowledgment for it or should we keep our philanthropy a secret?*

This is a personal decision and part of your charitable philosophy.

Some of our clients demand that their gifts be kept absolutely anonymous, while others want us to contact the charities and arrange proper and tasteful acknowledgments.

Whether you make gifts anonymously or want acknowledgment depends on your motivations, needs, and philosophy. There is no wrong thing to do in this regard.

◌ Where can I get assistance in putting my plan together?

It might be helpful for you to examine the giving habits of other individuals in your tax bracket. This information is readily available through the larger charitable organizations in your community or through your local community foundation.

Legal and financial advisors play a significant role in developing charitable giving plans, including the family charitable mission statement. Ask your accountant, attorney, and financial advisor for help in creating your charitable philosophy statement and giving program. At the very least, have one or more of your advisors review your plan before you implement it.

Financial Planning

◌ Is it important to the planning process to determine the amount of charitable funds that we will have available?

Determining the total amount of funds that you will have available for your giving program is critical. After choosing the causes you want to support, prepare your charitable budget. Your plan should be financially realistic and meet your personal comfort level and time horizons.

◌ What are the major financial issues I should consider as I prepare my charitable budget?

We suggest that you consider your charitable goals in terms of a coordinated plan, which includes these categories:

- *Financial planning:* Your current financial situation, the standard of living you wish to maintain over time, how much of your resources you will need to perpetuate that lifestyle, and which assets you can afford to give away

- *Tax planning:* The income and/or estate tax planning that you would like to accomplish
- *Estate planning:* The impact your proposed gifts to charity are likely to have on your ability to leave sufficient wealth to your family and other beneficiaries

Your goals in each category will assist you in determining the amount that you need to live on, the amount you will be comfortable giving to charity, and the planning strategies that your advisors will recommend that you use.

ℭ *Even if we look at the financial resources we have, how do we know how much we can give and still have enough to live on?*

If you have a strong interest in giving but need help deciding how much you can afford to give, you might consider investing in the services of a financial planner. A planner experienced in developing charitable giving models will take a comprehensive look at

- your income sources, such as pensions, Social Security, and investment distributions; and
- your expenses, capital risks, income needs, taxes, inflation, and expected investment performance over time.

From this information, he or she can assess your current financial situation, forecast the capital you will require to ensure your lifestyle, and then suggest the amounts that you could comfortably give away.

In addition, there are many different charitable giving strategies that allow you to make a gift during your lifetime but still receive income from the gift.

ℭ *How will we ever know how much is enough?*

This is a question commonly asked of professional advisors, even by the most affluent families. In general, it depends on your lifestyle, values, personal goals, and aspirations.

"Enough" is not always a decision relative to a dollar amount but rather a decision about your philosophy and desire for influence. Because so many of our clients ask us to help them get a handle on this very important issue, we often begin by having them complete a philanthropic questionnaire, which helps them come to terms with money as an emotional issue. This process allows them to explore how they and their families can make peace with money and the emotional charge associated with it to eventually determine how much is "enough" for them.

◌ *Do you counsel your clients to limit their giving?*

When our clients decide to give, they suddenly become liberated and overcome with an excitement to give unlimited amounts to everyone.

We do not necessarily limit their excitement or the size of their gifts. Instead, we help them create a comprehensive charitable plan so they can not only increase their financial resources to benefit their families, they can also enhance their charitable gifts to benefit charities.

Proper planning can increase the ultimate amount and benefits of any gift. Collaboration with your financial planner, attorney, accountant, and the planned giving officers of your charities is just as important in executing your giving strategies as it is in creating and monitoring your plan.

◌ *I own farmland that has been in the family for several generations, has a very low cost basis, and produces very little income. As part of our financial plan, can we convert some of it to an income-generating investment without losing 20 percent of the principal to long-term capital gain taxes?*

This is a common situation with farmland, highly appreciated and low- or non-dividend-paying stock, and older commercial real estate. If your financial planning goals are to increase income and reduce capital gain taxes, you can use a charitable remainder trust (CRT). With this type of trust, you give the property to a charity, but the property is held in a trust. You could also use a charitable gift annuity (CGA) and give the property directly to the charity. The benefits you would receive from either strategy are

- an immediate charitable income tax deduction,

- a deferral of capital gain tax, and
- an income for you.

We discuss these strategies in more detail in Parts Three and Four.

ᐒ *I own stock in a closely held corporation from which I do not receive income. Is there any benefit in donating this stock to a charity? If so, how would I do it?*

Again, a CRT or a CGA are accepted strategies to address your situation. With either strategy, you defer, and possibly avoid entirely, the capital gain taxes and generate an income for yourself and your family.

ᐒ *My husband and I are thinking about early retirement. How can we set up a guaranteed income stream for the 10 years between retirement and the time when Social Security benefits become available and then give the income-producing asset to charity?*

You can create a CRT to pay you and your husband a fixed sum from the donated property for any period you would like; in your case, 10 years. At the end of the term, the income interest expires (income payments stop) and the asset passes to charity.

ᐒ *Is there a way for me to use an asset to fund annual gifts to charity and still leave the asset to my wife?*

Yes, there are planning techniques, such as a charitable lead trust (CLT), that accomplish this result. A CLT is the reverse of the CRT. Under a lead trust, the donor transfers the asset to the trust, the trust makes distributions of income to charitable beneficiaries for a designated period of time, and the remainder passes to noncharitable beneficiaries such as your wife or others whom you name in the trust.

Passing Values and Teaching Responsibilities

ᐒ *How can I use my charitable giving to teach my children and grandchildren to appreciate money?*

Most of our clients either grew up with scarcity or experienced scarcity at some point during their lives and most of them created their prosperity through their own efforts, inheriting little or nothing. Most of our clients' children, however, have never known scarcity.

Exposing economically prosperous young people to the scarcity that others have experienced and involving them in charitable giving will hopefully teach them the blessings of wealth and privilege and the responsibilities that go along with their good fortune.

◌ Can you recommend a way to involve children and grandchildren in a family's charity?

Absolutely. We encourage our client families to have fun with their philanthropy.

Instead of writing checks to various causes in a haphazard fashion, help the kids identify their passions and focus their gifts on two or three causes they really want to support. Not only will they have more fun, but their gifts will have more impact.

Finally, encourage your family members to enjoy the socializing and networking that philanthropy creates.

◌ How can the family charity help our grandchildren learn about money management, business management, and investing?

Involving children and grandchildren in charitable giving often creates uncommon opportunities to share lessons—depending on the size and complexity of the fund—about money management, goal setting, working with others, managing others, investing, financial markets, planning, and many other skills that a parent or grandparent may not otherwise have the opportunity to share.

Even a fund of $1,000 offers a training ground for children who have had little or no experience with writing checks, managing money, and investing. The family fund will let children interact with each other and possibly with professional advisors, including an accountant, attorney, investment advisor, or a planned giving officer from the local community foundation or a particular charity.

◌ How can we use the process of "helping the community" to teach our children about accepting responsibility?

My family established a "family investment club" to teach the children about investing. One requirement of the investment club is that we must distribute 10 percent of the profits to charity annually.

The children must establish the guidelines for choosing the charitable recipients and then must meet to choose the charitable organization that will be the recipient that year.

You could, as part of your family goal, require that there be an annual family meeting to select a charity that will receive your gifts. You could require your children to visit the charity they want to benefit and that they meet some of the recipients of the charities' distributions. By doing this, they will be able to understand the needs firsthand. You may require that your children actively participate in the charities to which the family makes distributions. This process helps each child, or grandchild, to become involved in the community and in a purpose other than themselves. You can accomplish this through a private family foundation, a donor-advised fund (DAF) at the local community foundation, or through a supporting organization (SO).

ℭ𝔈 *Will participation in youth groups help our children to develop an understanding of the importance of charitable giving?*

Many of our clients encourage their children to participate in youth groups or religious organizations. Surveys suggest a close correlation between young people being active in charitable youth activities and their future giving and volunteering behavior. Membership in organizations such as Girl Scouts or Boy Scouts, church or synagogue groups, or student government helps create a sense of caring and community awareness.

ℭ𝔈 *How can my husband and I teach the values of giving and community service to our children?*

Teach by example. A 1999 survey conducted by Independent Sector notes that 69 percent of respondents who volunteered their time and 75 percent of those who made charitable contributions had parents who also volunteered their time and made charitable gifts.

If we want our children to learn these values, we must be willing to affirm our commitment to serve society by giving generously of our time and/or financial resources. Giving and sharing should be a normal part of your family's everyday life—take your children with you as you do volunteer work so they develop charitable habits and character.

For example, Marcia delivers Christmas food packages for her church to elderly people in the parish. She always takes her daughter, Katlyn, with her. Marcia tells the story that Katlyn was only 7 years old the first time she went. Katlyn moaned and groaned about going out in the cold and just didn't want to go. After the second delivery, Katlyn was having so much fun talking to the elderly recipients that she didn't want to stop. She was disappointed when there were no more presents to deliver and no more new people to meet. Now Katlyn can't wait until Christmas every year so she and her mom can make their fun rounds together.

    I have young grandchildren and would like to share some of the joys of charitable giving with them. Do you have any suggestions as to what would work for them?

We have clients who have seven grandchildren ranging in age from 8 to 18. Each year at Thanksgiving, grandma and grandpa send each grandchild $100 in cash, ask the grandchildren to do something for others with the money, and to report back at Christmas time what they did with their charitable dollars.

    Many of their grandchildren make it to their house for Christmas dinner, and, from what we hear, dinnertime is filled with fun and interesting stories. One of the younger granddaughters had her mother help her buy and blow up helium balloons that she took to the residents of a local nursing home. One 16-year-old grandson broke the neighbor's window and didn't tell anyone about it. He later felt guilty about that, so he put $100 in an envelope and left it in the neighbor's mailbox as an anonymous gift.

    What can we do to help our children understand the tremendous social responsibility they have with respect to our family wealth?

One of the best ways is for you to set up a family foundation and appoint your children to its initial board of directors or set up the foundation so they become its directors after one or both of you are gone.

    A family foundation provides a forum for your children to meet—at least once annually—and discuss the charitable allocations and distributions from the foundation's resources. It can provide your children with the opportunity to see and assess the various needs that are presented to the foundation. It also gives them an opportunity to make meaningful contributions to society.

If your children are on your foundation's board, they will also be responsible for deciding how its funds will be invested, which requires financial involvement and the opportunity to build investment acumen.

Parents can use DAFs and SOs to provide these same opportunities to their children.

Giving Family Members Prestige and Self-Esteem

℞ *Can our family's charitable giving help our children to establish a respected community identity of their own?*

A great way for you to help your children gain self-esteem and shape positive personal identities is to get them involved in community service.

As board members of a foundation or as decision makers with respect to other family charitable funds, your children become influential and as people who can influence charitable giving, they will receive invitations to community events for causes that range from the symphony to hospitals, parks, and the homeless. They will meet people and make the kinds of connections that enable them to become more significant players in your community.

℞ *Our son is not doing much with the opportunities we have given him. He is living in a small apartment in a bad part of town and doesn't appear to have much drive to do any better than the unsuccessful people with whom he associates. Do you think involving him in our charitable efforts can improve his chances for a productive life?*

Giving your son a direction is probably one of the kindest gifts you can give him. In our experience, children who seem unmotivated to do something with their lives are usually temporarily lost—wandering through life just waiting for someone to give them a direction because they don't have any idea what they can or should do—even though they would never admit that to you. Charitable involvement can do much for these children.

In your son's case, it could give him the opportunity to see that there are people in the world who need and appreciate even the smallest gift of time or money that he gives them. He will see meaningful results follow small, properly considered actions, which will encourage him to take larger actions that produce bigger and better results, until eventually he learns the value of accomplishment and has a direction.

ભ *Have you seen positive results after involving unmotivated children in charitable giving?*

Many years ago, we represented Stephen, a grandfather who wanted to get his grandson, Josh, involved in something that gave him an opportunity to meet the "movers and shakers" in the community. We recommended that Stephen create a family foundation and involve Josh in its administration. He did so, and the foundation hired Josh to evaluate grant requests from local charities. Their community's business, civic, and cultural leaders were on the boards of the charities, so Josh met and worked with many of them in the course of evaluating their requests.

After working for the foundation for a year and a half, a prominent business owner, whom Josh met through his foundation work, offered Josh a position that was a tremendous career opportunity. Josh accepted. As far as Stephen was concerned, the foundation had performed its primary purpose for Josh. But Stephen got even more than he expected: Josh continued to work for the foundation—without compensation—and eventually became its chairman. What is most interesting is that prior to his involvement with the foundation, Josh's parents considered him to be an unmotivated, problem child.

ભ *I was recently asked to join the planned giving committee of one of my favorite charities. Should I join?*

The invitation undoubtedly recognizes your accomplishments and expertise in business, philanthropy, or both. Some of our clients who have received similar invitations tell us that they find the experience to be meaningful for them.

A common goal of all planned giving committees is to identify prospective donors and to encourage charitable gifts. They are frequently committed to educating both their donor base and the public about the many financial and personal advantages of planned charitable giving—exactly what we're doing in *Giving*. By participating on the committee, you will likely gain insights into the charity's compelling need for fund development and its effective use of strategic planning.

Many charities use their planned giving committees as advisory boards where members can learn, grow, and matriculate to full board members. By having knowledgeable, accomplished individuals on their committees, charitable organizations have highly effective focus groups that can learn about and suggest solutions for the charity's needs.

Serving on a planned giving committee gives you opportunities to meet individuals who share common interests and goals, to gain personal prestige and visibility, and even to elevate your level of experience and expertise.

In short, the invitation recognizes your accomplishments and the respect others have for your abilities.

Leaving a Lasting Legacy

CR *How can I leave a legacy if I am not wealthy?*

To most people, the idea of leaving a legacy sounds like something only the Carnegie, Rockefeller, or Gates families of this world can do. This is not necessarily true. Mother Teresa helped millions of needy in India and in other countries and didn't have a dime of her own.

The size of the gift is not what characterizes a philanthropist. In fact, a national survey by Independent Sector found that people in the lowest income brackets tend to donate as much or more than their higher-net-worth counterparts (see chapter 1). While your estate may never be large enough to build libraries, it may be large enough to buy books for a library.

CR *Can you give me an example of what you mean by donating services to leave a legacy?*

Sure. Ted, one of our clients, began working for Habitat for Humanity when his friends dragged him out on a Saturday to help on a house. Ted got so caught up in that first experience of helping to build a home for a needy family that he now spends every weekend building homes for this organization. This activity has become a highly meaningful part of his life, and he takes great satisfaction in having increased his skills over the years, which he now uses to help even more people. Ted doesn't have a lot of money to contribute to charity but has nonetheless created his legacy by building homes for other families to live and flourish in for years to come.

Like Ted, many of our other clients have shown us that we do not have to make large gifts of money to create our legacies. We can visit nursing homes, hand out coats and blankets to the homeless on cold nights, teach the illiterate to read, mentor a child, be a big brother or big sister, or be involved in an infinite number of other worthy projects for which we can volunteer our time, empathy, and talents.

CR *I am interested in supporting specific charitable causes, but I do not have enough money to set up my own private foundation. Is there a way that I can establish my own charitable organization without much expense?*

You may wish to set up a donor-advised fund (DAF) at your local community foundation or at another charitable organization that sponsors DAFs. These funds are similar to private foundations but they avoid the red tape and arcane regulations associated with private foundations:

- Like a private foundation, you can make a contribution to the DAF, specify that the contribution remain segregated under your fund, and direct the community foundation or charity to use your contributions for the purposes in which you are most interested; but
- unlike a private foundation where you do all of the administration, the community foundation or charity invests and administers the DAF and files all of the necessary tax-related government reports, thereby relieving you of the costs and complexities of a private foundation.

CR *My wife and I don't have a lot of money but we do wish to leave a gift to our high school. Do you have any ideas?*

You should consider purchasing a life insurance policy on your joint lives and naming the high school as the beneficiary of the policy. The amount of the gift is the death benefit amount, but the cost of the gift is what you pay for the annual premiums. Depending on your ages, you may be able to purchase an insurance benefit ranging from $50,000 to $100,000 or more at a relatively small and very affordable cost.

Cℛ *My husband and I are both 70+ years old with no children. We would very much like to do something significant for our community but can't think of any special way to do so. Do you have any ideas for how we can make a unique impact on our community?*

A decade or so ago, clients of ours, Mike and Sarah, bought a large, vacant, retail facility and donated it to our community foundation to use as a youth center. Their gift spurred their friends and neighbors to join in with gifts of money and property, and the charity was able to transform the building into a place where teenagers "hung out" with their friends.

With the cooperation of a number of public youth-oriented charities and committed neighbors and parents, it is fully supervised at all times. The building contains computers for the youngsters to do their homework; has game, music, and study rooms; and has a large room for meetings and parties.

From the beginning, this project was applauded by the police, school counselors and administrators, youth leaders, and pastors and rabbis. Mike and Sarah and the supervisory leaders of the project receive countless inquiries from people all over the country who want to use this as a model for projects in their communities.

This project definitely had an immediate impact on our community, but the real results of Mike and Sarah's original contribution can only be measured by the number of youths who didn't and won't end up in trouble because they had a positive environment in which to spend time and by the number of troubled youths whose lives have changed because of the love, guidance, and direction of the handful of professional counselors and many, many community volunteers.

Tax Planning

Cℛ *What is the true after-tax cost of a charitable gift?*

Because your gift to a qualified charity is tax-deductible, your actual cost for the donation is reduced by your tax savings. For example, if you are in the 28 percent income tax bracket, the actual cost of a $100 donation is $72 ($100 less the $28 in tax savings). This same principle applies to federal estate tax as well.

ᙦ *I have paid income taxes all my life, and I am charitably inclined, but I don't want to pay a dime of estate tax upon my death. Do you have any recommendations?*

You may leave your estate to one of three beneficiaries: family, charity, or government. Depending on the size of your estate and the type of assets you own, you may have several options available to you (as outlined throughout this book) to accomplish your goals.

In general, a plan to reduce or even "zero-out" estate taxes will involve using the unified credit amount that is available to every person to maximize the tax-free amounts going to your family beneficiaries and to increase the amounts going to your charitable beneficiaries, which directly reduces the amounts going to your government beneficiary.

Given the current law, less than 2 percent of the people who die each year have taxable estates. Many of those do not actually pay federal estate tax because of the credits and deductions built into the system for passing estates to family members, while others do not pay them because of the charitable strategies they have included in their estate plans.

ᙦ *Our favorite charity is engaged in a massive capital campaign and we would like to make a significant contribution. With two children in college and two in private school, we have very little "free" cash. However, we do have several hundred shares of stock that were worth $10 per share when we received them from my husband's previous employer but are now trading in the high $80s. We recognize the severity of our capital gain tax problem and wonder what strategies you think we should consider to address it while benefiting our charity's capital campaign?*

You could do something as simple as giving all or a portion of your stock outright to your charity. If you do, your charity will be able to sell the stock capital gain tax–free, and you will receive an income tax deduction equal to the fair market value of the stock the day you transfer it to the charity. Depending on the amount and timing of your gift and your other financial goals, your advisors might also suggest using a charitable trust, a pooled income fund, or a charitable gift annuity.

ca I need help with my annual giving. I would like to make all of my gifts with appreciated stock, but that just isn't practical with smaller contributions. Is there one place I can go to make a single donation each year and then have them make all of my gifts?

Your local community foundation should be able to help in this area. You might consider establishing a donor-advised fund at your local community foundation. Each year, you could make one contribution of appreciated stock to this fund and provide the community foundation with a list of the charities you wish to receive donations. While the community foundation is not obligated under the law to give the money to your chosen charities, it is unlikely that it will not follow your wishes, as long as you have named legitimate charities. You can change your mind from year to year under a donor-advised fund; you are not locked into any specific charities or amounts.

chapter 3

Charities

QUALIFIED CHARITIES

Q Why do gifts to charities get special tax treatment?

Charities have become the third sector of our society, next to government and business. Charitable organizations do for the common good what no other entity will or can do. Charities exist to help society. Our government acknowledges charities' value to society by giving them special status, exempting them from taxes on most of the revenue they generate, and allowing taxpayers to take tax deductions for contributions to charities.

Q My tax advisor always refers to "qualified charities" when we talk about gifts to charity. What is a qualified charity?

When most people speak of charities, they are usually referring to organizations that are nonprofit and are devoted to charitable purposes. This is a fairly accurate description of a charity, but what many people do not understand is that the Internal Revenue Code (IRC) defines charities in many ways that dictate the tax treatment of the charitable organizations themselves and of the donations that

43

are made to them. The IRC contains a hierarchy of rules to define charitable organizations, and understanding how it classifies charities can be very confusing.

IRC Section 501(c) lists those types of organizations that are exempt from federal income tax. This list of the types of *tax-exempt* organizations is long and detailed. Now, here's the catch. Just because an organization is income tax–exempt under Section 501(c) does *not* mean that it is a charitable organization. There are many tax-exempt entities that have nothing to do with charity, for example, pension funds.

Tax-exempt organizations that operate to promote public welfare and public purposes are charitable organizations. The tax-exempt organizations that offer tax benefits to people who make donations are generally referred to as *qualified charities*. Most of the charities that we are familiar with and give money to—the United Way; the Juvenile Diabetes Research Foundation; your local hospital, college, or museum; and your local arts, education, and human services charities— are qualified charities. When you see the term *qualified charities* in this book, we are referring to those organizations that offer tax benefits to those who donate to them.

CR *What is a Section 501(c)(3) organization that my tax advisor refers to? Does a charity have to be a Section 501(c)(3) tax-exempt organization in order for me to receive the tax benefits of making a donation to a charity?*

No, not necessarily, but it is highly likely. Section 501(c)(3) is very broad and encompasses the vast majority of organizations that we perceive as charitable because they promote the public welfare and public purposes. However, some charitable entities, while not qualifying as tax-exempt under that particular section, can fall under other provisions of Section 501(c) or other IRC provisions and still offer tax benefits.

Remember, Section 501(c) controls whether an entity is exempt from paying federal income taxes. Other provisions of the Internal Revenue Code determine if a donation to a charity is income tax– deductible (IRC Section 170(c)), gift tax–deductible (IRC Section 2522(a)), or estate tax–deductible (IRC Section 2055(a)). The good news is that if you are not a tax advisor, you do not have to know the details of the Internal Revenue Code sections that apply to charities and charitable deductions. Your tax advisor must understand these details, however, to ensure that your donations get proper tax treatment.

Qualified for Charitable Income Tax Deductions

ଔ *I understand that for a donor to receive an income tax deduction for a gift to a charity, the charity must meet certain requirements. What requirements must a charity meet for me to receive an income tax deduction for donations I make to it?*

For income tax deduction purposes, the charity must fall into one of the categories set forth in the Internal Revenue Code. These categories include the following:

1. *States, possessions, or other political subdivisions of the United States.* Gifts made to these types of entities qualify for tax deductions only to the extent that a gift is made exclusively for public purposes.
2. *Corporations, trusts, community chests, community funds, or community foundations organized and operated exclusively for religious, charitable, scientific, literary, or educational purposes; or to foster national or international amateur sports competition; or for the prevention of cruelty to children or animals.* These entities and organizations must not have been disqualified for tax-exempt status.
3. *Organizations of war veterans and their auxiliary and affiliated entities.*
4. *Domestic fraternal societies, orders, and other associations or organizations operating under a lodge system, but only if the contributions or gifts are used exclusively for religious, charitable, scientific, literary, or educational purposes or for the prevention of cruelty to children or animals.*
5. *Certain companies that operate cemeteries.*

ଔ *Are there any other requirements that are important in order for a charity to be qualified for income tax deductions?*

Yes. For income tax purposes, the Internal Revenue Code requires that a qualified charity be created or organized in the United States; or in a possession of the United States; or under the laws of the United States, a state, the District of Columbia, or a possession of the United States. Further, no part of the organization's net earnings may benefit a private shareholder or individual. Finally, the organization cannot, as a substantial part of its activities, attempt to influence legislation.

ငာ *These rules sound very complicated. How can I be sure in advance that a charity is qualified under federal law so I can receive the tax benefits of my charitable donation?*

You should always investigate to ensure that the charity is qualified. One way to do this is to check that the charity is listed in IRS Publication 78, *Charitable Contributions: A Cumulative List of Organizations.* This publication lists many of the qualified charities and is available at many libraries or can be accessed online at the Internal Revenue Service's Internet website. The IRS updates this publication frequently, so make sure you have their most current one.

Most charitable organizations, other than churches and governments, must apply to the IRS to become qualified. You can request a copy of the charity's IRS determination letter directly from the charity to verify its status as a qualifying charitable organization for purposes of charitable income tax deduction. Be wary if the charity cannot readily furnish this letter. Also, keep in mind that even though a charity once received a favorable determination letter, its status as a qualified charity may have been subsequently revoked, so it is still important to check IRS Publication 78.

ငာ *What happens if I claim a charitable deduction for a gift I made to a qualified charity listed in IRS Publication 78 but subsequently discover that the charity lost its tax-exempt qualification?*

Taxpayers may generally rely on IRS Publication 78 for purposes of determining whether the charity is a qualified charity. Consequently, even though you made a contribution on a date when the charity was not qualified, the contribution will be protected as long as you were not actually aware of the revocation and did not participate in the activities that resulted in the revocation.

Taxpayers should check IRS Publication 78 at the time they make their contributions. If the charity is not listed in Publication 78 at the date the gift was made, the deduction may be disallowed.

Qualified for Charitable Gift Tax Deductions

CR *Do the same charities that qualify for an income tax deduction
qualify for the gift tax deduction?*

The Internal Revenue Code sets forth four classes of charities that
qualify for the gift tax deduction. They closely parallel those classes
of charities that qualify for the charitable income tax deduction that
we listed earlier in this chapter but are not identical. One difference,
for example, is that a taxpayer who makes a gift to a cemetery company will receive an income tax deduction for doing so but will not
receive a gift tax deduction. Also, to receive an income tax deduction
for a charitable donation, the donation must be to an organization
located in the United States. There is no such requirement for a gift
tax deduction.

The easiest and best way for you to ensure that the charity is
qualified for a charitable gift tax deduction is to check that the charity is listed in IRS Publication 78, *Charitable Contributions: A
Cumulative List of Organizations.*

CR *What does it mean if I don't receive a gift tax deduction?*

A gift made to a charity is treated the same as any other gift: it is subject to gift tax unless it somehow qualifies for an exemption. If a
donation does not qualify for a gift tax deduction, it is possible that
a taxpayer will have to pay a gift tax on the donation. This is not a
good result, so it is important that you are certain that the charity to
which you are making a donation is qualified and otherwise meets
the requirements for the charitable gift tax deduction.

Qualified for Charitable Estate Tax Deductions

CR *What is a qualified charity for purposes of an estate tax deduction?*

A qualified charity for estate tax purposes is similar to (but not
exactly the same as) a charity that meets the requirements for an
income tax deduction and for a gift tax deduction. The Internal
Revenue Code allows a charitable estate tax deduction for a transfer,
by reason of death, to a governmental unit within the United States;

or to an organization for religious, charitable, scientific, literary, or educational purposes; or to foster national or international amateur sports competition; or for the prevention of cruelty to children or animals. In addition, there are other tax-exempt organizations that qualify for charitable deductions in more specialized ways, such as organizations of war veterans and cemeteries. There is a restriction that the bequest cannot directly benefit a private person and the charity cannot be engaged in political activities.

Prior to making any distributions to a charity after your death, your trustee or personal representative should obtain from the charity the determination letter issued by the Internal Revenue Service showing that the charity is qualified for an estate tax deduction.

If the charity is not qualified or if a charitable gift given at death does not otherwise meet the requirements to qualify as a deductible charitable gift, it may still be possible to preserve the bequest as tax-deductible. If it is clear that a decedent was attempting to make a gift to charity that would be federal estate tax–deductible, it is possible that a court will interpret or revise the terms of the bequest or name another recipient (with a charitable purpose similar to the charity selected by the decedent) that is qualified so the gift would qualify for a charitable deduction.

TYPES OF CHARITIES

ᑲ *I understand that a qualified charity must be a tax-exempt organization that then must meet additional requirements so gifts qualify for income, gift, or federal estate tax deductions for the taxpayers. Are there any other categories of charitable organizations?*

Yes, there are. Generally, there are two major subcategories of qualified charities: public charities and private foundations. For taxpayers, the distinction between these types of charities affects the percentage and timing of the income tax deduction that a taxpayer receives. For charities, the classification of public or private affects the extent of regulation imposed by the Internal Revenue Code. Private foundations receive far more scrutiny from the Internal Revenue Service than do public charities.

Public Charities

CR *What are public charities?*

Public charities come in two basic types. The first type includes churches and organizations that are closely allied with churches, associations, and conventions of churches; schools; colleges; universities; hospitals; medical research organizations; and certain governmental entities.

If an organization does not fall within this first category, it may qualify in the second type of public charity if it meets the "public support test." The *public support test* requires that one-third of a charity's gifts and contributions come from a wide cross section of the general public, rather than from one person, company, or family. Admissions, sales, fees for services, and other forms of income do *not* count as public support. The public support test also requires that endowment and investment income may not exceed one-third of the charity's total support.

Community Foundations

CR *What are community foundations and are they public or private charities?*

The idea of a community foundation began in 1914 in Cleveland, Ohio, with The Cleveland Foundation. Today, community foundations can be found throughout the United States. *Community foundations* are public charities that exist to oversee charitable funds donated by members of a community and to invest in their own communities by making grants to local people and organizations.

A unique characteristic of community foundations is that they make it possible for whoever establishes a fund with the foundation to make certain their money serves specific charitable purposes. At the same time, a community foundation pools all of its funds for investment purposes, making it possible for individual, small funds to achieve economies of scale. For example, a community foundation might make a single grant for development of low-income housing that includes money from a half dozen different individual funds focused on the same issue.

☞ *Are there different types of funds that we can set up at a community foundation?*

The fund you set up at a community foundation can take many forms. The choice of how your fund is established is based on the amount of control you and your family wish to retain over the funds you have donated to the community foundation.

1. *Unrestricted option:* The option with the least control is the unrestricted option, in which the community foundation staff chooses the charities and the amounts to distribute for the fund that you create.

2. *Field-of-interest option:* With this option, you choose the types of charitable causes that you wish to support, then the staff at the community foundation decides which specific charities will receive distributions from your fund and the amount that will go to each charity. This option allows you to specify the type of charitable work that you wish to support while allowing you flexibility to adapt to future changes in the charitable organizations and the community they serve.

3. *Combination unrestricted and field-of-interest option:* You can combine the above two options by giving a percentage of your gift to specific charities and leaving a percentage undesignated.

4. *Restricted option:* You can specify the precise charities that are to receive benefits from your fund and the percentage that each will receive.

5. *Donor-advised fund:* The final option is a *donor-advised fund (DAF)*. A DAF is much like having a private foundation without the restrictions of a private charity and without your family being responsible for the entire administration of the fund. With a DAF, you, your spouse, and, if you choose, your children can "advise" the community foundation concerning the charities and specific projects you want to support. There are some limitations on what you can and cannot accomplish in a DAF. We'll discuss donor-advised funds in more detail in Chapter 18, Endowment Funds and Donor-Advised Funds.

☞ *Why do people donate to community foundations rather than creating private foundations or giving to existing charities?*

Setting up a fund with a community foundation is an inexpensive way to create your own giving vehicle—a "virtual" charity—without all of the extra paperwork and tax and legal hassles. The community foundation can help you research the charities that should receive grants from your fund, and, if you do not like to get inundated with solicitations, it could be a great way to give anonymously.

    I do want to help local charities, but there are other organizations I wish to benefit. Can I do both through my local community foundation?

This answer may vary depending on the community foundation, but, in our experience, most will allow you to make grants to any public charity within the United States. The focus of community foundations is to support charities within the local community, and they will certainly encourage you to have a substantial portion of your fund remain in the community that they serve. If you want to give to charities outside your area, check with the executive director of your local community foundation. Usually, he or she will be very flexible and do everything possible to meet your specific charitable goals.

Governmental Entities

    If we make gifts to governmental entities, would they qualify for the federal charitable income tax deduction?

Yes, you may make a gift to the United States or any state, the District of Columbia, a U.S. possession (including Puerto Rico), a political subdivision of a state or U.S. possession, or an Indian tribal government or any of its subdivisions that perform substantial government functions. However, to be deductible, your contribution to this type of organization must be made solely for public purposes.

    For example, you contribute cash to your county's sheriff's department to be used to purchase bulletproof vests. The sheriff's department is a qualified organization and your contribution is for a public purpose. You can deduct your contribution.

    I own real estate that has historical significance in my city and I can no longer afford to maintain it. I would like to donate it to my local city government to be preserved and used for public purposes. Will my gift be income tax–deductible?

Yes. Gifts to a government that are for legitimate public purposes, even when the gifts are restricted, qualify for charitable income tax deduction. Under most circumstances, even unrestricted gifts to the general fund of a government are deductible because the funds are used for public purposes.

Supporting Organizations

CR *I have heard of a type of charity called a supporting organization. Is this a public charity?*

Supporting organizations (SOs) are hybrid charitable organizations that, for most purposes, are treated as public charities. SOs use their revenue, gifts, or donations to "support" other public charities. Private individuals often create SOs to help specific public charities or specific charitable causes.

An SO is an alternative to a private foundation. It has many of the advantages of a private foundation without the restrictions. In addition, Congress affords SOs all of the tax advantages unique to public charities. We discuss supporting organizations in more detail in Chapter 17, Supporting Organizations.

Semipublic Charities

CR *What is a semipublic charity?*

A *semipublic charity* is a tax-exempt organization that does *not* qualify as a public charity but is not a private foundation either. Specifically, organizations for war veterans, such as the Veterans of Foreign Wars; domestic fraternal societies operating under a lodge system, such as the Fraternal Order of Eagles; and some cemetery companies are semipublic charities. Semipublic charities are qualified charities for purposes of income tax deductions.

Private Foundations

CR *What is a private foundation?*

A *private foundation* is a charitable organization that is supported by an individual, a family, a business, or other narrowly composed group, rather than by the public at large. These organizations are sometimes referred to as *family foundations*. Oddly enough, the Internal Revenue Code does not specifically define private foundations, referring to them as "organizations that do not meet the requirements of a public charity."

Private foundations are highly regulated under the Internal Revenue Code because they have been abused in the past by taxpayers. Complex rules surround their operation. Even so, the control offered by private foundations to those who create them makes them attractive to philanthropically motivated families and businesses.

People making contributions to private foundations can claim a federal charitable income tax deduction, as well as a gift tax deduction or an estate tax deduction. Private foundations come in a number of "flavors," the most common of which we introduce here. A detailed description of private foundations can be found in Chapter 16, Private Foundations.

Private Operating Foundations

CR *What is a private operating foundation?*

A *private operating foundation* actively uses its assets or income to conduct charitable activities, instead of passively encouraging charitable works by donating funds to other charities. For example, a private foundation that runs an animal shelter or soup kitchen is an operating foundation. For income tax deduction purposes, private operating foundations are treated as public charities even though they are not public charities as that term is defined in the Internal Revenue Code.

Private Nonoperating Foundations

CR *What is a private nonoperating foundation?*

A *private nonoperating foundation* does not actively carry on charitable functions; it supports charity by distributing its assets and earnings to other organizations that do actively carry on charitable activities. Nonoperating foundations are primarily *grant-making* organizations, meaning that they use the assets donated to them by a few people to further charitable causes.

"NONQUALIFIED" ORGANIZATIONS

Political Parties

◌ぺ Can my wife and I take a charitable income tax deduction for the contributions we make to political causes or candidates?

Gifts to political causes or to political candidates do not qualify for the charitable income tax deduction. This prohibition applies to gifts to corporations, trusts, community chests, and foundations that have been disqualified for tax exemption by reason of "attempting to influence legislation or which anticipate or intervene in a political campaign by a candidate for political office."

If you are concerned that a charity's activities in some way fall within that broad restriction, you should check with the organization to which you are considering making contributions and verify that it has not had its status as a qualified charity revoked.

Foreign Charities

◌ぺ Can my wife and I take an income tax deduction for our contributions to foreign charities?

Generally, you cannot. The Internal Revenue Code does not allow a charitable income tax deduction to donors for contributions they make directly to a foreign charity, even if the charity is tax-exempt.

That being said, there are treaties between the United States and other countries, such as Mexico and Canada, that qualify certain foreign charities for special treatment, allowing contributions to them to be income tax–deductible. Estates and trusts may obtain a charitable income tax deduction for contributions to foreign charities not organized under U.S. law. Also, this limitation applies only to the income tax deduction and not the charitable estate and gift tax deductions.

Many U.S.-qualified charitable organizations do sponsor work abroad, and contributions to such domestic organizations may, therefore, qualify for the charitable income tax deduction. Thus, a solution to identifying a qualified charitable organization may lie with you and your wife finding a domestic organization that furthers your charitable goals in the foreign country of your choice.

Be careful in choosing the U.S. charity. If it is merely a conduit for funds to a foreign charity, the income tax deduction may not be available. As long as the charity in the United States has some discretion as to how the contributions benefit the foreign charity, a charitable income tax deduction should be allowed.

CHOOSING AND MONITORING THE CHARITIES

Identifying the Charities and the Causes You Want to Support

◌Ꝛ How do people decide which charity to benefit?

Think of the qualities that you value most and be creative in perpetuating those qualities. Find a charity that values what you value. For example, if you love education, find a way to leave money for education in a way that's meaningful to you. We know a woman who gives money to a local parochial school with the instruction that the money is to be used to purchase uniforms for children who can't afford them. You may guess that her family was too poor to purchase uniforms when she was a child, and someone in the community was generous enough to pay for her uniforms. Her gift to that school continues the tradition.

Many people choose their churches, synagogues, temples, mosques, or other religious entities as their primary charity. Some give to their colleges or universities, and some give to help society in general. Those who do that often heed the advice of Andrew Carnegie, "The main consideration should be to help those that help themselves; to provide part of the means by which those who desire to improve may do so; to give those who desire to rise the aid by which they may rise...."

◌Ꝛ I want to make a charitable contribution, but I cannot decide which charity to make it to? What can I do?

You might consider your hobbies or how you like to spend your free time. If you enjoy music or the arts, there are many cultural institutions designed to promote those endeavors. If you are interested in scientific or medical research, there are many institutions dedicated to those pursuits. If you enjoy helping children, there are many charities dedicated to that cause, probably even in your own community. There is no shortage of worthwhile charitable causes; only a shortage of money.

℞ *I have very strong beliefs about certain issues that I want to advance during my lifetime. How do I choose a charity that will promote my value system?*

It is possible that your strong beliefs are shared by others who have already formed a charitable organization for the purpose of advancing this shared value system. With some research, such as contacting a national or international organization of charities or foundations, you could locate such an organization and contact a spokesperson directly. Also, many charities and foundations now have websites that you can review to get ideas about how to give and how to advance your values. The Center for the Study of Philanthropy and American Institute of Philanthropy are two informational websites that provide a variety of information about charities and giving.

℞ *How do I find specific charities?*

You could use the Internet. GuideStar has a database of more than 640,000 public charities and 60,000 private foundations. In addition, the BBB Wise Giving Alliance and the Center on Nonprofits and Philanthropy have searchable databases of entities that have filed for tax-exempt status with the Internal Revenue Service and also monitor and grade charities based on the amount of money spent on charitable programs and the cost of fundraising. And don't forget IRS Publication 78, *Charitable Contributions: A Cumulative List of Organizations,* that lists qualified charities. For additional information, see also Appendix B, Resources for Charitable Giving.

Once you identify qualified charities in which you are interested, you might also check for their websites. Many philanthropic organizations now have Internet websites to assist in their fundraising efforts. In other words, find out as much as possible about the organizations before you contact them to ask your questions.

One word of caution: Beware of charities with similar sounding names. It is easy to confuse one charity for another, so make sure that you are researching the correct charity.

◌⃝ *I've heard of an organization called Leave A Legacy. Is that a public charity?*

Leave A Legacy is not itself a public charity. It is a cooperative effort by charities to raise awareness among the public of the need for, and benefits of, charitable giving. Typically, Leave A Legacy is organized as a not-for-profit corporation, often on a statewide basis. Frequently, public charities in a community will form a local chapter.

Charities that participate in Leave A Legacy realize that they are not in competition with one another for a fixed amount of charitable donations but, rather, need to cooperate and collaborate to increase the total level of giving in their community. Educating the public in a community to make intelligent choices about how much to give and in what manner is the objective of Leave A Legacy. This educational task is too large for any one charity; therefore, combining efforts is the only way for these charities to make a significant impact.

◌⃝ *Are there specific questions I should ask a charity when deciding whether it is worthy of my support?*

Yes, there are several general questions that are always appropriate. Regardless of whether the charity is large or small, you should call the charitable organization that you are considering and speak to the executive director or development coordinator. Keep in mind that giving locally may mean that you are unable to evaluate the charity the same way that you could evaluate a national or international charity. Save the Children and United Way may be easily researched; your local church or community foundation may not be.

Your local charity probably doesn't have a fundraising department, glossy brochures, and reams of statistics at its disposal. However, a meeting with one of the directors should provide you with enough specific information for you to make your decision.

You may want to ask the person you meet with about the specific goals of the charity (maybe even ask for a copy of the mission statement) to confirm that the goals of the charity are similar to the goals you wish to promote. Make sure you are comfortable with the answers, and ask for all written materials that show the charity's goals over the next 1, 5, or 10 years. Even a small charitable organization should have a brochure or other written information available.

You probably want to explore the methods that the charity uses to meet its goals, to be sure that you approve of their actual work. And, of course, you always want to compare the overhead costs of the particular charity to other, similar charities. The Internet has been particularly helpful in this regard, and there are many wonderful websites that can provide hard statistics on either the specific charity in question or other charities doing similar work. Table 3-1 contains a more detailed list of questions you might use to evaluate charities.

TABLE 3-1   Questionnaire for Evaluating Charities

☐   What problem does the charity seek to address?

☐   Does it fall within the charitable purpose(s) of our family charitable philosophy?

☐   Can I make a meaningful donation to assist the charity?

☐   Will the donation be enough?

☐   Does my gift have to extend for more than 1 year?

☐   Is the charitable organization efficient?

☐   Is the charity worthy of receiving the funds?

☐   Are there any other charities that address the same need but are worthier?

☐   Does the charity have a current tax-exempt status?

☐   Is this charity run by experienced people with a track record for getting things done?

☐   Does the charity spend most of its money on the problem at hand rather than on administration, promotion, or collection of funds?

☐   Can I monitor my gift?

☐   Will I be able to follow through to see that my donation is used as promised?

℘ I was recently approached by a local charity to make a planned gift. What can I do to verify that it is a worthy cause?

A site visit is a good place to begin your due diligence effort. Observe the staff at work. The staff should be friendly and the premises should appear efficient and organized. If the charity is a service provider, such as a rehabilitation center or a homeless shelter, use the site visit as an opportunity to inquire and observe. Is your first impression positive? The cause must feel good to you.

Another insightful opportunity may be a visit with members of the charity's board of directors and top executives. These people must be actively involved in the stewardship of the organization and should possess the necessary background and experience to manage and direct the organization effectively. Inquire as to how many board members have actually made financial contributions to the organization. Be wary of investing in a charitable cause whose board members seem relatively distant from or indifferent to the organization's programs and services.

Review the organization's financial records. Ask for a fully audited financial statement prepared by an independent certified public accountant. Look over the current year's operating budget. Ask to review tax returns. The charity should be able to assure you that your gift will be used wisely.

If you are being asked to support a particular project, such as a capital campaign, review the written strategic plan. If the plan is well conceived, the needs, goals, and time frame will be well documented. Without a formalized plan, there could be confusion and waste.

Volunteer your time and skills to help the organization. This is a good way to meet the staff and other volunteers. Through these contacts, you will learn more about the cause that you are being asked to support.

Monitoring the Charities

℘ Can I place conditions on my charitable gift to assure its effectiveness?

Yes. As a donor or potential donor, you have some opportunity and ability to control your gift. A committed not-for-profit will try to meet your demands, if it is possible under its philosophy and administrative capability. Securing charitable gifts is extremely competitive and most charities are sensitive to their potential donor's wishes. Your gift is significant to the charity. Reasonable conditions should encourage the organization to operate more efficiently or serve more effectively.

As more business people are becoming philanthropic "investors," they are becoming actively involved and demanding a voice in the operation of charities. Many of today's active philanthropists are younger. These young business people have acquired their wealth through their own skills and hard work and not by the luck of an inheritance. In many cases, successful business philanthropists consider their charitable activities a second career. They are hands-on and demand that the organizations they support be accountable.

If your goal is to support a particular project of a charity, be sure the projections and promises are well conceived and researched. You will make the charity and the project far more effective if you simply insist on a sound businesslike foundation.

cR *After the September 11, 2001, attacks on the World Trade Center, many people were upset with how the money donated to the victims was being distributed. I want to know that the money I give goes to help needy people and is not wasted on administrative costs. Is there a way that I can make sure that my charitable donations are used in the way I want?*

Those events brought to light some unsettling statistics about how a sampling of charitable institutions spend our money, with some admitting that up to 90 percent of our donations may go in fees for paying telephone solicitors.

Evaluating your charity's efficiency isn't rocket science, but it can be a daunting task. Just as you did when you were choosing the charity, you can start by checking out the organization with the local charity registration office (usually a division of your state's attorney general's office) and with your local Better Business Bureau (BBB). After that, watchdog organizations such as GuideStar, the Urban Institute National Center for Charitable Statistics, and the BBB Wise Giving Alliance can provide additional information. For instance, a recent search of a favorite charity using the BBB Wise Giving Alliance website provided this information: the charity's stated purpose, the kind of programs it sponsors, its management and fundraising methods, tax status, financial status, and a pie chart displaying administrative and fundraising expenses as they relate to program expenditures and total assets. By contrast, a random search of an unfamiliar charity produced a warning stating that the organization had refused to provide current information regarding its finances, programs, and management.

You can also check to see the amount or percentage of each dollar that goes directly to charitable work on the charitable organization's required annual Form 990. The GuideStar and Urban Institute websites provide the latest 990 forms for more than 61,000 private foundations and more than 200,000 public charities. Charities and foundations are required to complete this form annually, and this information must be made available to potential donors upon request. Many forthcoming charities also post their financial information on their websites.

The specific information provided on the Form 990 and in a charity's annual report (call and request a copy of the report) will give you a good idea of how the charity works, who runs it, and where and how it spends money to address its concerns and run its operation. You should also be able to see the major expense categories, including program services, management and/or operation, and fundraising.

Finally, don't be afraid to call a charity and ask the tough questions you want answered. If the charity is not listed with the BBB Wise Giving Alliance, ask why it isn't and suggest that you would feel better donating to an organization that is more accountable as to how it plans to use your money.

For contact information for the organizations discussed above, see Appendix B, Resources for Charitable Giving.

chapter 4

Required Elements
for a Charitable Gift

*Are there specific requirements that I should be aware of before I
make a charitable gift?*

Yes, if you wish to take an income and gift tax deduction for your
lifetime gift or an estate tax deduction for a gift of property from
your estate at death, your gift must meet specific requirements. The
requirements are

- the gift must be made to a qualified charity, which we discussed
  in chapter 3;
- the gift must be a completed gift, that is, it must be *irrevocable*—
  once you give it, you cannot take it back;
- there must be a clear intention by the donor to make a gift,
  often called "donative intent";
- the gift must be in an appropriate form;
- there must be "delivery" of the gift, either actual or constructive;
  and
- there must be acceptance of the gift.

DONATIVE INTENT

CR *Why is donative intent important?*

Donative intent means that the donor, the person who makes the gift, makes it without the expectation of receiving anything of value in return. If the donor has an expectation of receiving something in exchange for the gift, the transaction is more like a purchase than a gift; therefore, the gift may not qualify for a charitable income tax, gift tax, or estate tax deduction. Part of the gift may qualify for an income, gift, or estate tax deduction if part of the gift was completely charitable and the donor did not have an expectation of receiving something of value in return for making the gift.

CR *My father has Alzheimer's and is in very poor health, and I have his power of attorney. He and I never discussed charitable giving, but he has a lot of money that he'll never spend. The American Cancer Society is very important to me. I can't afford to make any charitable gifts right now, so can I make donations to this worthwhile charity from my dad's bank account?*

Following through on your idea could cause some problems. A person who holds the power of attorney of another is pretty much restricted to the actions that are authorized in the power of attorney. Unless the power of attorney specifically states that you, as the holder of the power of attorney, can make charitable gifts and if your father never made such gifts before, it is likely that the Internal Revenue Service (IRS) will not allow the gifts as charitable deductions. Without specific language in the power of attorney, there would certainly be a question of intent, because someone who is mentally disabled cannot, by definition, have donative intent.

Also, if your father's will or trust names other heirs, they may dispute your authority to make the gifts. You are under a duty to care for your father's property in a prudent manner. You could end up in a very costly lawsuit with other heirs who feel that you gave away their inheritance.

CR *My accountant just told me that the IRS disallowed the income tax deduction for that fancy cocktail party and dinner that I*

went to last year. The event was for a charity and I paid a bun-
dle for the ticket. Why can't I deduct the price of the tickets?

When the IRS and federal courts decide whether a charitable donation qualifies as a gift, they make that determination based on
whether the gift was made out of a "disinterested sense of generosity."
Simply put, they want to know if you made the gift out of the good-
ness of your heart (which is deductible) or because you would get
something in return (which isn't deductible). If the value of the
ticket to the party was $100, your $100 donation (or some part of it)
wouldn't be deductible, because you made the gift in anticipation of
receiving something in return, which you got—cocktails and dinner.
Usually, in these situations, the charity will tell you in advance how
much of the ticket price is deductible as a charitable donation.

FORMS OF GIFTS

CR *What kinds of property can we give to charity?*

Although we primarily think of gifts in terms of cash, charitable gifts can
take many forms. They can take the form of intangible property, such
as stocks, bonds, securities of all types, and promissory notes. They can
take the form of tangible property, such as jewelry, furniture, clothes,
collections, boats, recreational vehicles, and motor vehicles. They
can take the form of real estate, both vacant land or with structures.

Even though charitable gifts come in many forms, there are reasons why some types of gifts are more appropriate than others. For
example, the Internal Revenue Code restricts the deductibility of
some forms of gifts. So, if you're interested in taking an income tax
deduction for a charitable gift, make sure the gift qualifies for such
treatment. Also, charities are often cautious about accepting some
types of gifts because they may have some problems attached to
them that would subject the charities to liability if they were to
accept the gifts. For example, charities are cautious about gifts of real
estate because the property might have environmental problems for
which the charity would be liable. In this respect, charities do not
have to accept all gifts.

If you intend to make a gift that may be unusual in form or that
may be subject to a liability of any kind, you should consult your tax
advisor to make sure the gift will be tax-deductible and otherwise

appropriate for charity. Once you have confirmed this with your tax advisor, make sure the charity will accept it.

❧ Can I donate my stock options to charity?

There are two kinds of stock options, incentive stock options (ISOs) and nonqualified stock options (NQSOs). ISOs generally cannot be transferred and, therefore, should not be donated to charity.

Most NQSO plans do not allow for the options to be transferred. You will need to read your stock option agreement to see if you can transfer NQSOs. Even if the plan allows it, you need to be careful about the tax consequences.

❧ Can I donate valuable antiques and paintings to a charity?

You may donate valuable antiques and paintings, but there are some considerations. First, you will probably need to obtain an appraisal to determine the fair market value of the property. You must find an individual qualified to appraise that particular article. Second, to maximize the amount of your deduction, you will need to be sure the charity receiving your property can use it. That is, the type of property you give must be related to the purpose or function of the charity. In the case of a painting or antique, for example, donating the item to a museum will provide a larger income tax deduction than donating it to the American Red Cross. Third, if you are donating works of art that are copyrighted, the copyright must be donated to the charity as well.

❧ Can I transfer my individual retirement account to a charity during my lifetime?

You can transfer your individual retirement account (IRA) to a charity as a lifetime gift but, unfortunately, you will have to take a taxable withdrawal from the IRA to make the transfer. President Bush has proposed legislation that would permit IRA owners to make lifetime transfers of IRAs to charity in some circumstances, but Congress had not enacted this proposal as we wrote *Giving*. You may, however, transfer the IRA at your death by naming a qualified charity as the beneficiary of the IRA. Due to its tax-exempt status, a qualified charity will not incur an income tax on the proceeds of the IRA as a noncharitable beneficiary would.

Can I give a life insurance policy to a charity during my lifetime?

Yes, you may contribute your life insurance policy to a charity, but there are some considerations. You must change the beneficiary designation on your policy to the name of the charity and you must irrevocably transfer the ownership of the policy to the same charity. If it is an existing policy, you will receive a charitable deduction for the cash surrender value of the policy (cash value less any loans on the policy) in the year you make the transfer. When you pay the premiums on the policy, you may deduct the premium payments as charitable contributions in the year you pay them.

You will need to check your state's law to determine whether charities in that state are permitted to own life insurance policies on their donors. New York is one state in which they cannot, and there may be others. As with all gifts that involve transfers other than cash, you should consult your tax advisor to find out what you can and cannot do in making a charitable transfer.

I am unable to make a cash contribution to my church of an amount as large as I would like. Alternatively, I work several hours each week at the church doing general maintenance and groundskeeping. May I deduct the value of services I provide to my church?

The Internal Revenue Code does not allow a charitable income tax deduction for a contribution of services. However, a deduction is usually allowable for your out-of-pocket expenses, such as mileage, associated with the services that you perform for your church.

I serve on the board of a local charity. How much can I deduct for the value of the services I contribute?

Nothing. You are not allowed a charitable income tax deduction for services rendered to a charity. Don't let that discourage you. Keep up the good work, because your charity needs you.

Can I give the university that my grandson attends funds to pay for his tuition through a scholarship fund? Is this a charitable contribution?

No. If you pay tuition directly to the university on your grandson's behalf, you are making a gift to your grandson, not to the school. Gifts to individuals, no matter how appropriate and necessary, are not deductible charitable contributions.

○ᴙ *Are my expenses in making a charitable gift deductible?*

There can be a number of expenses associated with making a charitable gift, such as appraisal fees, accounting fees, and attorney fees. All expenses in making a charitable gift are deductible, but only to the extent they exceed 2 percent of the donor's adjusted gross income.

METHODS OF
DELIVERING GIFTS

○ᴙ *I've never even thought about making a charitable gift before now and I don't know much about it. What is the best way to make a charitable gift?*

There are numerous possibilities for making charitable gifts, ranging from direct gifts of cash or property to the charity; to contributing through a local community foundation; to delaying, or deferring, the contribution through conduits such as gift annuities or charitable remainder trusts; all the way to setting up your own family foundation (and they can take several forms). Only you can decide which strategy is best for you and your family based upon your own unique circumstances and objectives, as recommended to you by your advisors.

Outright Contributions—Immediate Delivery

○ᴙ *I do not physically have possession of my stock certificates; my broker has them in an investment account. How do I make the gift of stock to my charity?*

Your broker can set up a temporary account for the charity so you can move the stock from your account to the charity's account. Once you've made the transfer, the charity can do whatever it wants with the stock—leave it in the account or instruct the broker to sell the stock and mail the charity a check.

CR *We have some land that has been in the family for many years. Some of it is rough acreage, good for animals and birds but not for farming. None of our children will be returning to the farm, so we want to sell the good farmland. Can we have the rough land set aside for wildlife use so others can enjoy it?*

Yes. You could place a conservation easement on that land to restrict the use and development of the property. Conservation easements are discussed further in Chapter 15, Planning for Real Estate.

Deferred Contributions—Future Delivery

CR *How do I transfer property at my death?*

To qualify for a charitable estate tax deduction, there must be a valid and effective transfer of property by a trust maker's revocable living trust or by a testator's valid will. Gifts to charities by the trust maker's or the testator's beneficiaries are not deductible from the decedent's estate because they are not transfers from the decedent.

Not only must there be a valid transfer at the death of the trust maker or the testator, but the trust or will must specifically state the object and purpose of the charitable gift. If the trust or will fails to specify the charitable beneficiary or fails to limit the bequest to strictly charitable purposes, no charitable estate tax deduction will be allowed. However, the trust maker or testator can clearly state a charitable purpose and authorize his or her trustee or executor to select a charity to receive the bequest.

Other types of qualifying transfers can be estate tax–deductible. We will discuss these transfers in more detail in Chapter 12, Charitable Estate Planning.

CR *How do I name a charity as a beneficiary in my will or trust?*

A good start would be to contact the charity directly to determine the formal name of the charity, whether the charity will accept your gift, and in what form. That may seem strange, but we were recently consulted by the executor of a will that contained a bequest of a substantial amount of money to Alcoholics Anonymous. When the executor contacted AA to arrange for completion of the gift, he was told that AA only accepted gifts from its members and only up to

$2,000. The executor will now have to petition the court to name another charity to receive the money, and what started as a generous gesture by the decedent is now derailed. Either you or your attorney can contact the charity.

Remember, if you want your estate to receive a charitable deduction for your gift, the charity must be qualified; that is, it must be approved as a charity that meets certain requirements found in the Internal Revenue Code. So checking on their status would be your second step.

Here are some examples of how to craft a charitable bequest to a charity:

- *Percentage:* I give, devise, and bequeath to the University Hospital Foundation, located at 111 First Street, Los Angeles, California, five percent (5%) of the residue of my estate.
- *Dollar amount:* I give, devise, and bequeath to the University Hospital Foundation, located at 111 First Street, Los Angeles, California, the sum of ten thousand dollars ($10,000.00).
- *Specific property:* I give, devise, and bequeath to the University Hospital Foundation, located at 111 First Street, Los Angeles, California, all of my right, title, and interest in the real property located at 2021 Second Street, Palm Springs, California. The legal description of the property is Lot 15, of Tract 921, as recorded in book 22, pages 1–4, of the county recorder of said county.

℞ *Can I just name a charity as the beneficiary of a life insurance policy?*

Yes, you can.

Partial-Interest Gifts—Current or Future Delivery

℞ *Can I make a charitable gift of less than an entire interest in a particular piece of property?*

Although a transfer of a "partial interest" in property may be accomplished legally, care must be taken because there are strict tax laws that govern the deductibility of such gifts. Examples of gifts of a partial interest would be a donor wanting to give the family farm or personal residence to charity but still live there during his or her lifetime or a donor who would like to retain the income from an investment for a period of years and then give the principal to charity.

A properly prepared charitable remainder trust, a gift of a remainder interest in a residence or farm, or a gift to a pooled income fund are examples of tax-deductible methods by which a person may accomplish a gift of a partial interest. Experts in estate planning can accomplish the goal of transferring a partial interest in property to a charity and obtaining the tax deductions, so make sure that you consult with your tax advisor before making such a gift.

Charitable Remainder Trusts

CR *What is a charitable remainder trust?*

A *charitable remainder trust (CRT)* is an irrevocable split-interest trust. The donor can transfer assets to the CRT either during the donor's lifetime or upon his or her death. It is a split-interest trust because there are two classes of beneficiaries, noncharitable and charitable, who have an interest in the gift. The noncharitable beneficiaries receive distributions of income from the CRT either for life or for a term of years. When the noncharitable beneficiaries pass away or the term of years ends, the remaining assets of the CRT are distributed to the charitable beneficiaries. We discuss charitable remainder trusts in detail in Chapter 8, Charitable Remainder Trusts and Alternatives.

Pooled Income Funds

CR *What is a pooled income fund?*

A *pooled income fund* is similar to the charitable remainder split-interest trust in which a noncharitable beneficiary retains the income interest and the remainder interest passes to a charity at the noncharitable beneficiary's death. The major difference is that the donor does not create or control this trust. Instead, the pooled income fund must be maintained by the public charity to which the irrevocable remainder interest is contributed. The instrument governing the fund must require that the property contributed to the fund be commingled with, as well as invested or reinvested with, property contributed by other donors. Property contributed to pooled income funds is limited to cash and publicly traded securities. We discuss pooled income funds in more detail in Chapter 8, Charitable Remainder Trusts and Alternatives.

Charitable Gift Annuities

CR *What is a charitable gift annuity?*

A *charitable gift annuity* is an arrangement whereby you transfer cash or other property to a qualified charity in exchange for a commitment by the charity to pay you a specified amount (an "annuity") each year for a specified term or for the remainder of your life.

The arrangements for gift annuities vary widely, from annuities payable over a fixed period to annuities payable over the life of a single annuitant or survivor annuitants. The donor can structure payments to begin immediately or at a future date. He or she can also set the frequency of the payments so they may be received annually, semiannually, quarterly, monthly, or more frequently.

The transaction is both an acquisition of an annuity and a charitable contribution because the value of the property you transfer to the charity exceeds the value of the annuity. Your charitable contribution, and your charitable income tax deduction, is the value of the property less the value of the annuity. We also discuss charitable gift annuities in Chapter 8, Charitable Remainder Trusts and Alternatives.

Charitable Lead Trusts

CR *What is a charitable lead trust?*

A *charitable lead trust (CLT)* is an irrevocable split-interest trust that is essentially the reverse of a charitable remainder trust. After the donor contributes assets to the CLT, the trust makes distributions of income from these assets to one or more charitable beneficiaries for a specific period of time. At the end of that period, the remaining CLT assets are distributed to the noncharitable beneficiaries who may be the donor, the donor's family, or others. We discuss charitable lead trusts in detail in Chapter 9, Charitable Lead Trusts.

Bargain Sales

ℭ *Can I get a deduction if I sell property to a charity for less than fair market value?*

Yes. This transaction is known as a *bargain sale.* When you make a bargain sale to a qualified charity, the excess of the fair market value of the property over the sales price is a charitable contribution to the charity.

ℭ *Why would someone want to make a bargain sale to a charity?*

Often a donor is in a position to donate only part of the property to a charity. A bargain sale is one way to make a partial-interest gift because it is both a sale and a gift. The donor would still have to pay income taxes on the difference between the sale price and his or her cost basis in the property. The value exceeding the sale price is the gift portion. In a carefully constructed transaction, the charitable deduction can offset all or most of the tax due on the sale portion.

Here's an example. Joseph retired and moved to sunnier climes but still owned a rental property in his hometown. It became increasingly burdensome to continue to manage the property, but the tax bite on a sale was unattractive. Joseph felt that the hometown hospital had done a wonderful job of caring for his mother and he wanted to do something for the hospital in return and in her memory. Joseph could not afford to give the property away just to avoid the taxes on a sale. Instead, he sold the property to the hospital's charitable foundation for half of its value and received a charitable income tax deduction for the other half, because the deduction for the half of the property that he donated offset the gain (over Joseph's cost basis) on the half that he sold. The final result was that Joseph paid no tax on the sale. It is hard to put a value on the satisfaction of making a gift, but Joseph was happy and satisfied with the transaction, because he was able to make a gift in memory of his mother and receive his sale proceeds free of income tax.

Loans

ℭ *I made a charitable gift a couple of years ago and am carrying over the income tax deduction. I cannot deduct any additional charitable gifts this year but would like to help my favorite charity. Is there a method for me to give additional amounts to charity and receive some financial benefit?*

You could consider giving a below-market or interest-free loan. As a general rule, loans that do not carry a sufficient rate of interest result in negative tax consequences to the borrower and debtor, but there is an exception to this general rule for loans made to charity, up to a maximum of $250,000 at any time during the tax year. Under this exception, you could make an interest-free loan to your charity and not have to recognize the foregone interest as income.

While you will not receive an income tax deduction for the loan, you are still helping your charity with minimal financial impact to you because you are reducing your taxable income: you are lending funds to the charity that you might otherwise be investing and creating taxable income for you.

❧ *Can you give me an example of how this interest-free loan can help me to make a gift to charity and still get tax advantages?*

Sure. Let's assume that the local YMCA wants to add on to its pool center. Guy and Cindy have already made maximum charitable contributions to a capital campaign for the YMCA but really want to help in this remodeling project that will cost the YMCA $500,000. Guy and Cindy lend the YMCA $250,000 for a period of 4 years at zero interest. This $250,000 was in a 6 percent CD earning $15,000 annually. Guy and Cindy are in the maximum 39.6 percent tax bracket, so they will save $5,940 each year in income tax. They no longer have the $250,000 earning income; the YMCA has the $250,000, which it can use to help pay for the pool remodeling.

DONOR'S RESTRICTIONS
ON THE CHARITY'S USE
OF THE GIFT

❧ *Is it possible for my gift to revert to my family if it is not used by the charity in the manner I specify?*

Yes, it is possible, perhaps even common, but not necessarily desirable, to have your charitable gift revert to family members if your wishes are not met. Perhaps the best example of this involves the Woburn Baptist Church of Woburn, Massachusetts. In the mid-1800s, the Woburn Baptist Church held its services in the top floor of a block of buildings on the main street of Woburn. Most of the churches in the community had similar arrangements. The building in which the Baptist church met was owned by a church's member, and she left it to the congregation on her death with the provision that if the building ever ceased to be used by the church for its services, the building would revert to her heirs. Over the years, the character of downtown Woburn changed, and, as the street became a busy thoroughfare and as commercial activity increased, the other churches left the downtown area for new buildings. The Woburn Baptist Church did not, because the congregation did not want to lose the value of their building. As the building became a less and less attractive place to worship, the membership declined until the congregation ceased to exist. At that point, the building reverted to the family. The family sold the building and distributed the proceeds to a large number of heirs, all of whom were born long after the donor died and few of whom had ever heard of her existence. The moral of this story is that a reversion may not have the desired consequences.

If the donor had left the building to the church with the provision that the church could sell the building as long as it reinvested the proceeds in a new church, the congregation might still be active today. Instead, the gift of love that she intended to support her church led to its demise.

PART TWO

Fundamentals of Charitable Tax Deductions

To ENCOURAGE PEOPLE TO GIVE TO CHARITY, CONGRESS, LONG ago, chose to authorize tax deductions for charitable gifts to acknowledge that charities take a great burden off the government. In the end, the more we Americans give to charity, the less the government has to provide through tax dollars. This simple idea has grown into a series of rules that are confusing, not only to the general public but also to most tax practitioners.

Charitable giving in the face of a slowing economy and the tragic events of September 11, 2001, demonstrates the fundamentally charitable nature of the American people. While our contributing authors submitted answers suggesting that charity should be done for its own sake—and in our experience and in that of the hundreds of advisors we mentor, people who give are *not* primarily motivated by taxes—it is still important that you understand the basics of charitable deductions for income, estate, and gift tax purposes when you are considering a planned giving program.

More questions arise about the income tax deductibility of charitable gifts than any other aspect of charitable giving, and a great number of those questions are in chapter 5. Our contributors' answers cover all aspects of the income tax effects of charitable giving, especially as they relate to the percentage limitations and technical rules.

Interestingly, the questions that clients ask our contributing authors indicate that clients who are involved in charitable giving are quite sophisticated—although they may not know all the details, they have a firm grasp of the income tax implications of charitable giving. Clients seem interested in one topic in particular: whether a gift of appreciated stock to charity is superior to a gift of cash. These questions were submitted at a time when the stock market was particularly volatile. The implication is that people still own a great deal of highly appreciated stock and are considering giving it to charity. We are quite heartened by this interest in giving stocks to charity; it demonstrates a continuing interest by many people to support charitable causes even in times of economic uncertainty.

Chapter 5 goes a long way in taking the mystery out of the rules surrounding the income tax deductibility of charitable gifts. Those taxpayers with a philanthropic bent will appreciate how these questions and answers put those rules in perspective.

Federal gift and estate taxes have been the subject of a great deal of controversy and debate, culminating in the Economic Growth and Tax Relief Reconciliation Act of 2001 (EGTRRA, or the 2001 tax act). Unfortunately, the 2001 tax act has done a disservice to the public, as well as to planning professionals. Rather than reforming or clarifying federal estate and gift taxes, it has made responsible planning more difficult than ever before. While the federal estate and gift tax laws in effect prior to the 2001 tax act were not perfect, this new law has created such a degree of uncertainty that people are afraid to plan. This reluctance to plan is understandable; however, it is also dangerous. The danger arises because no planning—or living with an outdated plan—may result in higher taxes for many people with taxable estates. It may even result in unintended heirs receiving inheritances while disinheriting those who should have received that property.

Our contributors, in an effort to dispel uncertainty and motivate people to plan, offer a number of questions and answers that give an overview of the new law and contrast it to the old law. Charitable giving can play a significant role in estate planning, and our contributors introduce some of the fundamental concepts for lifetime charitable giving and testamentary (at death) transfers to charity. With chapter 6 as a foundation, you should be able to understand how both lifetime and testamentary gifts to charity affect the federal estate and gift taxes that they may be liable to pay. After reading the chapter, you will certainly understand that now, more than ever, estate and wealth strategies planning is critical to you and your family and you will understand how charitable giving can in fact compliment your plan.

Because charitable contributions often involve property rather than cash, Congress and the Internal Revenue Service are very concerned about establishing the value of charitable gifts and making sure that charities actually receive the donations. To accomplish these objectives, the Internal Revenue Code and its regulations contain numerous rules that must be meticulously complied with by taxpayers who seek to deduct charitable contributions. Chapter 7 describes the rules that govern the valuation and substantiation requirements for charitable contributions. And, because many gifts will be deductible according to their fair market value, our contributing authors submitted questions and answers that address fundamental rules about valuation and those elements that constitute fair market value. They also offer excellent suggestions about appraising different types of property.

In addition to the valuation issues, the clients of our contributing authors ask regularly about record keeping for income tax–deductible charitable contributions; and it's no wonder. The rules are different for small, medium, and large gifts. Many of these rules apply to all gifts, but some apply only to gifts that fall within a particular value range. Making sense out of the rules can be a Herculean task, which our contributing authors were up to.

This chapter is a wonderful summary of the principles of valuation and the substantiation rules. While you may not be an expert after reading this chapter, you will certainly have a better perspective of what it takes for a charitable gift to qualify for an income tax deduction and an appreciation of why your tax preparer asks for so much information.

chapter 5

Federal Charitable
Income Tax Deductions

℧ *What does it mean to get a federal charitable income tax deduction?*

Congress enacted the first income tax deduction for charitable gifts in 1917 as part of the first Internal Revenue Code (IRC). Individual taxpayers were allowed charitable deductions for contributions or gifts "to corporations or associations organized and operated exclusively for religious, charitable, scientific, or educational purposes, or to societies for the prevention of cruelty to children or animals...."

Since then, Congress continues to encourage charitable giving by adding more charitable contribution income tax deductions. Presently, IRC Section 170 provides that, for federal income tax purposes, an individual who itemizes his or her deductions on Schedule A is permitted to deduct from adjusted gross income (AGI) charitable contributions made if the requirements of Section 170 are satisfied. As we'll see below, these requirements include percentage limitations for the deductions, the types of organizations to which the deductible charitable contributions are being made, and the types of property interests being donated.

∝ *What is the purpose of the income tax deduction for charitable gifts?*

Although many people investigate the tax ramifications of charitable giving, few make gifts solely because of the tax benefits. People make gifts for much deeper reasons, most often because they want to benefit society in some way. Nevertheless, income tax deductions are available to encourage and reward charitable giving.

∝ *I feel funny deducting my charitable contributions. Shouldn't charitable giving be motivated solely by the spirit of giving?*

The federal government has long recognized the inefficiencies of distributing the tax dollars earmarked for the public good to the right places through our federal tax system. As a result, Congress passed laws to motivate people to give to charity. If you do not wish to take advantage of this right, that is your decision. However, the government encourages and rewards charitable giving by offering incentives in the form of tax deductions.

LIMITATIONS ON THE FEDERAL CHARITABLE INCOME TAX DEDUCTION FOR INDIVIDUALS

∝ *May I deduct 100 percent of my charitable contribution against my income taxes?*

Yes, up to a point. Since 1917, the deduction for charitable contributions has been limited to a percentage of the donor's income. These so-called percentage limitations have been modified from time to time by Congress, reflecting its intent to encourage or discourage certain kinds of contributions to particular charities. The limitations, though, are so generous that they usually only affect deductibility of larger gifts.

In some cases, the entire charitable income tax deduction may not be used in the year of the contribution because of limitations on the deduction. These limitations are based upon the type of organization to which the gift is made, the type of property given, and the manner in which the gift is made. The impact of these limitations can be disappointing to the uninformed. In the final analysis, the only way to determine how much charitable income tax deduction you can use in any year is to "run the numbers." Your professional advisors will be able to do this for you in advance of making the gift.

CR *What are the limitations for deducting charitable gifts?*

While there is no limitation on the amount you can give to charity in a year, there is a limitation on how much is income tax–deductible in 1 year. An individual donor's charitable deduction is limited in any tax year to an amount not greater than 20, 30, or 50 percent of his or her contribution base (defined in the next answer). A taxpayer's deduction for a charitable gift will fall under one of these three percentage limits, determined by

- whether the donation is made "to" or "for the use of" the charity,
- the type of charity that receives the donation, and
- the type of asset given by the taxpayer.

To the extent that any limitation prevents full use of the deduction in the year of the gift, the taxpayer may carry over the deduction for up to 5 additional years.

Table 5-1 at the end of this chapter contains a summary of these limitations to help in your review of this chapter.

Contribution Base

CR *What is a donor's contribution base?*

A donor's *contribution base* is defined as the donor's AGI, not including any net operating loss carry-back deduction. For those who do not claim a net operating loss carry back, which is a majority of all taxpayers, the contribution base is the same as AGI.

Cost Basis

CR *What does the term cost basis mean?*

Cost basis is the cost of the asset plus certain capital improvements less depreciation or depletion. When capital assets are sold, there is generally a tax on the difference between the cost basis of the asset and its sales price. Depending on the nature of the asset, a gain can be taxed at ordinary-income tax rates (ordinary-income property), at short-term capital gain rates (essentially ordinary rates), or at long-term capital gain rates (long-term gain property).

If you are considering making a charitable gift of anything other than cash, you should know what your cost basis of that asset is. This knowledge is especially important if one of the cost-basis rules of charitable giving applies to the property you are giving away. If you do not know the cost basis of an item of property, the presumption is that your basis is zero, which may mean no income tax deduction is allowable. To avoid this, always keep track of how much you paid for and when you acquired property and what and when you received property as a gift or bequest.

"To" or "for the Use of" the Charity

Cℜ *What is the difference between making a gift "to" or "for the use of" a charitable organization?*

A gift "to" a charitable organization is one that is given outright to the charity for its immediate use.

In contrast, a gift "for the use of" a charitable organization is a gift of an income or other interest in property that is almost always held in a trust. An example of a gift "for the use of" a charitable organization is a gift of property to a charitable lead trust (CLT). A CLT pays income to a charity for a period of time. When that time ends, the principal of the CLT is distributed to noncharitable beneficiaries, who are named by the trust maker. Such a gift to a charity would be considered a gift "for the use of" the charity, because the charity's interest is the income interest only.

Cℜ *How does a donation "to" or "for the use of" the charity affect the charitable income tax deduction?*

If property is held "for the use of" a public charity, the allowable deduction is limited to no more than 30 percent of the donor's contribution base versus 50 percent in most instances for a donation "to" the public charity.

Type of Charity

Public Charities

ଔ *To what charities can I make charitable contributions and receive the 50 percent deduction?*

The 50 percent deduction limitation applies to charitable organizations commonly referred to as public charities. Public charities, for purposes of the 50 percent limitation, include the following:

- Churches
- Educational institutions, such as primary, secondary, preparatory, and high schools; colleges and universities; and organizations that benefit certain state and municipal colleges and universities
- Hospitals and medical research organizations and facilities whose principal purpose or function is medical or hospital care medical education, or medical research
- Governmental units
- Organizations that normally receive a substantial part of their support from state or federal governments or the general public
- Private operating foundations
- Supporting organizations
- Distributing and common-fund private nonoperating foundations

Most charities, other than private nonoperating foundations and semipublic charities, are treated as public charities for purposes of calculating charitable income tax deductions.

Private Foundations

ଔ *What is my income tax deduction for a gift to a private foundation?*

The income tax deduction for a gift to a private foundation has a ceiling of 20 percent, 30 percent, or sometimes even 50 percent of your contribution base, depending on the type of property you contribute and the type of private foundation receiving the donation.

◌ My attorney tells me that there are two types of private foundations. What are they and how are donations to them treated for income tax purposes?

There are two types of private foundations: private operating foundations and private nonoperating foundations. The primary difference between the two has to do with their activities. Generally, a private operating foundation actively carries on charitable activities, such as operating a homeless shelter. A private nonoperating foundation simply makes grants out of its assets to other charities.

Private operating foundations, for purposes of deducting donations, are treated like public charities. Cash contributions to private operating foundations, many of which are family foundations, are eligible for the 50 percent tax deduction, just like public charities. Gifts of capital gain property are eligible for the 30 percent limitation just like public charities.

Private nonoperating foundations have a different set of deduction rules. Gifts of cash, ordinary-income property, and short-term capital gain property to a private nonoperating foundation are eligible for the 30 percent limitation. The 20 percent limitation applies to any gift of long-term capital gain property made to a private nonoperating foundation.

There are two exceptions to this rule. *Common-fund* and *distributing private foundations* are nonoperating foundations, but gifts to these two types of foundations have the same deduction limitations as gifts made to public charities.

◌ Do I receive an income tax deduction if I donate long-term capital gain property to a private nonoperating foundation?

Yes, you would receive a charitable income tax deduction up to 20 percent of your contribution base. The deduction would be based on your cost basis in the land (i.e., what it originally cost you). The exception to this rule would be a donation of publicly traded securities, which would be based on the fair market value of the securities on the date of the donation.

Supporting Organizations

ℭℛ *What are the income tax deduction limits for contributions to supporting organizations?*

Supporting organizations are public charities for deduction purposes. Cash contributions are limited to 50 percent of the donor's contribution base; and deductions for contributions of long-term capital gain property are based on the property's fair market value up to 30 percent of the donor's contribution base.

Semipublic Charities

ℭℛ *What is a semipublic charity? What are the percentage limitations for donations to semipublic charities?*

As a reminder, this category includes organizations of war veterans (and some affiliates), domestic fraternal organizations, and certain cemetery companies. Contributions to semipublic charities are limited to 30 percent of the donor's contribution base, except for contributions of long-term gain property, which are limited to 20 percent of the donor's contribution base.

Type of Property

ℭℛ *Does the type of property I contribute affect my income tax deduction?*

Yes, it does. The Internal Revenue Code basically classifies donated property as one of the following types:

- cash;
- ordinary-income property, including short-term capital gain property;
- long-term capital gain property; or
- tangible personal property.

There are also special rules that apply to some types of stock, life insurance, and annuities.

Cash

∾ *To what extent are cash gifts deductible?*

A donor making a cash gift to a public charity can deduct up to 50 percent of his or her contribution base. Similarly, cash gifts to private nonoperating foundations and to semipublic charities are deductible at 30 percent of the donor's contribution base.

∾ *I want to give my alma mater a sizable gift and plan to make a pledge of $250,000, payable in cash over 5 years. Can I deduct the full pledge in the year I make it?*

No. As an individual, you are a cash-basis taxpayer and can only deduct contributions that you actually pay during a given tax year.

Ordinary-Income Property

∾ *What does ordinary-income property mean in the context of charitable giving?*

Ordinary-income property is defined as any property that, if sold, would generate income that is taxed at either ordinary-income or short-term capital gain tax rates. Examples of ordinary-income property are the inventory of a business, U.S. savings bonds, or any investment that has not been held long enough to be taxed at the long-term capital gain tax rate.

∾ *If I donate ordinary-income property to a charity, what is the tax deduction?*

When you give ordinary-income property to a charity—it doesn't matter if it is a public charity or a private foundation—the value of the donation for calculating your deduction is limited to your cost basis. If you give ordinary-income property to a public charity, your deduction is the amount of your cost basis in the property up to 50 percent of your contribution base. If you give it to a private foundation or a semipublic charity, your deduction is limited to 30 percent of your contribution base.

QR *If my wife and I contribute appreciated property that we've had for less than 1 year, will we be able to deduct the full fair market value of the property?*

Appreciated capital gain property that you have owned for 1 year or less is "short-term capital gain property," which is taxed as ordinary-income property, and is deductible only at its cost basis, at the same percentage limitations as for gifts of cash.

QR *Can I donate U.S. savings bonds to charity?*

Series E, EE, H, and HH are the most common varieties of savings bonds; however, they are not particularly attractive as charitable donations while you are alive. If you transfer ownership of the bonds to a charity, you will have to pay income tax on all of the income that has accumulated. You are better off making charitable contributions of appreciated stock or real estate, because you can usually deduct the entire value of the gift without paying tax on any long-term gain.

After your death, however, these bonds become very attractive sources for a charitable bequest. If you leave the bonds to charity at death, the income tax on all of the accrued income is forgiven and your estate will also get a charitable estate tax deduction. Consequently, you get to "double dip."

To get this favorable outcome at your death, you must provide specific instructions in your will or trust that the bonds are to be given outright to a charity. This is a simple but extremely important requirement. If you fail to comply with this requirement, your estate will have to pay income tax on all of the accrued income and it would not be able to claim the offsetting charitable income tax deduction for the donation to the charity. You can obtain detailed information about U.S. savings bonds at the U.S. savings bond Internet website: www.publicdebt.treas.gov/sav/sav.htm.

QR *I have a $100,000 face value, whole life insurance policy that I purchased when my children were very young. I no longer need this life insurance because my children are adults now and financially independent. Is there a way for me to give this policy* *to a charitable organization and receive an immediate charitable income tax deduction for the gift?*

Yes. If you make an irrevocable assignment of the life insurance policy to the charitable organization, you will be allowed a federal charitable income tax deduction for the fair market value of the policy or the net premium paid, whichever is less.

ભ *If I make an irrevocable assignment of my life insurance policy to a charity, can I deduct future premiums paid on that policy?*

Yes, and you will receive an annual income tax deduction for the net premiums that you pay in the future.

Long-Term Capital Gain Property

ભ *What is long-term capital gain property for purposes of charitable giving?*

Long-term capital gain property is property that is held for more than 1 year and, if sold, generates income that is taxed at the long-term capital gain rate. Most investment assets, such as real estate, securities, and property used in a trade or business, are long-term capital gain property.

ભ *If my husband and I contribute appreciated property that we've had for 10 years, will we be able to deduct the full fair market value of the property?*

Appreciated property that you have held for *longer* than 1 year is long-term capital gain property and is subject to several different rules:

- Your contributions to public charities are deductible for their full fair market value up to 30 percent of your contribution base or, if you choose, they are deductible for your cost basis in the property up to 50 percent of your contribution base.
- Your contributions to semipublic charities are deductible at their fair market value but are limited to 30 percent of your contribution base.
- Your contributions to private nonoperating foundations are

deductible at their cost basis but only up to 20 percent of your contribution base. However, qualified appreciated stock that you contribute to a private nonoperating foundation is deductible for its full fair market value up to 20 percent of your contribution base for the year.

ൟ *I have been told that I can choose either fair market value or the cost basis as the value for a donation of long-term capital gain property to a public charity. What does this mean?*

For donations of all long-term capital gain property to public charities, instead of using the fair market value of the property as the value of the contribution and a 30 percent deduction limitation, by election, you may use the property's cost basis as its value and be eligible to deduct up to 50 percent of your contribution base.

ൟ *Why would I elect to limit a charitable deduction for long-term capital gain property to my cost basis?*

It sounds a little silly at first, but if you have a high basis in the property—that is, there has been little appreciation in the property's value since you purchased it—it may be better to limit the deduction to cost basis and increase your percentage limitation to 50 percent of your contribution base.

ൟ *What if the fair market value of the property we want to contribute has decreased to less than what we paid for it?*

In a capital-loss situation, your deduction will be limited to the property's fair market value, as opposed to its cost basis. When this happens, it is generally advisable to sell the property, take the tax loss (which you would lose if you contributed the property to the charity), and then contribute the proceeds to the charity. For example, let's say you purchased stock 2 years ago for $10,000 and the stock is now worth $6,000. You are considering donating that stock to the local chapter of the YMCA. If you give the stock to the YMCA, your charitable deduction is limited to $6,000, its fair market value on the date of your gift. You would waste the $4,000 loss in the stock. In this instance, it would be better to sell the stock so you can claim the loss on your income tax return, then give the cash to the YMCA.

CR I've heard that if I give publicly traded stock to a private foundation, it is deductible at its fair market value rather than at my cost basis. Is this true?

It is true. Appreciated publicly traded stock is deductible at its fair market value, up to 20 percent of the donor's contribution base. This special rule for publicly traded stock is the exception to the general rule that long-term capital gain property contributed to a private foundation is valued at its cost basis for purposes of the charitable income tax deduction.

CR What is the advantage of giving appreciated stock over just writing a check?

You can give much more to the charities of your choice by giving appreciated stock. Because you receive a tax deduction for the amount of your gift and also avoid paying capital gain taxes on the stock, it costs less for you to donate stock than cash; thus, you can donate more stock. Let's look at an example.

Assume you are in the 36 percent federal income tax bracket and the tax on capital gains is 20 percent. If you give cash to charity, you receive a tax deduction for the gift. Your net out-of-pocket expense to make the gift is $6,400.

Cash gift	$10,000
Less:	
Tax saved on deduction	3,600
Cost of gift	$ 6,400

Contrast that result with giving an equal amount of stock that cost you $2,500. Your actual out-of-pocket cost for making the gift in the form of stock would only be $4,900.

Stock gift	$10,000	
Less:		
Tax saved on deduction	3,600	
Capital gain tax avoided	1,500	($7,500 × 20%)
Cost of gift	$ 4,900	

Under this scenario, you could donate $3,500 more in stock to charity (total $13,500) at approximately the same cost as a $10,000 gift of cash.

Stock gift	$13,500	
Less:		
Tax saved on deduction	4,860	
Capital gain tax avoided	2,200	($11,000 × 20%)
Cost of gift	$ 6,440	

⋒ Is stock the only kind of appreciated asset that would be advantageous to give to charity instead of cash?

Publicly traded stock is the most common type of appreciated asset that is donated to charity. There are three reasons for the popularity in giving stock. First, over time, stock has been one of the most highly appreciating assets. Second, stock is easy to transfer. Many people hold their stocks in accounts with brokerage firms. It is simple to have the brokerage firm make the transfer. Finally, publicly traded stock is easy to value. No appraisal is necessary as long as the stock can be valued on an established market.

Other assets, such as real estate, closely held stock, or nonpublicly traded investments, require an appraisal. Appraisals can be costly and difficult, thereby reducing the benefits that may make it more advantageous than giving cash.

Gifts of tangible personal property, such as artwork or other collections, can also be difficult to value. In addition, if gifts of tangible personal property are donated to a charity and the property is not used for or related to the charity's charitable purpose, the deduction is limited to the cost basis of the property.

For these reasons, stock is by far the better type of asset to donate to charity in lieu of cash, if it is possible to do so. However, it is always wise to explore all of your alternatives with your tax advisors to determine which assets are best suited for you to donate in your particular situation.

⋒ Are there any restrictions if I want to contribute property with a mortgage on it?

A charitable contribution of debt-encumbered property, made during your life, may result in adverse income tax consequences to you, as the donor.

When property that is subject to debt is transferred to charity, certain rules, known as *bargain-sale rules,* apply. Under these rules, you are considered to have received proceeds from a sale in the amount of the debt, regardless of whether the charity agrees to assume the debt. The gain that you have to realize on the sale is allocated between what you have theoretically sold and what you have contributed. The amount contributed is essentially the difference between the fair market value of the property and the debt on it.

> *Can you give me an example of how you have to allocate the capital gain in a bargain sale?*

Sure. Jerry Williams contributes to a public charity a parcel of real estate that he has held as an investment for 5 years. On the date of the transfer, the property has a fair market value of $250,000, a cost basis of $150,000, and a mortgage of $100,000.

Under the bargain-sale rules, Jerry is considered to have received $100,000 in sale proceeds, the amount of the outstanding mortgage, even though he did not actually receive any cash in the transaction. Jerry's allowable contribution deduction is $150,000, the excess of the fair market value over the debt. In determining gain on the transaction, Jerry must allocate 60 percent, or $90,000, of his cost basis to the contribution portion of the transaction ([$150,000/ $250,000] × $150,000). The remaining 40 percent, or $60,000, of his cost basis is allocated against the $100,000 sales portion of the gift, yielding a long-term capital gain of $40,000 ($100,000 − $60,000) on the transaction.

> *I'm considering giving some rental property to a charity. Over the years, I've taken substantial income tax deductions for depreciation of the property. Will that affect my deduction?*

It might. The Internal Revenue Code requires taxpayers to *recapture* certain depreciation deductions when they sell a depreciated asset. Recapture means that the gain that would otherwise be taxed as a capital gain is converted into ordinary income and taxed at 25 percent. In the context of a charitable gift, the IRC requires taxpayers to reduce the value of the donated property by any amount that would be treated as ordinary income if sold.

For example, Tony contributes a duplex to a church. The property has a fair market value of $60,000 and an adjusted basis of

$10,000. At the time of the contribution, Tony had owned the property for several years as rental property and, over the years, had taken depreciation deductions totaling $20,000 on the property. If Tony had sold the property at its fair market value at the time of the contribution, $20,000 of the $50,000 gain would have been recaptured and $30,000 would have been long-term capital gain. Tony's contribution of $60,000 would be reduced by $20,000.

CR *Does a donation to a charity in exchange for a charitable gift annuity result in an upfront deduction?*

A *charitable gift annuity (CGA)* is a contract between a charity and a donor under which the donor donates property to the charity and, in return, the charity promises to pay a periodic, fixed amount over the life of the donor, or donors in the case of a married couple. The donor is allowed to deduct, in the year he or she purchases the CGA, the difference between the fair market value of the property he or she contributed to the charity and the present value of the annuity. The present value of an annuity is based on the age(s) of the annuitant(s) and a rate of return usually determined by the American Council of Gift Annuities. If the entire deduction cannot be used in the current year, the donor can carry the deduction forward up to 5 additional years and take the deduction against future income.

CR *How do I determine which percentage limitations apply to a CGA?*

CGAs are almost exclusively provided by public charities, so the 50 percent limitation applies to CGAs that are purchased with cash and 30 percent for CGAs that are traded for long-term capital gain property.

Tangible Personal Property

CR *What is tangible personal property?*

Tangible personal property includes works of art, collections, manuscripts and papers, and other items of property that are not real property and are not intangible property. Examples of *intangible property* are stocks, bonds, partnership interests, and other assets that are not valuable in and of themselves but represent ownership in something else.

ᐁ I have a significant art collection and I would like to begin giving the collection to charity during my life. Would I get a tax deduction for such a gift?

Yes, you would receive an income tax deduction for a lifetime contribution of the artwork to a qualified charity. The amount of your deduction would depend on

- the type of charitable organization,
- what the organization would do with the artwork, and
- how you would be taxed if you were to sell the artwork.

The amount of your deduction would depend on whether the charity was a public charity or a private foundation. If the contribution is to a public charity, the charity must be able to use the artwork for a related purpose for you to receive the full fair market value deduction for the gift. In other words, the charity must use the art in a way that is consistent with its charitable purpose. If it is long-term capital gain property, you would be entitled to receive the full fair market value deduction, limited to the 30 percent limitation.

ᐁ I have a painting that I would like to give to a local charity. It would look great in its reception area, and perhaps the charity could sell it some day. Can I deduct the value of the painting as a charitable contribution?

Under the Internal Revenue Code, a donor who donates tangible personal property to a public charity, where the charity does not use the property for a purpose that is related to its charitable purposes, may only deduct the cost basis of the property, not its fair market value. The donation does, however, qualify for the 50 percent limitation.

Contributions of tangible personal property whose use is unrelated to the exempt purpose of a private foundation are deductible at cost basis and qualify for the lower 20 percent limitation.

It appears that your painting would not be used for your charity's exempt purposes, so your deduction would be limited to your cost basis. Perhaps you should consider giving your painting to an art museum, which has the collection and preservation of works of art as its exempt purpose. If you have owned the painting for more than 1 year, you would be able to deduct the fair market value of your painting, although your deduction will be limited to 30 percent of your contribution base.

ᝊ I am a painter and a local art museum has asked me to donate one of my paintings to the museum. The museum values this painting at $100,000. The painting is directly related to the museum's purpose. Do I get a $100,000 charitable deduction?

No. Because you created this property, it is considered ordinary-income property and your deduction is limited to your cost basis. The fact that the painting is related to the museum's purpose is irrelevant in this instance.

ᝊ What if I give the American Cancer Society my old Thunderbird that's been in my garage for the past 10 years and is worth about $25,000? Can I deduct that as if it were cash?

Not necessarily. If you give your car to the American Cancer Society and it sells the car to obtain money for cancer research, the amount of your charitable deduction will be for your cost basis, because the Cancer Society can't use your car to fulfill its primary purpose. However, if you donate your car to the Salvation Army and it gives the Thunderbird to a needy family to use for transportation, you would probably get the full fair market value deduction, because the car was used to fulfill a primary purpose of the Salvation Army.

LIMITATIONS ON THE FEDERAL CHARITABLE INCOME TAX DEDUCTION FOR ENTITIES

ᝊ What are the annual limitations for charitable donations by businesses?

Businesses come in a number of different forms, so the limitations differ. Generally, businesses that file an income tax return and pay taxes separate and apart from their owners, such as C corporations, have one set of rules. Businesses, such as S corporations and partnerships, that are *pass-through* entities, meaning they do not pay federal income taxes separate and apart from their owners, have different rules.

ᗡ *I own a C corporation. Are the deduction rules the same for contributions that my corporation may make?*

No. The rules governing deductibility of charitable gifts for C corporations are significantly simpler than for individuals. Contributions by C corporations are eligible for deductions of up to 10 percent of their adjusted taxable income, regardless of the type of property it is donating or the type of charity receiving the donation. A 5-year carryover is available. C corporations on the accrual basis may, in some instances, deduct contributions in the current tax year even though they are not making the payment until the following tax year. Corporations may not, however, deduct contributions to semipublic charities.

As with individuals, corporations can only deduct ordinary-income and short-term gain property at their cost basis. Special rules apply in the case of contributions of inventory and qualifying scientific equipment to educational and scientific organizations.

ᗡ *What are the rules for deducting charitable contributions for an S corporation or partnership?*

Partnerships and S corporations are pass-through entities. They do not pay income taxes at the entity level but pass their tax items through to partners and shareholders. Thus, contributions by partnerships and S corporations are allocated and passed through to the individual partners and shareholders who take the deductions on their individual returns as if they had made the contributions.

ᗡ *Are there nontax reasons why a business would want to make charitable gifts?*

Many businesses find that charitable giving is an essential part of their public relations programs and a way for them to participate in local community activities. Quite often, businesses will "lend" employees to charitable activities such as food or clothing drives or community fundraising events.

⟨ℛ What about charitable contributions by my trust or estate? Are they deductible for federal income tax purposes?

Provided the trust or estate is authorized to make the distribution to charity, an estate or trust may deduct income that is distributed to qualified charitable organizations during the estate's or trust's tax year up to 100 percent of its gross income for the year. If your personal representative or trustee makes a proper election, the charitable gift can be made within 12 months after the end of the tax year and still be deductible for the prior year. Because the deduction can equal the estate's or trust's gross income for the year, there is no unused deduction to carry forward to future years.

If it is a *grantor trust* (a trust that does not file a separate tax return but whose tax items appear on its grantor-maker's return), the grantor may take an income tax deduction for distributions made by the trust to qualifying charitable organizations. As an individual taxpayer, the grantor is subject to all of the percentage limitations and other rules governing deductibility of charitable gifts.

CALCULATING FEDERAL CHARITABLE INCOME TAX DEDUCTIONS

⟨ℛ Can you give me an example of how to calculate these limitations?

We can give you a couple of examples:

- William and Cindy have a contribution base of $100,000 in 2002 and give $60,000 in cash to their church and the Salvation Army during the year. Both charities are public charities, so the 50 percent limitation applies. Their charitable income tax deduction for 2002 is $50,000 (half of their contribution base), even though they contributed $60,000 during the year.

- This example is the same as the one listed above, except William and Cindy make their charitable contribution to the Veterans of Foreign Wars, which is a semipublic charity. Their charitable income tax deduction for 2002 is $30,000 (30 percent of $100,000).

CR In both of these examples, the donations exceeded the contribution base. Could William and Cindy use the excess deduction later?

Yes. In the first example, they were eligible for a deduction of $50,000 in the year they made the donation and could carry over $10,000 up to 5 years. If their contribution base dropped to $50,000 in the second year, their deduction would be 50 percent of that, or $25,000. For subsequent years, the calculation is similar. Their carryover is good for 5 years after the year in which they made the gift. If they do not use the carryover during that time, they lose it.

CR This year I made contributions to both public and private charities. Some of the contributions qualified for the 50 percent limitation and others for the 30 percent limitation. How do I determine the deduction to which I am entitled?

For any year in which you make contributions to both public and private charities, the 50 percent public charity limitation and the 30 percent private charity limitation must be blended to determine the overall percentage limitation for the year. To determine the final deduction amount, the 30 percent limitation is calculated as the lesser of 30 percent of the donor's contribution base or the excess of 50 percent of the contribution base over the amount of 50 percent contributions.

For example, let's assume that you have a contribution base of $90,000 and made charitable contributions to public and private charities of $25,000 each. The entire $25,000 gift to the public charity is deductible because it is within the 50 percent limitation of the contribution base ($90,000 × 50% = $45,000). You have an excess of $20,000 ($45,000 available, less $25,000 used, equals $20,000 excess).

Thirty percent of your contribution base is $27,000 ($90,000 × 30% = $27,000). Because the $20,000 excess amount is less than the $27,000 of available 30 percent limitation, only $20,000 of the charitable contribution to private charities is deductible for the year. You may carry forward for as long as 5 years the $5,000 that you were not able to deduct this year.

CR Where are my charitable contributions found in my federal income tax Form 1040?

Charitable contributions are itemized deductions taken on Schedule A.

Under present law, if you do not itemize your deductions, you cannot take a charitable income tax deduction. However, legislation now pending in Congress would permit single taxpayers who do not itemize to deduct up to $400 a year for charitable donations and married couples filing jointly to deduct up to $800 a year.

‰ *I made a large contribution to charity last year and was not able to use all of it, even though I met the percentage limitation. How did that happen?*

If you earned a large amount of income last year, your deduction was likely "phased out" by a provision of the Internal Revenue Code. Generally, taxpayers whose adjusted gross incomes exceed a certain amount must reduce the amount of otherwise allowable itemized deductions by the lesser of 3 percent of the excess of adjusted gross income over that amount or 80 percent of the amount of otherwise allowable itemized deductions.

In 2002, a married couple with a gross income exceeding $137,300 is subject to this rule. This amount is adjusted each year for inflation. This limitation itself will be phased out of existence from 2006 through 2010.

‰ *May I make a gift to charity on December 31 and deduct the full amount from that year's taxes?*

The date on which the gift is completed determines in which year the gift is deductible. The most common end-of-year gifts are by check. For gifts of cash paid by check to be deductible within the year in which you make the charitable gift, you must be able to prove that:

- there was a delivery of the check to the charity, without any conditions, within the taxable year;
- the charity presented the check at your bank in a timely manner; and
- the bank paid the check upon presentation.

If these conditions are met, the check "relates back" to the date you delivered it to the charitable organization.

A gift of stock is usually not completed when you give the

instructions to your stockbroker; it is completed only when the stock is received by the charity's stockbroker or by the transfer agent so there is no longer any opportunity for you to take back the stock or get any benefits from it.

There are technical rules with regard to the proper transfer of different kinds of assets. You should consult with your tax advisor so you take the correct steps to ensure that your gift is complete by December 31.

ℂ঺ *When is the best time of year to make a charitable gift?*

Congress has placed no limits on when charitable gifts must be made, other than some time during the taxable year. For most of us, the taxable year is anytime before December 31. Therefore, we control the timing of our giving in the following ways:

- Generally, for gifts of income-producing property or property you use, it is best to make your contributions toward the end of the taxable year. That way, you have the use of the property for most of the year before you make the contribution.

- For other types of property, such as property with a value that might change during the year, you might want to consider making the gift when you think the property value is at its highest so you can maximize the value of your deduction.

- Finally, for property that you are paying to store or that is taking up space in or around your home and its value is not likely to increase with age (such as a used vehicle), you might want to make the contribution sooner rather than later.

TABLE 5-1 Summary of Federal Charitable Income Tax Annual Deduction Limitations

Type of property	All public charities and:			Private nonoperating foundations	Semipublic charities
	Supporting organizations	Private operating foundations	Pooled income funds		
Cash					
Amount deductible	cost basis	cost basis	cost basis	cost basis	cost basis
% limitation	50	50	50	30	30
Ordinary income					
Amount deductible	cost basis	cost basis	cost basis	cost basis	cost basis
% limitation	50	50	50	30	30
Short-term capital gain					
Amount deductible	cost basis	cost basis	cost basis	cost basis	cost basis
% limitation	50	50	50	30	30
Long-term capital gain, in general					
Amount deductible	FMV*	FMV	FMV	cost basis	FMV
% limitation	30	30	30	20	20
Long-term capital gain with election					
Amount deductible	cost basis	cost basis	cost basis	N/A†	N/A
% limitation	50	50	50		
Tangible personal property unrelated to charity's purpose					
Amount deductible	cost basis	cost basis	cost basis	cost basis	cost basis
% limitation	50	50	50	20	20

*FMV = fair market value.
†N/A = not applicable.

chapter 6

Federal Estate and Gift Tax Deductions

FEDERAL ESTATE AND
GIFT TAXES

ᔑ *I thought the estate and gift taxes had been repealed. Why are we still talking about them?*

The Economic Growth and Tax Relief Reconciliation Act of 2001 (EGTRRA, or 2001 tax act) does gradually repeal the federal estate tax and make adjustments to the federal transfer tax system. However, it is unclear whether the federal estate tax will actually be repealed.

Under EGTRRA, the federal estate tax is reduced over a 9-year period ending in 2009. Then the federal estate tax is repealed for persons who die in 2010. EGTRRA actually expires in 2011, and the law as it stood in 2001 prior to EGTRRA is reinstated. Congress does have the option to repeal the federal estate tax permanently after 2009, but has not done so yet. In fact, in 2002, Congress twice failed to pass legislation to make the estate tax repeal permanent.

The federal gift tax remains intact, and the exemption amount for taxable gifts is $1 million. Unlike the federal estate tax applicable exclusion amount, the gift tax exemption does not go up in increments.

TABLE 6-1   Maximum Estate and Gift Tax Rates under EGTRRA

Year	Tax rate (%)
2002	50
2003	49
2004	48
2005	47
2006	46
2007–2009	45
2010	0/35*
2011	55†

*Estate tax repealed/there will still be a federal gift tax with a top rate of 35%.
†EGTRRA expires and estate and gift taxes return to pre-EGTRRA rates.

Thus, the federal estate and gift tax systems are no longer completely unified as they were before EGTRRA.

As we discussed earlier, EGTRRA may not do all it was intended to do. Many political and economic experts believe that this law is unlikely to survive through several congressional changes and one, or potentially two, presidential administrations. It is almost certainly going to be revised or even repealed. Individuals embarking on the process of planned giving should do so within the context of their financial, tax, and estate planning goals to preserve their wealth for themselves and their families while they support their cherished causes.

QR *So what are the new estate and gift tax rates under the 2001 tax act?*

Under the old law, prior to the 2001 tax act, the maximum estate and gift tax rate was 55 percent, except for some large estates that were taxed at 60 percent. Under the new law, the maximum estate and gift tax rates are as shown in Table 6-1.

QR *What are the new exemption amounts?*

The 2001 tax act increased the applicable exclusion amount (AEA) for estate tax, as shown in Table 6-2.

TABLE 6-2   Federal Estate Tax Applicable Exclusion Amount under EGTRRA

Year	Amount
2002	$ 1,000,000
2003	1,000,000
2004	1,500,000
2005	1,500,000
2006	2,000,000
2007	2,000,000
2008	2,000,000
2009	3,500,000
2010	0/1,000,000*
2011	1,000,000[†]

*Estate tax repealed/$1 million gift tax exemption.

[†]EGTRRA expires and AEA returns to pre-EGTRRA levels.

It looks like the applicable exclusion amounts listed in this table apply only to the federal estate tax. Are there any changes to the federal gift tax exemption?

Table 6-2 applies only to the federal estate tax. The gift tax exemption amount increased to $1 million in 2002 and remains at that amount. EGTRRA does away with complete unification of estate and gift taxes. The result is that lifetime taxable gifts are subject to tax if they cumulatively exceed $1 million. Assets in excess of $1 million that you own at death may also be exempt from federal estate tax, depending on the year of death. However, lifetime gifts up to $1 million count against the applicable exclusion amount for estate tax.

For example, if Susan makes taxable gifts of $300,000 in 2002 (and has not made any taxable gifts prior to this), Susan uses $300,000 of her $1 million lifetime gift tax exemption amount. If Susan dies in 2006, the scheduled $2 million estate tax applicable exclusion amount will be reduced by the $300,000 gift tax exemption that Susan used during her life. The resulting $1.7 million of applicable exclusion for federal estate tax is applied to offset Susan's estate tax. Assets that Susan owns in excess of $1.7 million will be subject to federal estate taxes.

It is important to keep in mind that EGTRRA does *not* repeal the gift tax as of 2010. The gift tax remains in place—possibly to make sure that taxpayers do not give away too many of their assets before 2011 to avoid the estate tax later, in the event that Congress does not extend EGTRRA and the old tax law comes back in 2011.

○ℛ *Did the 2001 tax act affect the annual gift tax exclusion?*

No. Individuals can still make annual lifetime gifts that are gift tax–free ($11,000 in 2002) to any number of recipients.

For example, if you have a daughter who is married and has three children, you could give $55,000 in annual exclusion gifts every year ($11,000 each to your daughter, your son-in-law, and the three grandchildren). If you are married, your spouse could do the same, making a total of $110,000 in annual exclusion gifts from both of you. As you can see from this example, you can remove large amounts from your estate without paying any gift taxes or using any of your lifetime gift tax exemption amount. The annual exclusion amount is indexed annually for inflation but will increase only in $1,000 increments.

○ℛ *Are there likely to be further changes to the tax law?*

We would pose historical statistics to answer this question. Commerce Clearing House (CCH), the oldest publisher of tax law information, regularly tracks, reports, explains, and analyzes tax law for professionals and the Internal Revenue Service. Consider their statistics:

- The estate tax was initiated in 1916 and has never been interrupted.
- Between 1986 and 2000, there were approximately 6,559 changes to the Internal Revenue Code.
- The 2001 tax act created 441 changes and added 14 new sections to the IRC.
- The 2001 tax act is the first real decrease in tax rates since the 1986 Tax Reform Act—and then in 1990, Congress raised the rates again.

○ℛ *Do you believe that the estate tax will be repealed?*

Most professionals believe that we will never see a full repeal of the estate tax. The demand for social services between now and 2010 will increase exponentially over today's needs, and it is likely that the federal government will have to expand rather than contract its income sources.

Given that elimination of the estate tax will only affect a small percentage of estates—approximately 2 to 3 percent of the population—Congress's attention will most likely have to focus on the first wave of the 77 million retiring baby boomers and their concomitant drain on Social Security and other governmental safety nets.

Many educated and politically savvy professionals suggest that Congress will simply and quietly let the 2001 tax act expire at the end of 2010 and allow the estate tax to return in full force very much like it was in 2001.

CR *If our estate is less than the applicable exclusion amount, do we still have to plan our estate under the new law?*

Although repeal of the estate tax was technically enacted in the 2001 tax act, it is not scheduled to occur until 2010. That's two presidential and four congressional elections away; time for many more tax changes to intervene. Also, the tax act contains its own "sunset provision" that reinstates the pre-2001 tax act limits in the year 2011, unless Congress intervenes and extends it.

In reality, the new law is very complex and, while these tax changes may relieve you of some transfer tax concerns, they may generate others. Changes in the law necessitate a review of your estate plan with your advisors to ensure that it not only is and remains current but to allow you take advantage of new opportunities created from the new law.

GENERATION-SKIPPING TRANSFER TAXES

CR *What is the generation-skipping transfer tax and why should I care about it in the context of charitable giving?*

The *generation-skipping transfer (GST) tax* applies when you make gifts or bequests in your estate plan to someone who is more than one generation below you; for example, a gift to your grandchild.

Any property that will not be subject to estate or gift taxes as it passes from one generation to the next may be subject to the GST tax, which is imposed on the transferred property at a flat 50 percent rate. This tax is *in addition to* all other estate or gift taxes imposed on the transfer.

Each taxpayer has a GST tax exemption that he or she can use to avoid paying the tax. In 2002, the exemption is $1.1 million, with increases to come in future years. Under the 2001 tax act, the GST tax rate will gradually decrease as the estate tax rates drop. In 2010, the GST tax, along with the estate tax, will be repealed for 1 year until 2011, at which time the GST tax will return with a top rate of 55 percent.

Grandparents can combine GST tax planning with some charitable planning techniques to maximize the use of their GST exemption.

CAPITAL GAIN TAXES AND STEP-UP IN BASIS

What is a step-up in basis and why is it important in estate planning?

Generally, an owner's cost basis in an asset is what he or she initially paid for the asset, plus the cost of any improvements to that asset. The basis is the starting point for computing any gain or loss on the sale or exchange of the asset. For example, let's assume you own an asset that you purchased some years ago for $10,000 (your cost basis) that is now worth $50,000. If you sell the asset today, you have a capital gain of $40,000 on which you would owe an income tax.

Let's suppose you give this asset to your daughter. Because you are still alive when you make the gift, your daughter "steps" into your shoes and "inherits" your $10,000 cost basis as her cost basis. She would have the same $40,000 taxable gain if she were to sell the asset.

Now, let's assume, instead, that you leave the asset to your daughter at your death and it is prior to 2009. Her cost basis in the asset is "stepped-up" to $50,000, the market price as of your date of death. If your daughter were to sell the asset at that time, she would owe no income taxes. If she sells it later, she will owe income taxes only on the gain above the $50,000 stepped-up value.

ন্ন What if I die after December 31, 2009? Don't the step-up-in-basis laws change when the federal estate tax is repealed?

Under EGTRRA, beginning January 1, 2010, the date-of-death *step-up-in-basis* system is replaced with a *carryover-basis* system. This new system provides that the heir not only inherits the asset but also inherits the same basis that the decedent had prior to the decedent's death.

The new carryover-basis law does provide partial relief by allowing a limited step-up in basis for certain assets that were owned by the decedent at his or her death. Beginning in 2010, a decedent's administrator can increase the basis of property owned by the decedent by $1.3 million. Additionally, qualified spousal property is entitled to an additional $3 million increase in basis. *Qualified spousal property* is generally defined as any property that passes outright to a spouse or any property passing to a spouse in trust that would have qualified for the marital deduction against estate tax. With proper planning, spouses have the opportunity to obtain a total basis increase of $4.3 million on the deceased spouse's estate.

ন্ন This $4.3 million step-up seems to be pretty generous. Are there any hidden traps?

Single people, including widows and widowers, and people who may not want a substantial amount of assets to pass to a surviving spouse will not be able to qualify for the full $4.3 million step-up. Complex planning will be required to ensure that a person's planning desires are achieved with the new step-up-in-basis rules.

In addition, the step-up rules do not apply to all assets. Property that creates income in respect of a decedent is excluded. *Income in respect of a decedent (IRD)* is income generated by an asset in the decedent's estate but on which he or she did not pay the income taxes during life. The most common examples of IRD property are qualified retirement plans, individual retirement accounts, nonqualified deferred compensation plans, U.S. savings bonds, and installment notes. IRD property created income tax problems for heirs even before passage of the 2001 tax act; at least this is one area in which it didn't create a new negative effect.

THE CHARITABLE GIFT
TAX DEDUCTION

Isn't the gift tax deduction for a gift to charity the same as the income tax deduction?

The two taxes have their own rules. The gift tax deduction is different from the income tax deduction but, for practical purposes, the rules are virtually the same in most situations.

How do I calculate the gift tax deduction for direct charitable gifts?

Assuming that you made a qualifying transfer to a qualified charity, your gift tax deduction is the same amount as your income tax deduction. The major difference is that you always use 100 percent of your gift tax deduction in the year the gift was made; there is no percentage limitation as there is for the income tax deduction. You file a gift tax return for the taxable year that you made the charitable gift and take the full deduction on that return. (See Chapter 5, Federal Charitable Income Tax Deductions.)

THE CHARITABLE ESTATE
TAX DEDUCTION

Can I make a gift to a charity when I die?

Yes, you can designate anyone you want to receive what you have when you die, including a charity.

Are charitable contributions deductible from estate taxes?

Yes. The Internal Revenue Code allows a deduction from a decedent's gross estate for gifts to qualifying charities for public, charitable, and religious uses. The policy underlying the estate tax deduction is to encourage charitable giving through bequests (gifts of property by will or living trust) and other transfers of the decedent's property occurring on account of death.

☞ *How is the charitable estate tax deduction calculated?*

The charitable estate tax deduction equals the value of the transferred property based on the value included in the donor's gross estate. In other words, the deduction can never be larger than the value of the property that is passing to the charitable beneficiaries. The value of the bequest is deducted from the donor's gross estate.

☞ *Why is a charitable estate tax deduction so important?*

To the extent that you give any portion of your estate to charity, it reduces the value of the estate and, thus, reduces the estate tax. You can even eliminate all estate taxes by giving to charity the amount of your estate that would be subject to estate taxes—sometimes referred to as "zeroing-out" your estate tax.

As an example, Brian dies in 2002 when the federal estate tax applicable exclusion amount is $1 million and his gross estate, for estate tax purposes, is valued at $1.1 million. By making a $100,000 bequest to charity in his will or living trust, Brian reduced his taxable estate to $1 million and saved, roughly, $39,000 in estate taxes.

☞ *At my death, will my estate receive a federal charitable estate tax deduction if I name a charity as the beneficiary of my life insurance policy?*

Yes. Although the death benefit of the policy will be included in your gross estate, no estate tax liability will result from the inclusion because of the offsetting charitable estate tax deduction.

chapter 7

Valuing and Substantiating Contributions

VALUING CHARITABLE CONTRIBUTIONS

CR *Will the Internal Revenue Service require proof of a charitable donation or just take my word for it?*

In the event of an examination, the IRS requires that you be able to substantiate your charitable donations. So, be sure to keep reliable records of your contributions to charity each year. The IRS also requires different types of substantiation depending upon the amount of your donation and whether the donation was of cash or property.

Fair Market Value

CR *When my accountant does my taxes, he asks me for the fair market value of the property I gave to charity. What does fair market value mean?*

Fair market value (FMV) is the price a property would sell for on the open market or, as it is defined in the regulations for the Internal

Revenue Code, "the price at which the property would change hands between a willing buyer and a willing seller, neither being under any compulsion to buy or sell and both having reasonable knowledge of relevant facts." When you sell your house and you and the buyer agree on a price, that is the fair market value of the house. If you buy stock, the FMV of the stock is the price quoted on the stock exchange.

If you give used clothing to a charity, the FMV of that clothing would be the price typical buyers actually pay for clothing of the same age, condition, and style. Usually, such items are worth much less than what you originally paid for them.

The IRS also requires you to reflect any restrictions you may have put on the use of the donated property in your determination of FMV. For example, if you donate land and restrict its use, the FMV must reflect the restriction, even if your land would have a higher FMV if it could be used for any other purpose without the restriction.

Tangible Personal Property

CR *I give used household items, furniture, and clothing to charitable causes and church rummage sales. How do I determine a fair value of these items?*

The Salvation Army and other charities occasionally compile a list of suggested values for such items and make the list available to the general public. You can also use the prices from local thrift shops if you wish to do your own survey.

CR *I purchased a hand-crocheted christening gown at a charity auction. On the bid sheet and on my receipt, the charity showed the value as "priceless." What can I deduct on my income taxes, if anything?*

Enjoy your rare find. Unless you can convince the charity to give you an actual value for the gown, you may take no charitable contribution deduction. The charity probably had as difficult a time valuing the item as you are having, because it is hard to price the many hours of labor that went into making this item. However, it is the charity's responsibility to set a value, even when the donor does not. If you do establish the fair market value for the gown, you can only deduct the difference between the FMV and what you paid, assuming, of course, that what you paid was greater.

ભ *What if I donate a used car or a boat to charity? How would I research the FMV of these assets?*

There are regularly published guides that provide complete dealer sale prices or dealer average prices for most types of vehicles. They report prices for each make, model, and year of used automobile, recreational vehicle, boat, and aircraft. They also provide estimates for making adjustments for unusual equipment on the vehicle, unusually high mileage, and physical condition. The automobile *Blue Book* is an example and the one that most people are probably familiar with. You can pick up these guides at most banks, credit unions, or finance companies.

As for boats, unless it's a small, inexpensive craft, the FMV of a boat should be based on an appraisal by a marine surveyor, because a boat's physical condition is so critical to its value. Also, if the car is a rare, collectible vehicle, it should be appraised by a professional appraiser.

Publicly Traded Securities

ભ *I would like to satisfy my annual stewardship obligation to my church through a gift of stock. The value of the stock changes with fluctuations in the market. How do I determine the value of this gift?*

The deduction for a charitable contribution of publicly traded stock is determined by its value at the time of its delivery. Note that state law controls when delivery takes place. Therefore, the value of the stock on the day the donor delivers the stock certificate to the charity, or its agent, is the deductible amount of this gift. If the donor delivers the stock certificate to his or her bank or broker as agent, the gift is completed on the day the corporation transfers the stock on its books. Consequently, the value on that day determines the stock's value and the corresponding deduction. For securities held in a "street account" at a brokerage firm, the contribution occurs when the brokerage firm transfers the shares to the charity's account, either at that same or another brokerage firm.

For stocks that are regularly traded on an exchange, the value is the average of the highest and lowest quoted selling price for that day. If there were no sales on the valuation date, you determine FMV by taking the average price between the highest and lowest sales prices on the nearest date before and on the nearest date after the valuation date.

Real Estate

CR *How is the value of my gift of real estate established?*

For tax purposes, the fair market value of real estate is the amount a willing buyer would pay a willing seller in an arm's-length transaction if both had reasonable knowledge of the property. There are many specific IRS rules that apply to the determination of the fair market value of real property. An appraisal will establish the FMV. However, the appraisal requirements are detailed and complex when the value of the property exceeds $5,000. The Internal Revenue Code sets forth detailed regulations for substantiating your deductions that can be summarized as follows:

- You must obtain a qualified appraisal not earlier than 60 days before you transfer the property to the charity and dated no later than the due date of your tax return.
- The appraisal must be performed by a "qualified" appraiser who cannot be the donor or the charity, or anyone connected with them.
- You must file with your tax return Form 8283 on which Section B, Appraisal Summary, has been signed by the appraiser and also by a representative of the charity.
- The appraiser requirements, which are listed on Form 8283, are ironclad. A word of caution to you and the appraiser: You must follow the IRS rules to the letter or you will not get a charitable deduction for the gift.
- The charity is required to complete Form 8282 if it sells or disposes of the real estate within 2 years after it receives the gift.

CR *I have a tract of unimproved wilderness property that I would like to donate to a charity. All of the property surrounding my tract is being developed. I would like this property to be used only as a youth camp. Will this affect the deductibility of this gift?*

The highest and best use of your property (the use that would generate the highest FMV) is probably not as a youth camp, depending, of course, on the type of development going on around it. The property may be more valuable if it were developed consistent with the surrounding property. The amount of your charitable deduction is limited to the FMV of the property at the time of the contribution, taking into account your restriction that it only be used as a youth camp. Your restriction is likely to reduce the value of your contribution.

Other Property

∞ *I know that gifts of real estate need to be appraised for purposes of taking a charitable income tax deduction. Do I need an appraisal if I give other kinds of property to a charity?*

Except for cash and publicly traded securities, a "qualified" appraisal is required if the value of the gift exceeds $5,000. There are detailed rules about what information the appraisal must contain. The appraisal requirements apply to gifts made to both private foundations and public charities.

Appraising Hard-to-Value Property

∞ *How do I get an appraisal for personal property, such as artwork or antiques?*

Auction houses that specialize in antiques or artwork will usually make appraisals for a fee. For other types of property, search for appraisers in the Yellow Pages or on the Internet for sources that provide estimates of value.

If you claim a deduction of $20,000 or more for donations of art, you must attach a complete copy of the signed appraisal to your tax return. If you donate a piece of art that has been appraised at $50,000 or more, you can request a Statement of Value for that item from the IRS to minimize any dispute as to the value of the item. According to existing law, this process is supposed to be available to taxpayers prior to donating the artwork. However, the current IRS procedure applies only to artwork that has already been donated, severely limiting the usefulness of this procedure.

If the property that you are donating to charity has substantial value and you want to avoid a prolonged controversy with the IRS if they examine your income tax return or gift tax return, find the best appraiser you can. You may pay a little more, but a good appraisal will serve as a good insurance policy that will help protect against the IRS questioning the value of a donated asset.

SUBSTANTIATING CONTRIBUTIONS

CR *How do I substantiate donations?*

For cash donations (payment by check, credit card, or payroll deduction), the records you need to keep depend on whether you contributed less than or more than $250. For contributions other than cash, your record-keeping requirements depend on whether you contributed property valued at less than $250, valued between $250 and $500, valued above $500 but not more than $5,000, or valued in excess of $5,000.

Cash Contributions under $250

CR *I'm a sucker for the Salvation Army buckets during the holidays. I probably put more than $200 in cash into the buckets between Thanksgiving and Christmas last year. Will the IRS take my word for it?*

Not likely. This is one time when the requirements may dampen your holiday spirit. You made several contributions over a number of weeks, and none of the gifts amounted to more than $250. For contributions under $250, the IRS requires one of the following:

- A cancelled check or account statement that shows the transfer of funds by check, electronic transfer, or credit card, with the amount and date posted and payee clearly indicated
- A written receipt or letter from the charity with the charity's name, amount given, and date indicated
- Other reliable written records that include the same information as above

This last option may help you in your casual contributions to the Salvation Army and others. You should regularly keep a written record, perhaps in your appointment calendar, of the amounts and dates of your contributions and the names of the charities. This log should be completed around the same times you make your donations.

Contributions of Property Other Than Cash Valued at Less Than $250

❧ *How do I substantiate a charitable contribution of property valued at $250 or less?*

The Internal Revenue Service requires written records for property contributions, even if the value of the property is $250 or less. In fact, the records required for these modest charitable donations are identical to those required for donations of $5,000 or less. To make sure that your smaller charitable donations will be allowed, your records should contain the following information:

- Name and address of the charity
- Date and location of contribution
- Description of property in reasonably sufficient detail
- A receipt from the charity containing the above information
- The FMV of property contributed; the method used to determine it; and, if an appraisal was used, a copy of the appraiser's report
- In the case of ordinary-income property or capital gain property, the adjusted basis of the property and how the reduction was calculated
- If the taxpayer contributed a partial interest in the property in the current year, the amount the taxpayer is claiming as a deduction, the amount he or she claimed in prior years for interests in the same property, and the name and address of each charity to which those donations were made
- The terms of any agreement or understanding placing conditions or restrictions on the charity's use, sale, or other disposition of the property

CR *The record-keeping requirements for smaller gifts seem a bit extensive. How can I easily substantiate gifts of used clothing, household items, old furniture, and the like?*

Most of the requirements listed above don't apply in this context. Just make an inventory or listing with a description of the nature and condition of each item you give to charity. Then, place the value that you would expect to receive at a garage sale if you were to sell the item. For items with higher values or large numbers of items, you may wish to take a photograph of the items or the entire group. Keep the photographs and a copy of the receipt you received from the charity for your records.

Contributions in Excess of $250

CR *How do I substantiate a charitable contribution of cash or property in excess of $250?*

A charitable contribution deduction will be disallowed for any contribution of $250 or more unless the taxpayer can substantiate the gift by a timely written acknowledgment from the charity. The charity's written acknowledgement must include the following information:

- The amount of cash contributed and a description of any property other than cash that was contributed
- Whether the charity provided any goods or services in consideration, in whole or part, for any cash or other property contributed
- A description and a good estimate of the value of any goods or services, other than intangible religious benefits, that the charity provided, if any
- A statement of any intangible religious benefits provided by the charity

The charity's acknowledgment may be by letter, postcard, or computer-generated form. If the taxpayer makes more than one contribution of $250 or more to a charity during a tax year, the taxpayer may substantiate the contributions with one or more acknowledgments.

Goods and services include cash, property, services, benefits, and privileges. Goods and services are deemed to be provided in consideration for a payment to a charity if the taxpayer receives or expects to receive goods or services in exchange for the payment. If a taxpayer makes a payment to a charity in exchange for goods or services, a deduction is allowed only to the extent that the payment exceeds the value of the goods or services and the taxpayer intends a gift of the excess.

Last, but not to be overlooked, get written acknowledgment from each charity on or before the date you file your return for the tax year in which you make the contribution, or the due date (including extensions) for filing your return, whichever comes first.

What proof do I need for cash contributions made through payroll deductions?

For a contribution of $250 or more from a single paycheck, keep a pay stub, W-2 form, or any other document supplied by your employer that shows the amount withheld and the purpose. Additionally, obtain a pledge card or other document from the charity stating that no goods or services were provided, either in whole or in partial consideration, for your donation.

Contributions of Property Valued Between $500 and $5,000

What proof do I need for a charitable deduction of property worth between $500 and $5,000?

You need a written acknowledgment of your donation from the charity, as required for any donation to charity for $250 or more, as well as records that show the following:

- How you obtained the property (purchase, gift, bequest, inheritance, or exchange)
- The approximate date you acquired the property or approximate date that you substantially completed it if you created, produced, or manufactured the property
- For property other than publicly traded securities, the cost of the property or other basis of valuation if you've owned the property for less than 12 months; and the same information, if available, if you've held the property for more than 12 months

If you are unable to substantiate the approximate date when you obtained the property or substantiate its cost basis and have a reasonable explanation (for example, albeit an extreme one, your house burned down taking all your property records with it), include a statement to that effect with your tax return.

Contributions of Property Valued Over $5,000

℞ *I made a contribution of property worth $7,000 to a charity. What are the requirements for substantiating deductions associated with this amount?*

In addition to the requirements described above for property of lesser value, deductions for certain charitable contributions of property in excess of $5,000 must be substantiated by a qualified appraisal. The appraisal must be performed no earlier than 60 days prior to the contribution and received by you before the date that your income tax return is filed or due, including extensions. You must also attach a completed appraisal summary to your income tax return.

You do not need a qualified appraisal if the property that you contributed is nonpublicly traded stock valued between $5,000 and $10,000 or certain publicly traded securities for which market quotations are not readily available. Also, no qualified appraisal is needed if the property is donated by a C corporation (other than a closely held corporation or a personal service corporation) or is inventory or other property that is donated by a closely held corporation or a personal service corporation and is considered a "qualified contribution" for the care of the ill, the needy, or infants.

℞ *How do I substantiate a charitable contribution of nonpublicly traded stock or certain publicly traded securities valued at more than $5,000?*

When a taxpayer donates nonpublicly traded stock valued at more than $5,000 but less than $10,000, or publicly traded securities for which quotations are not readily available on an established market, the following requirements apply:

1. First, the taxpayer must attach a partially completed appraisal summary to the income tax return on which the deduction is claimed.

2. Second, the taxpayer must maintain records containing the following information:

- The name and address of the charity

- The date and location of the contribution

- A description of the property and its value, the name of the issuer, type of security, and whether the security is regularly traded on an exchange or over the counter

- The FMV of the property at the time the taxpayer made the contribution

- The taxpayer's cost basis

- If the taxpayer is contributing less than the entire interest in the property, the total amount being claimed for the tax year and the amount claimed as a previous deduction

- The terms of any agreement or understanding entered into by or on behalf of the taxpayer relating to the use, sale, or disposition of the property contributed

3. Third, the taxpayer must obtain a contemporaneous written acknowledgment from the charity.

CR *What are the requirements of an appraisal summary?*

An *appraisal summary* is a summary of a qualified appraisal and is signed and dated by the recipient of the property, as well as by the qualified appraiser. It must be filed with the tax return on which the property is claimed as a deduction. The appraisal summary is required to contain the following information:

- The name and taxpayer identification number of the person giving the gift
- A detailed description of the property
- A summary of the property's overall condition
- The manner and date of acquisition of the property by the person giving the gift (e.g., purchase, exchange, gift, or bequest)
- The adjusted cost basis of the property
- The name, address, and taxpayer identification number of the recipient of the gift

- The date on which the gift is made
- An explanation of any consideration associated with the gift
- The name, address, and other identification of the qualified appraiser
- The appraised fair market value of the property on the date of the contribution
- Certain other declarations by the qualified appraiser

 What do I do with the full qualified appraisal if I don't have to attach it to my tax return?

You must maintain the qualified appraisal for an unspecified period of time characterized as "...so long as it may be relevant in the administration of any Internal Revenue law."

 What happens if I take a charitable deduction but don't have an appraisal done?

The IRS may deny your deduction for your charitable contribution and you may be subject to a penalty if you substantially overstate the value of the property that you contributed. The penalty is 20 percent of the tax deficiency resulting from the incorrect valuation and, in some situations, higher.

 I would like to make charitable contributions of books valued at $2,000, $2,500, and $3,000 to three colleges. Consequently, the total of the gifts exceeds the $5,000 threshold, requiring an appraisal. Do I have to have three separate appraisals prepared?

A separate appraisal is required for each item of property that is not included in a group of "similar items of property." Similar items of property are of the same generic category or type, such as a stamp or coin collection, paintings, photographs, books, land, buildings, clothing, jewelry, furniture, electronic equipment, household equipment, toys, kitchenware, china, crystal, or silver. Your books constitute similar items of property so you would only have to have one appraisal prepared.

PART THREE

Trusts for Charitable Planning

Part Three provides a thorough introduction to charitable trusts and their uses in planned giving. The charitable trusts described in this part start with the trust maker-donor transferring property to the trust. Professionals refer to these charitable trusts as *split-interest trusts* because there are two different classes of beneficiaries who benefit from the trusts at different times. Depending on the type of trust, a charity is either a beneficiary when the trust commences (a lead beneficiary) or when the trust terminates (a remainder beneficiary). The other beneficiary—the noncharitable beneficiary—is often the trust maker-donor.

Our contributing authors have found that the charitable planning strategy that most often suits the needs of their clients and provides them with the greatest level of flexibility is the charitable remainder trust (CRT). The CRT comes in several versions. These versions and two alternative strategies that are closely related to the CRT are discussed in chapter 8.

A CRT provides a stream of payments to the noncharitable beneficiaries for a specified term; the assets remaining in the trust at the end of the trust term are then donated to charity. The trust maker is often the sole noncharitable beneficiary. A CRT is a very flexible planning strategy and can be set up either during your life or at your death through your will or trust. Most trust makers utilize a lifetime, or *inter vivos,* CRT in order to receive a charitable income tax deduction for the gifts to the CRT. Trust makers often fund a CRT with highly appreciated assets, and the trustee, in turn, sells the assets and reinvests the sale proceeds in a diversified portfolio that will provide the trust maker with a stream of payments for a designated term, which is often the trust maker's life. Because a CRT is a tax-exempt trust, it pays no income taxes on the capital gains realized on the sale. In most cases, the trust maker is better off financially by contributing the highly appreciated asset to the CRT and receiving the payments from the trust than by selling the asset directly and reinvesting the after-tax proceeds of the sale.

CRTs are irrevocable trusts, meaning that they can't be changed, and people are often concerned about making gifts to trusts that they cannot later change. Clients regularly ask if they can retain some control over their CRTs. As our contributors explain, clients are usually pleasantly surprised by the degree of flexibility that they can build into their CRTs. Still, there are some strict requirements for CRTs, and our contributors do a fine job of explaining those rules in a concise, understandable fashion.

As Part Three of *Giving* explains, a CRT can be a powerful tool for people who want to make substantial gifts to charity while also benefiting themselves financially. Business owners who want to sell their companies, working couples who need to save more for retirement, and investors who need to diversify their portfolios can use a CRT to benefit themselves and their favorite charities at the same time. Because of the versatility and power of CRTs, our contributing authors invested a great amount of effort explaining them and their benefits. Their energy was well spent—in our experience, CRTs are probably the most popular planned giving tool used today.

Chapter 8 concludes with discussions of charitable gift annuities and pooled income funds. These two planned giving techniques offer benefits similar to those offered by a CRT but without the expense and effort of creating and managing a CRT. For people who want to make a gift of property to charity but need the income from that property, pooled income funds and charitable gift annuities are appealing alternatives to CRTs. There are drawbacks to each strategy, and these drawbacks are discussed at the end of chapter 8.

Chapter 9 covers the charitable lead trust (CLT). CLTs may also be either lifetime or testamentary trusts. The CLT is the reverse of the CRT in that the CLT beneficiaries who receive the income stream are charitable organizations and, at the end of the trust's term, the assets remaining in the trust pass to the noncharitable beneficiaries. A CLT is somewhat more restrictive in terms of what the trust maker may do once the trust has been established. Depending on the terms of the trust and the trust maker's other goals, the trust maker may or may not receive a charitable income tax deduction for donations to a CLT. Despite this limitation, CLTs can be extremely effective tools for passing wealth to succeeding generations with minimal estate or gift taxes. These topics are discussed in chapter 9.

Our contributors address the issues that are common to all charitable trusts in chapter 10. Because these trusts serve a public, charitable purpose, they are, to some extent, regulated like public charities. While the rules governing trusts are complex, our contributors do a marvelous job explaining them. These rules are essentially intended to prevent people from using charitable trusts in an abusive fashion that is ultimately unfair to the charitable beneficiaries. When viewed in this light, most of the rules are based on common sense. In our experience and that of our contributors, these rules do *not* deter genuinely, charitably motivated people from using these trusts.

In chapter 10, our contributors also discuss the types of assets that are best to donate to these charitable trusts and the problems associated with particular types of assets, such as closely held stock or debt-encumbered property. A final issue in this chapter is the timing of the transfer of assets to a charitable remainder trust. Chapter 10 discusses matters that require the attention of professional advisors to avoid, or at least minimize, problems even before they develop.

chapter 8

Charitable Remainder Trusts and Alternatives

OVERVIEW OF CHARITABLE REMAINDER TRUSTS

CR *What is a charitable remainder trust?*

Charitable remainder trusts (CRTs) were introduced in the Tax Reform Act of 1969. Since then, they have become increasingly popular because of the charitable, financial, retirement, and estate planning opportunities they afford taxpayers.

A charitable remainder trust is an irrevocable *split-interest* trust because it pays a percentage of trust principal to named individuals and then distributes what is left, the "remainder," to charity. The split is between individual beneficiaries and a charity or charities as *remainder beneficiaries.*

CR *When can I set up a CRT?*

Remember that you can give gifts during your lifetime or at your death. You can do this with charitable remainder trusts in the following ways:

- You can create a CRT, transfer assets to it during your lifetime, and receive an immediate charitable income tax deduction. This is called an *inter vivos* charitable remainder trust.
- You can include provisions in your will or your living trust that create a charitable remainder trust after your death, at which time your executor or trustee will transfer the assets to it and your estate will receive an estate tax deduction. This is called a *testamentary* charitable remainder trust.

Whether the CRT is *inter vivos* or testamentary, your charitable trust must provide an income stream to one or more noncharitable beneficiaries for a specified term and, at the end of the term, the trustee of the CRT must distribute the balance of the trust assets to one or more charities.

◌ *Why must the trust be irrevocable?*

Charitable remainder trust arrangements must be irrevocable to meet the requirements of the Internal Revenue Code for charitable income, gift, and estate tax deductions.

◌ *Why should I consider establishing a charitable remainder trust?*

While there are a number of financial benefits to creating a charitable remainder trust, your primary reason should be a commitment to charitable giving.

A CRT is first and foremost a gift to charity. With a charitable remainder trust, you can convert your tax dollars that the government spends at its discretion (social capital) into charitable gifts that you make to support your favorite causes and organizations and, in addition, provide you with financial and tax-saving benefits.

◌ *How large an estate should I have before I consider using a charitable remainder trust?*

It isn't so much a matter of estate size as it is a matter of your desire to give to charity within the context of your specific financial circumstances and goals.

THE *INTER VIVOS* CHARITABLE REMAINDER TRUST

Q̃ Can you give me an example of how an inter vivos *CRT works?*

Figure 8-1 is a diagram of how an *inter vivos* CRT works. In this simple example, Mrs. Smith creates a charitable remainder annuity trust that will pay her for life and, at her death, pay the charity the remainder. By donating the remainder interest to charity during her lifetime, Mrs. Smith generates a substantial tax deduction (which she can use to offset other taxable income).

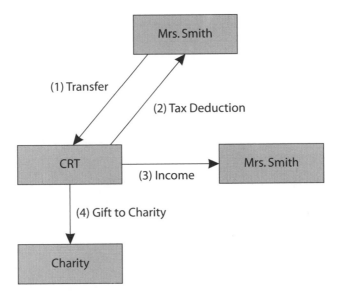

Step 1: Mrs. Smith transfers property worth $100,000 to the trust; trustee may sell and reinvest property to generate higher income.

Step 2: Mrs. Smith receives a current charitable income tax deduction.

Step 3: Mrs. Smith receives 7 percent of the value of the trust each year for life.

Step 4: When Mrs. Smith dies, the charity will receive the remainder of the assets in her trust.

Figure 8-1   Charitable remainder trust

Purposes for Using an *Inter Vivos* CRT

✩ *What tax deductions does a contribution to an* inter vivos *CRT give me?*

Your contributions to an *inter vivos* charitable remainder trust will qualify for charitable income, gift, and estate tax deductions.

When you make a gift to an *inter vivos* CRT, you create a charitable income tax deduction equal to the present dollar value of the remainder interest ultimately going to charity. Said another way, you receive a charitable income tax deduction for the property's projected value—original value, minus all payments to noncharitable beneficiaries, plus undistributed income and growth—ultimately going to the charity at your death or at the end of the stated term, calculated in today's dollars.

You can use the charitable income tax deduction in the year you create the trust; and, if it exceeds the maximum allowable deduction in that calendar year, you can carry over any unused amount for 5 years to use against your future income.

✩ *Is it likely that the changes to the estate tax laws in 2001 will diminish the need for charitable remainder trusts?*

It is not likely that the Economic Growth and Tax Relief Reconciliation Act of 2001 (EGTRRA, or 2001 tax act) will adversely affect the use of charitable remainder trusts because the CRT is used as often, if not more often, for income tax planning as it is for estate tax planning.

✩ *What are the main advantages of creating a CRT?*

There are several categories of advantages for using a CRT as a strategy for making charitable gifts. These are:

Charitable philosophy: A CRT allows you to
- receive recognition for the gift during your life, even though the charity will not receive the gift until later, and
- leave a legacy to your favorite charities or possibly to your own foundation.

Financial planning: A CRT allows you to
- receive a current charitable income tax deduction for the present value of the property that will eventually go to the charity,
- diversify your portfolio by selling the donated asset and reinvesting the proceeds,
- increase your income beyond what the original asset was generating for you, and
- avoid paying capital gain tax immediately upon the sale of highly appreciated property (e.g., real estate, stock, etc.) that you transfer to the trust.

Estate planning: A CRT allows you to
- receive an estate tax deduction for the value of the gift you make to the charity and
- potentially increase the amount you leave to your heirs at your death through the income and estate tax savings.

Control: A CRT allows you to
- control, with certain restrictions, investment of the trust assets and
- protect your charitable trust principal from the claims of creditors.

Reduce Income Taxes and Increase Income

✑ *How can a CRT increase my income?*

With a charitable remainder trust, you can convert a non-income-producing asset, such as appreciated real estate, to income-producing assets, such as bonds or preferred stock, without paying an immediate capital gain tax on this conversion of your portfolio. This is so because the CRT is a tax-exempt trust—it is exempt from the payment of income taxes, including capital gain taxes. Thus, the CRT has 100 percent of the sale proceeds to reinvest rather than the sale proceeds net of capital gain taxes, which would be the case if you sold the property yourself. After you transfer the appreciated property to the CRT, the trustee of the CRT can sell the property and immediately reinvest the sale proceeds in income-producing investments.

The combination of the charitable income tax deduction for

making the gift to the CRT and the gross sale proceeds being available for investment will almost always result in a higher income for the income beneficiaries.

CR *Can you give me an example of how a charitable remainder trust can increase my income?*

Let's suppose that Susan and Richard have stock in their portfolio that they purchased years ago for $10,000. Let's further assume that the stock is worth $110,000 in 2002. If they sold the stock for $110,000, they would have to realize an immediate capital gain of $100,000, which would result in a $20,000 capital gain tax (20 percent in 2002), leaving them $90,000 to reinvest. If Susan and Richard then purchased an investment worth $90,000 that earned a 7 percent return, they would receive $6,300 in annual income.

In contrast, if they contributed the stock to a CRT and the trustee of the trust sold the stock, the trustee would have the entire $110,000 available to invest in that same 7 percent vehicle and Susan and Richard would receive $7,700 annually.

Reduce Estate Taxes

CR *Why would I create a charitable remainder trust and give away property? I want my money to go to my family, not charity.*

When used in conjunction with other estate planning vehicles, a charitable remainder trust can result in your family getting more at your death than they might have received if you had not contributed assets to the CRT.

CR *How could this possibly result in my children receiving more rather than less of our property?*

If your estate will be subject to estate tax, your children will receive your assets less the federal estate tax, which will be due soon after you die. Assuming your estate is in a 50 percent estate tax bracket, your children will receive only one-half of the value of your property.

When you give an asset to a charitable remainder trust, you remove the asset from your estate and essentially eliminate any estate tax that might be due on that asset at your death.

Yes, you reduced or eliminated the estate taxes your children would have to pay but you also gave part of their inheritance to charity. Stay with us. Remember, when you give assets to a CRT, you receive a charitable income tax deduction. If that deduction is significant, it generates a tax savings that puts additional cash in your pocket. If you use that cash to purchase a life insurance policy in conjunction with a wealth replacement trust (also called an irrevocable life insurance trust), the proceeds of the life insurance, which could be of equal or higher value than the asset you donated, go to your children totally free of federal estate tax at your death. We discuss this strategy in detail in Chapter 12, Charitable Estate Planning.

⊘ Can I provide for my family through a CRT?

Yes, you can provide an income stream to a family member or friend. For example, we have a client who created a CRT for his grandchildren for a term of 20 years. At the end of the 20-year term, the balance will be divided into two shares: one share will go to a local university to establish a faculty chair in honor of his deceased wife and the other share will go to organizations that train Seeing Eye dogs.

Using this strategy, he not only supports his grandchildren through school, beginning careers, and much more; but he also achieves his philanthropic goals by supporting his favorite charitable causes and by establishing a legacy in memory of his wife.

Disadvantages of the CRT

⊘ The charitable remainder trust sounds too good to be true. What are all of its potential disadvantages?

There are some potential disadvantages to a charitable remainder trust; but, whether any of these is a disadvantage in actuality depends upon your goals and your specific circumstances. For example,

- Your gift is irrevocable, thus you lose full access to the property if your circumstances change.
- The property that you contribute to the charitable remainder trust will not go to your family at your death. Whatever is in your charitable remainder trust, at your death or at the end of the term of years specified in the trust agreement, will go to the

named charity or charities. But it is important to realize that not all of the property would necessarily pass to your family anyway, due to estate taxes.

- You can be as speculative with your personal investments as you want. However, as the trustee for a charitable remainder trust, you must exercise the prudence a reasonable person would exercise in preserving principal. This may be a more conservative standard of investing than you are willing to accept.

- You will incur certain administrative costs, such as accounting and trustee's fees, for a charitable remainder trust that you will not incur if you maintain the investment outside of a CRT.

- You could be effectively converting your long-term capital gains into ordinary-income gains, which are taxed at higher rates.

Types of *Inter Vivos* and Testamentary Charitable Remainder Trusts

ᕦ *What are the types of charitable remainder trusts?*

There are two basic types of CRTs (with variations on the second):

1. Charitable remainder annuity trust (CRAT)
2. Charitable remainder unitrust (CRUT):

   a. Net-income-only charitable remainder unitrust (NIOCRUT)
   b. Charitable remainder unitrust with net income makeup (income deferral) provisions (NIMCRUT)
   c. Charitable remainder unitrust with "flip" provisions (FLIPCRUT)

Each trust dictates a specific payment option arrangement and has different requirements, as we discuss below.

Charitable Remainder Annuity Trust

ᕦ *What is a charitable remainder annuity trust?*

A *charitable remainder annuity trust (CRAT)* is a charitable remainder trust that pays the noncharitable beneficiaries, at least annually, either a fixed dollar amount or a fixed percentage of the initial value of the assets transferred to the trust. It is described as an "annuity trust" because the amount of the annual payment does not change. The annuity amount must be at least 5 percent of the value of the original assets contributed to the trust but may not be more than 50 percent of that value.

ℚ *Can you give me an example of how the CRAT works?*

Let's say you create a CRAT to which you will contribute $500,000 of highly appreciated stock. You establish the CRAT to pay you annually for life 7 percent of the fair market value of the contribution—or you can state it as an annuity amount of $35,000 ($500,000 × 7 percent). At your death, the trust will distribute the remaining assets to your charity.

If your CRAT investments earn exactly $35,000 each year and the CRAT distributes the $35,000 to you each year, at your death, your charity will receive the exact amount you contributed, $500,000. However, if your CRAT investments earn $50,000 each year, you will continue to receive $35,000, the CRAT will retain the $20,000 annual excess to reinvest, and your charity will receive more than $500,000.

ℚ *What if the trust investments earn less than the $35,000 required annuity payment?*

The trustee will distribute principal. If the CRAT investments earn less than $35,000 in a year, you still receive $35,000—the difference having to be made up from trust principal—and your charity ultimately receives less than $500,000. The trustee may have to sell investments to make up the difference and you cannot contribute additional property to a CRAT to help earn the deficit.

Thus, the long-term effect of electing to receive an annual return greater than the amount the trust earns is that the trust principal will continually decrease.

ℚ *Can I ever make additional contributions to my CRAT?*

No. Once you fund a CRAT, you cannot contribute additional assets later; the annuity amount is fixed and your income tax deduction is established. You could, however, create and fund additional CRATs in later years.

◌ *Are there any drawbacks to a CRAT?*

Because the dollar amount of the payment is fixed at the time the donor-trust maker creates the CRAT, there are two drawbacks:

1. the noncharitable beneficiaries do not benefit from any appreciation of the value of the trust's assets and
2. inflation may erode the purchasing power of the annuity payments.

◌ *What are the advantages of a CRAT?*

A major benefit is that the income beneficiaries are protected from a decrease in the value of the trust assets. As such, a CRAT is often beneficial for individuals who want to be able to count on a fixed income and to be free from market fluctuations and risk.

◌ *In your experience, to what type of investors does a CRAT appeal?*

The CRAT appeals to older donors who prefer fixed, predictable annual payments.

Charitable Remainder Unitrust

◌ *What is a charitable remainder unitrust?*

A *charitable remainder unitrust (CRUT)* pays a fixed percentage of trust assets *valued annually.* This means that the actual dollar amount that the beneficiaries receive is adjusted annually to reflect the increase or decrease in the value of the trust's assets. This is the major distinction between a CRUT and a CRAT in which the income payment is fixed permanently on the initial value of the trust.

For example, if the initial contribution to the CRUT is valued at $100,000 and the payout rate is 6 percent, the first year's payment is $6,000. If the trust has a net return of $10,000—after payment of the $6,000—in that first year, the trust at the beginning of the second year is valued at $110,000 and the second year's payment would be $6,600.

ℭ *What would happen if the CRUT didn't earn anything during that first year?*

If the CRUT doesn't earn any income or appreciate in value in the first year, the trustee would have to use principal to make the payment. This would reduce the value of the trust principal in the next year, thus reducing the unitrust payment in the second year. Alternatively, the donor-trust maker could contribute additional assets during the year to try to earn enough to make that payment.

Table 8-1 demonstrates how a CRUT works.

ℭ *Can we make additional contributions to the CRUT?*

Yes. Another distinction between the CRUT and the CRAT is that you *can* make additional contributions to your CRUT and you are entitled to an income tax deduction for each additional contribution.

ℭ *What are the benefits of the unitrust?*

The CRUT provides a hedge against inflation because the annual payment is calculated on the trust assets, which are valued annually.

ℭ *When should I consider a CRUT over a CRAT?*

You should consider a unitrust if you believe that the value of your trust investments will increase over time and are comfortable with some risk and a fluctuating annual payment.

TABLE 8-1   Example of a Charitable Remainder Unitrust with a 10 Percent Payout Rate

Trust year	Annual trust value	Payment amount	Principal growth/(loss) and income	Net change to annual trust value
1	$1,000,000	$100,000	$100,000	$ 0
2	1,000,000	100,000	150,000	50,000
3	1,050,000	105,000	90,000	(15,000)
4	1,035,000	103,500	200,000	96,500
5	1,131,500	113,150	100,000	(13,150)

○א What are the different variations of the unitrust?

There are three variations of the charitable remainder unitrust:

1. Net-income-only charitable remainder unitrust (NIOCRUT)
2. Charitable remainder unitrust with net income makeup provisions (NIMCRUT)
3. Charitable remainder unitrust with "flip" provisions (FLIPCRUT)

Net-Income-Only Charitable Remainder Unitrust

○א What is a net-income-only charitable remainder unitrust?

A *net-income-only charitable remainder unitrust (NIOCRUT)* is a variation of a CRUT in which the trust distributes annually the *lesser* of the stated unitrust payout rate or the net income of the trust. If the net income of the trust assets is insufficient to make the stated annual unitrust payment, the beneficiaries simply receive the lower income payment. The difference between the stated unitrust payment and the income the beneficiaries actually receive is lost.

For example, if the unitrust payout rate is 8 percent and the fair market value of the trust's assets is $500,000, the unitrust amount is $40,000. If the trust's income for the year is only $30,000, the beneficiaries receive the $30,000 income earned because it is less than the stated $40,000 payment amount. If the trust's income for the year is $50,000, the beneficiaries receive $40,000, the unitrust amount, because that amount is less than the trust's income for that year.

Because of the greater benefits that can be received through the NIMCRUT, the NIOCRUT is an estate planning strategy that is seldom used.

Charitable Remainder Unitrust with Net Income Makeup Provisions

○א What is a charitable remainder unitrust with net income makeup provisions?

A *charitable remainder unitrust with net income makeup provisions (NIMCRUT)* is a special type of CRUT, similar to a NIOCRUT, but with an added advantage. As with the NIOCRUT, the beneficiary of a NIMCRUT in a given year is entitled to the *lesser* of the stated payout rate or the trust's income. However, the terms of the NIMCRUT provide that if the trust does not earn sufficient income to make the unitrust payment, it can make up the shortage in the future when the trust earns *more* than the unitrust amount. In other words, the trustee uses excess income to make up for shortages from previous years.

ℭℛ *What constitutes net income?*

The trust document and local law determine the definition of what constitutes *net income.* Local law, in most states, means the Revised Uniform Income and Principal Act, which states that income should include interest, dividends, rents, royalties, and the discount element of original issue discount obligations. Many states provide that reasonable expenses to maintain the trust, including, but not limited to, administrative and management expenses, can be deducted from the trust income to come up with net income.

ℭℛ *Why would I want to use a NIMCRUT?*

Although it might be the right time for you to sell a highly appreciated asset, you may not need the income from the CRT at some later time, such as when you retire. If the trustee of the NIMCRUT invests the trust assets for growth rather than for income, the trust is unlikely to earn enough to make the required unitrust payments. Each year that the trust fails to make the unitrust payment, it owes the beneficiary more and more in later years. At the same time, the assets in the trust are growing in a tax-free environment, so the trust principal is also increasing in value.

When you decide that you do need the income, the trustee could convert the growth investments into interest- or dividend-paying investments and you could then take the aggregate value of all those past deficits in future years.

For example, Carol created a NIMCRUT in 1998 with a 5 percent unitrust payout rate and funded the trust with $200,000. Table 8-2 shows the results, year by year. As you can see, when the trust earned more than the unitrust amount in 2000, the trust paid Carol the $12,000 unitrust amount for the year, plus an additional $5,000 to "make up" the prior shortfalls.

TABLE 8-2 Example of a NIMCRUT with a 5 Percent Payout Rate

Year	Annual trust value	5% of value	Trust income	Actual payment	Cumulative deficit owed
1998	$200,000	$10,000	$ 8,000	$ 8,000	($2,000)
1999	220,000	11,000	8,000	8,000	(5,000)
2000	240,000	12,000	18,000	17,000	0
2001	240,000	12,000	11,000	11,000	(1,000)
2002	250,000	12,500	13,000	13,000	(500)

ℚ *What are the benefits of a NIMCRUT?*

A NIMCRUT offers donors all the benefits of any other CRT, plus two more:

1. Donors can transfer a non-income-producing asset like real estate to the trust and hold it there while searching for a buyer. While waiting for a buyer, the trust has no obligation to distribute cash to the donor.

2. Donors can also defer receiving payments from the trust by investing in growth assets that produce little income. If those assets appreciate over time, the donor will be rewarded with larger unitrust payments later when the trustee sells the assets and invests the proceeds in assets that generate income.

Charitable Remainder Unitrust with "Flip" Provisions

ℚ *What is a charitable remainder unitrust with flip provisions?*

A charitable remainder unitrust can be drafted to start out as a NIMCRUT (CRUT with net income makeup provisions) when the donor-trust maker makes the initial contribution. It can then switch, or "flip," to a regular CRUT upon a "triggering event." These unitrusts are known as *charitable remainder unitrusts with flip provisions (FLIPCRUTs)* and can accommodate differing needs of a trust maker at different phases of his or her life.

The triggering event for the flip to occur can be

- a specific date;

- a person reaching a certain age;
- the occurrence of a specific event—not in the discretion of the unitrust income beneficiary—such as a birth, death, marriage, divorce, or retirement;
- the sale of an unmarketable asset owned by the trust (an *unmarketable asset* is defined as an asset other than cash or cash equivalents, such as real estate, business interests, and closely held stock).

The flip from a NIMCRUT to a CRUT occurs the first day of the taxable year after the triggering event.

♋ When is a FLIPCRUT used?

Donors who want to contribute real property to a charitable remainder trust often use a FLIPCRUT.

For example, let's assume that you contribute a $500,000 parcel of vacant land to a FLIPCRUT with the provision that it switches to a CRUT upon the sale of the property. The trustee of the trust does not sell the property for 2 years, so there is no income to pay and the trust owes you 2 years' worth of unitrust payments. The trustee sells the property in the third year, which triggers the flip to a regular CRUT, and invests the sale proceeds in income-producing assets that will now generate enough income to make the stated unitrust payments. Depending on the timing of the sale and your wishes, you may or may not receive the makeup amount from prior years.

♋ Can I use a FLIPCRUT to generate funds for my retirement?

The FLIPCRUT can be used to create additional retirement funds for the donor and his or her spouse. The plan is as follows:

1. Your attorney drafts the FLIPCRUT with a provision stating that the "triggering event" is the age at which you plan to retire.
2. As the donor-trust maker, you regularly contribute funds to the trust over several years, with each contribution generating an income tax deduction.
3. The trustee invests the trust assets in a portfolio that aims at producing capital appreciation over a period of years rather than in income-producing investments, so the annual trust income will be zero or a small amount.

4. The year after you reach the stated age, the trust flips to a standard unitrust and thereafter pays the unitrust amount to you and your spouse as the income beneficiaries.

Because the trust principal was allowed to grow tax-free through the choice of investments and by your taking minimal or no payments prior to retirement, the trust should generate a significant income for you when you retire.

Rules for *Inter Vivos* Charitable Remainder Trusts

Gifts to CRTs Are Irrevocable

℞ *Since the charities named in my charitable remainder trust will not receive anything until the end of the trust term, can I change my mind and terminate the trust?*

No. Even though the charities you named in your trust do not receive their remainder distributions until sometime in the future, the transfer of property that you made to the trust constitutes an irrevocable gift that you cannot take back. Thus, as you consider creating a charitable remainder trust, it is important that a primary reason for doing so is to benefit charity and not solely for the tax benefits or the payments that you may receive.

Trust Maker Can Retain Rights to Revoke Certain Interests in the Trust

℞ *Even if the gift is irrevocable, is there anything about the trust that I can later change?*

Even though charitable remainder trusts are irrevocable, they do provide trust makers with extensive flexibility. For example, the maker of a CRT can

- change the trustees;
- change the charitable beneficiary, and, if there are multiple charitable beneficiaries, change the percentages of the remaining trust principal that each will ultimately receive; and

- reserve the right to revoke the payments passing to other non-charitable beneficiaries at the maker's death, thereby transferring the property to charity sooner.

What's important to note is that these rights are *not* automatic; your attorney must draft provisions in the CRT document to give you this flexibility. Even the standard forms issued by the Internal Revenue Service and used by many charities do not include these provisions.

ℭ *Can I set up my CRT to stop income payments to my daughter if she remarries?*

Yes. The regulations governing CRTs permit the trust maker to terminate payments to noncharitable beneficiaries upon the occurrence of a qualified contingency. A *qualified contingency* is a provision in the trust document directing that a noncharitable beneficiary's interest in the trust will terminate upon the happening of a specified event or occurrence, which may be sooner than the payments would have terminated had the event or occurrence not happened.

Income Beneficiaries

ℭ *Who are the typical noncharitable beneficiaries of a charitable remainder trust?*

The income beneficiaries can be almost anyone; however, those commonly named are the donor-trust maker and his or her spouse.

Trustees of Charitable Remainder Trusts

ℭ *Who can be the trustee of a CRT?*

Most trust makers name themselves and their spouses as the trustees of their CRTs. As trustees, they can retain control of their trust assets during their lifetime. If they do not wish to be involved in the administration of the trust, they will name a corporate, or institutional, trustee. If donors choose to act as their own trustees, they may be required to name a special independent trustee in their trust documents to perform specific trustee duties.

ᐊ *What is the role of an independent trustee?*

An *independent trustee* is someone who makes decisions in the following situations:

- when the trust maker is contributing an asset that is difficult to value,
- when the trustee must make a decision to distribute income derived from a variable annuity owned by the CRT, or
- when the terms of the CRT authorize the trustee to "spray" or "sprinkle" the annuity or unitrust amount to the noncharitable trust beneficiaries "at the trustee's discretion."

The independent trustee must truly be independent, meaning that the trustee *cannot* be related to, or controlled by, or employed by the trust maker.

ᐊ *Who do you recommend that we name as the trustee of our charitable remainder trust, and why?*

CRTs are technical documents that must closely follow the law. They are also particularly complicated with regard to accounting issues. If the trust is not properly administered, there can be adverse tax consequences for the donor, including subsequent disqualification of the trust as a CRT.

Because of the experience required with investments, accounting, and government reporting, we usually recommend a corporate trustee (a bank or trust company that specializes in managing trust assets) to act as sole trustee or as a cotrustee with our clients. Alternatively, we suggest that if our clients choose to act as sole trustees, they use the services of a trust administrator to handle the accounting and reporting tasks. The ultimate choice of a trustee or administrator is best made in consultation with your professional advisors.

Term of the Trust

ᐊ *How do I structure the term of my CRT?*

You set up the trust to pay the annuity or unitrust for the life of a beneficiary or for a term of years (not to exceed 20). You have several common scenarios to choose from:

■ You can establish the CRT to pay to one beneficiary for his or her lifetime only. When the beneficiary dies, the trustee will distribute the remainder of the assets to the charity.

■ You can establish the CRT as a "joint-and-survivor" payment, which means that the CRT will pay to two or more beneficiaries for their lives, until the death of the last beneficiary. At that time, the balance of the funds will pass to the charity or charities. Although you can use this option for any individuals, you would usually use it for husband and wife beneficiaries.

■ You can establish the CRT to pay to one or more beneficiaries for a specific number of years—not to exceed 20. Thereafter, the trustee will distribute the remainder of the assets to a charity.

✸ Can I combine a term of years with a life term?

Yes; however, the permitted combinations are tricky and you really need to be careful if you intend to establish this type of payment formula. In short, you cannot have a lifetime payment for one beneficiary and tack on a term of years for a second beneficiary. You may, however, have a term of years for one beneficiary and then a lifetime payment period for another individual if the second individual is alive at the time the CRT is created. Here are some illustrations of these rules:

Example 1:   It is *not* permissible for a CRT to provide income payments to Corey for his life, and upon his death, to Laura for a term of 10 years.

Example 2:   It *is* permissible for a CRT to provide income payments to Ann for her lifetime or for 20 years, whichever period is shorter.

Example 3:   It *is* permissible for a CRT to provide income payments to John for 10 years and then to make the payments to Debbie for her lifetime, if Debbie is living at the time the CRT is created.

Having described these term options, it is important to mention that the choice of term is inextricably linked to the choices of payout rate, age of the beneficiaries (life expectancy), amount of income tax deduction that the donor-trust maker desires, and a couple of statutory requirements for payout rates and the amount left for charity. We discuss these variables and their relationships in the balance of this chapter.

ᗡ *Typically, what term do people select in their CRTs?*

The most common term is for a CRT to pay income to the trust maker for his or her life and, depending upon the age of his or her spouse, for the spouse's lifetime as well.

ᗡ *I want to make sure that my charitable remainder trust pays me an income stream for the rest of my life. However, if I were to die soon, I would want my children to receive something from my charitable remainder trust. Is there a way for me to accomplish both objectives?*

Yes. You can include provisions in your trust to pay you the income stream for your life, no matter how long you live, and, if you die within a certain number of years (up to 20), to pay your children the annuity or unitrust amount for the remainder of the term of years.

Minimum/Maximum Payment Requirements

ᗡ *How much income can I get from my charitable remainder trust? Are there any restrictions that I need to know about?*

The Internal Revenue Code requires that the annuity and unitrust payout rates be a least 5 percent but not more than 50 percent per year, although this maximum payout rate rarely comes into play. Most CRTs carry a single-digit payout rate. Whether you take 5, 6, 7, 8, or any other percent, for that matter, it is totally a function of

- the amount of income tax deduction that you want,
- how much money you want during the term of the trust, and
- the current interest rate environment (the higher the rate on mid-term treasury bills, the higher your payout rate can be without violating the 10 percent rule described later in this chapter).

If you do not need the cash to live on, you would probably choose a low payout rate to maximize your income tax deduction. However, if you need a certain amount of funds each year to live on or to pay the premiums on a life insurance policy for a wealth replacement strategy, you would select a payout rate large enough to cover those expenses.

Keep in mind that the earnings and appreciation in excess of the annual payout amount grow tax-free inside the trust. In some CRUT cases, this results in the noncharitable beneficiaries receiving a greater sum over the trust term with a lower payout rate than they would have received with a higher rate.

ᝍ *Is there an annual dollar limit on how much I can take from my charitable remainder trust?*

There is no dollar limit on how much you can receive from your CRT annually. Only the maximum 50 percent limitation and the 10 percent rule (explained below) limit the amount that you can receive.

ᝍ *Is there a certain amount that must be left in the trust for the charity?*

To qualify as a charitable remainder trust, the present value of the amount *expected* to pass to charity must be at least 10 percent of the initial contribution. Professionals refer to this as the *10 percent test.* Put another way, your income tax deduction for an *inter vivos* CRT must be at least 10 percent of the value of the assets that you transfer to the trust.

For example, if you contribute $500,000 to a CRT, your deduction must be at least $50,000 or the trust does not qualify as a CRT and you won't be entitled to any income tax deduction. (We explain how to calculate the deductions later in this chapter.)

Keep in mind that the actual amount that eventually passes to the charity when the noncharitable interest expires is irrelevant for purposes of this rule. The payout rate, the trust term, the age (life expectancy) of the beneficiaries, and the applicable federal rate (an assumed rate of return prescribed by the government) combine to determine whether the present value of the remainder will be at least 10 percent to meet this test.

For example, a 30-year-old prospective donor might not be able to create a CRT for his or her life. Even if the trust pays only the required 5 percent minimum, the donor's life expectancy is so long that it is mathematically impossible to comply with the 10 percent test.

If you have an existing CRUT and want to make additional contributions, new contributions must also satisfy the 10 percent rule. You should check with your accountant, financial advisor, and attorney before you make additional contributions to your CRUT.

CR *Are the limitations on a charitable remainder annuity trust the same as the limitations on a charitable remainder unitrust?*

A charitable remainder annuity trust must meet the same requirements explained above for the charitable remainder unitrust. The CRAT, however, has an additional requirement. A CRAT pays a constant percentage of the trust assets, valued when they were initially contributed to the CRAT, no matter how much the trust assets grow or decline in value. Therefore, if the trust's investments do not perform well over time, a CRAT might eventually run out of funds and there is nothing in the end for the charity.

To avoid this result, the mathematical possibility that the CRAT will be exhausted before distribution to the charity cannot exceed 5 percent. For example, if your accountant determines that there is a 6 percent probability that there will be nothing left in the CRAT for the charity at the end of the term, you cannot establish the CRT under the terms used for this calculation.

CR *I want to name my wife and me, and then our children, as the income beneficiaries of our charitable remainder trust. Can I do that?*

Maybe. The rules described previously may prevent you from implementing your plan. One factor that determines the projected amount that the charitable beneficiary will receive is the term of the trust—how long the charity must wait for the charitable remainder trust to end. Therefore, if the joint life expectancies of the four of you is so long as to make the present value calculation less than 10 percent, you cannot name your children as income beneficiaries for their lives and still have your CRT qualify.

Permissible Payment Periods

CR *How often will I receive payments from the charitable remainder trust?*

You will receive payments from your CRT in any periodic term that you designate. You must receive payments at least once per year, but you may also elect to receive them monthly, quarterly, or semiannually and at the beginning or end of the period. You provide for the payment frequency in the original trust, and the payments will continue on that schedule during the entire term of the trust.

Charitable Remainder Beneficiaries

ରେ *What kinds of charities can I name in my charitable remainder trust?*

Your charities must be qualified charitable beneficiaries, which could be public charities, supporting organizations, donor-advised funds, or private foundations.

ରେ *Can I name more than one charity as beneficiary of my charitable remainder trust?*

You can name one or any number of charities as beneficiaries of your charitable remainder trust; there are no limitations on this. You may also allocate the trust remainder to the beneficiaries in unequal amounts.

ରେ *Can I change my mind later as to which charity will receive the property in my charitable remainder trust at my death?*

Yes; however, the trust agreement itself must contain a provision that gives you or someone else the right to make this change. You can give the power to change beneficiaries to yourself, the trustee, or to other income beneficiaries. This flexibility allows the CRT to support specific causes even though the identity of the organizations furthering those causes may change over time.

ରେ *I would like to set up a CRT now and name several public charities as the remainder beneficiaries. If I decide to set up a private foundation in the future, can I change the CRT beneficiary to be the private foundation?*

As we have indicated, to be able to change beneficiaries, you must create your CRT to allow this flexibility. Second, your CRT must not limit the choice of possible charitable remainder beneficiaries to public charities. As a rule, most CRTs are drafted with this as a built-in limitation.

However, there are adverse income tax consequences that result when this flexibility is drafted into the trust. The percentage limitation for donations to private foundations is lower than for donations to public charities, and, by reserving the right to name a private foundation as the remainder beneficiary, you will be required to use the lower percentage limitation even if you *never* set up your foundation and the property eventually passes to public charities.

Tax Consequences of the *Inter Vivos* CRT

Income Tax Deductions

∝ *What kind of tax benefits will I receive if I establish a charitable remainder trust?*

You will receive an income tax deduction equal to the present value of the interest that will pass to charity upon termination of your charitable remainder trust.

There are limitations on the amount of charitable income tax deduction that you may take in the year of the contribution, but you may carry forward any unused deduction for the next 5 years.

∝ *What factors control the amount of a CRT income tax deduction?*

In addition to the usual limits for charitable income tax deductions, the deduction for a contribution to a CRT is determined by

- the term of the trust—that is, the number of years that the charity must wait to receive the remainder;
- the fair market value of the asset you contribute;
- the CRT payout rate;
- whether the trust is a CRUT or a CRAT;
- the frequency of the payments; and
- an assumed rate of return published monthly by the government called the *applicable federal rate.*

∝ *Can you give me an example of how the deduction is calculated?*

Yes. Let's say that Harold, age 60, established a CRAT in 1999 with a 7 percent payout for his life, to be paid quarterly. He contributes $300,000 to the trust. The applicable federal rate in the month he funds the trust is 7 percent. Based on the IRS tables, the present value of Harold's annuity interest is $213,901. The value of the remainder interest is, therefore, $86,099 ($300,000 − $213,901). This is the amount of Harold's income tax deduction, which also passes the test of being at least 10 percent of the initial contribution.

ᏅᎡ *Why can't we take the full fair market value of the contribution as an income tax deduction?*

Because you and/or other beneficiaries are retaining the annuity or unitrust interest for a period of time, you are not giving the entire amount to the charity. The amount of the deduction is, therefore, the value of the remainder interest that will pass to charity at the end of the term.

Gift Taxes

ᏅᎡ *What are the gift tax consequences associated with setting up a charitable remainder trust?*

To fully understand the various tax considerations associated with setting up a charitable remainder trust, remember that all CRTs consist of two distinct interests: a noncharitable annuity (CRAT) or unitrust (CRUT) interest and a charitable remainder interest. The gift tax considerations are different for each interest.

ᏅᎡ *What are the gift tax consequences for the interest going to the noncharitable beneficiaries?*

When you name anyone other than yourself or your spouse as an income beneficiary of a CRT, you are making a taxable gift to that person. In this instance, the amount of your gift will be equal to the present value of the unitrust or annuity payments. While you may not have to actually pay any tax because of your gift tax exemption, you will use up a valuable portion of that exemption.

If the beneficiary is immediately entitled to the unitrust or annuity payments, the gift qualifies for the annual gift tax exclusion of $11,000 per donee (in 2002), and the amount of the gift will be reduced by that exclusion when calculating the gift tax. When you name your spouse as a beneficiary, the unlimited marital deduction applies, so you do not use up any of your gift tax exemption or annual exclusion. The unlimited marital deduction provides that most gifts to a spouse are exempt from estate and gift taxes.

⌘ Does the remainder interest going to charity create a gift tax?

With respect to the remainder interest, a charitable gift tax deduction is allowed for gifts to qualified charitable organizations. Thus, if the CRT is properly drafted and the named charitable beneficiaries are qualified organizations, there will be no gift tax on the remainder interest.

⌘ If I set up the CRT to pay me during my life and then my children after my death, what are the gift tax consequences of that transaction?

This arrangement will create a gift to your children. The amount of the gift will be equal to the present dollar value of their future payments. Unfortunately, this gift would not qualify for the $11,000 annual gift tax exclusion because the children do not receive an immediate benefit from the trust—it is a future gift.

⌘ Is there any way I can get around this "gift of a future interest" to my children?

You can avoid it by including a provision in your CRT document that gives you the right to cancel the children's right to the payments and accelerate the donation of the trust balance to the charitable beneficiaries. Retention of this right will ensure that the gift will be "incomplete" for gift tax purposes and, therefore, avoid current gift taxes. However, the value of the children's interest will be subject to federal estate taxes when you die.

Estate Taxes

⌘ What are the estate tax consequences of a CRT?

The present value of the charitable remainder interest qualifies for the federal charitable estate tax deduction and reduces the taxable estate; however, it may not eliminate all estate taxes.

If the CRT continues after the death of the trust maker or the trust maker's spouse, the interest for the spouse is protected from federal estate tax by the unlimited marital deduction.

If the CRT annuity or unitrust income stream is payable to a nonspouse beneficiary after the maker's death, the present value of the unitrust or annuity interest is included in the maker's estate and will be taxed based on the value of the interest.

෬ *If my wife and I create a trust for our lives and then for the life of our adult daughter, will we avoid estate tax on this gift to charity?*

Not entirely. In fact, there may be a substantial tax to pay. Assuming you die first, at your death, the gift is not a gift to your wife alone—it is a gift to your spouse and daughter, which means it is not protected by the unlimited marital deduction. The value of all of the property in the trust will be included in your estate. The charitable estate tax deduction will have to be calculated as of the date of your death. If your daughter is young, the present value of the CRT income stream going to her over her life expectancy could be pretty substantial. The younger she is, the less will be the value of the gift passing to charity, and your charitable estate tax deduction will be small.

Your estate must pay tax on the difference between the value of the assets in the trust and the value of the remainder interest passing to charity.

Generation-Skipping Transfer Taxes

෬ *Are there any tax consequences arising from naming my grandson as one of the beneficiaries of my charitable remainder trust?*

The distributions to your grandson are a type of generation-skipping transfer (GST) and will be subject to a GST tax unless you allocate enough of your lifetime GST tax exemption to the trust in an amount equal to the value of your grandson's interest in the trust. You must allocate the GST exemption at the time you create the trust. However, if you are also a beneficiary of the CRT, you will not be able to allocate your GST tax exemption during your lifetime due to the *estate tax inclusion period* rules of the Internal Revenue Code.

We discuss generation-skipping transfer taxes and methods of using the GST tax exemption in Chapter 12, Charitable Estate Planning.

Taxation of Trust Income

ଔ *Will my CRT pay capital gain or income tax?*

Because CRTs are generally tax-exempt, the trust will not recognize income when the CRT sells stock, real estate, or other appreciated assets. Similarly, a CRT does not pay income taxes on the income it earns unless it has "unrelated business taxable income" (see Chapter 10, Issues Common to All Charitable Trusts). Although the CRT is exempt from paying income taxes, the payments you receive from the trust are taxable income to you.

Income Taxation of CRT Payments

ଔ *Are the payments that I receive from my CRT taxed and, if so, how are they taxed?*

The trustee must keep track of the different types of income in the trust. These different types of income are like layers of colored sand in a jar, and your trustee will pay the trust income to you based on the layer it's in. Amounts paid from a CRT are taxed on a "worst (income) in/first (income) out" (WIFO) basis as prescribed by law. Trust distributions are characterized based on the type of income, and are distributed in the following order:

- *First, as ordinary income, to the extent that the trust has ordinary income for the current year and any undistributed ordinary income from prior years:* The trustee will first pay to you all of the ordinary income that it earns. If it does not earn sufficient ordinary income to pay your unitrust or annuity amount, it will start digging into the capital gain layer.

- *Second, as long-term capital gain, to the extent that the trust has capital gain for the current year and any undistributed capital gain from prior years:* The capital gain that you did not immediately recognize when the CRT sold the asset retains its character. If the trustee dips into this layer, you will report the proceeds on your tax return as capital gain.

- *Third, as other income (e.g., tax-exempt income from municipal bonds), to the extent that the trust has other income for the current year and any undistributed other income from prior years:* Don't count on getting any; it seldom gets distributed.

- *Fourth, as a tax-free return of principal from the trust's corpus:* Only after the beneficiaries have recognized all of the CRT's income, both ordinary and capital gain, from current and prior years as taxable income can they treat the distributions as non-taxable return of principal.

○ॠ *Can you give me a simple example of how this accounting system works?*

Yes.

Example 1:   If you have a CRT with a fixed payout rate of 6 percent and the trust earns 7 percent ordinary income and 2 percent long-term capital gain income, all of the income you receive will be ordinary income.

Example 2:   If the CRT earns 5 percent ordinary income and 4 percent long-term capital gain income, to make the 6 percent payment, the trustee will have to pay you 5 percent from the ordinary income layer and 1 percent from the long-term capital gain layer.

Example 3:   Let's assume that Patrick establishes a CRAT with an 8 percent payout rate on his initial contribution of $250,000, or $20,000 to Patrick annually. As a tax-exempt trust, the CRT is not taxable on any of this income. Table 8-3 demonstrates how this four-tiered tax works.

○ॠ *Why does the IRS insist that the distributions be accounted for with four-tiered accounting?*

The obvious intent of this four-tiered accounting system is to characterize the distributions in a manner that will force beneficiaries to pay the highest income tax on the distributed amounts.

TABLE 8-3   Example of Four-Tiered Income Taxation of CRAT Payments

	Trust earns income of:	Patrick's $20,000 payments characterized and taxed as:
Year 1	$ 8,000 dividend 30,000 capital gain 12,000 tax-exempt	$ 8,000 ordinary income 12,000 capital gain
Year 2	$15,000 tax-exempt	$18,000 capital gain not distributed in year 1 2,000 tax-exempt
Year 3*	$20,000 interest	$20,000 ordinary income
Year 4	$17,000 interest	$17,000 ordinary income 3,000 tax-exempt interest not distributed in year 1

*CRT switches portfolio to U.S. bonds.

Tax Consequences of Early Distributions to Charity

ભ *I set up a CRUT a number of years ago. I don't need the payments now and would like to see the charity get the money instead. Is this possible?*

Yes, you can accelerate the gift to charity if you are willing to give your entire remaining unitrust interest to the charity. You will be entitled to a charitable income and gift tax deduction for the year of the transfer in the amount of the present value of the remaining unitrust interest.

ભ *What if I want the charity to get half of the money in my CRUT now and half of the unitrust payment I've been receiving. Can that be done?*

Yes. This is known as a "partial acceleration." Since the value of the unitrust is determined annually, after the trustee distributes one-half of the trust property to the charity, future unitrust payments will be based on the value of the remaining trust property, taking into account any depreciation or appreciation that may have occurred with the remaining trust property. Because the charity received the property earlier than originally anticipated, you will be entitled to an additional income tax deduction. To provide you with this option, your attorney must include language in the original document permitting you to accelerate the charity's interest in the trust.

While the law is not clear, partial acceleration is most likely *not* permitted with a CRAT. Since the amount of the annuity payments is set when you fund the trust, a premature distribution to the charity doesn't reduce the annuity amount. This makes it possible for the trust fund to run out of money, which is in violation of the 5 percent probability exhaustion rule discussed earlier.

Choosing the Appropriate Payment Option

Cℛ *Can you compare the results of using the different types of CRTs?*

Yes. Tables 8-4 and 8-5, which appear at the end of this chapter, illustrate the differences between the various charitable remainder trusts.

Cℛ *Why would I choose one over the other?*

The answer depends, in large part, on how much you need for an income stream during the term of the trust and how much market volatility you can tolerate. For example, if it's essential that you have a predictable income stream from the trust to maintain your standard of living, the charitable remainder annuity trust is more likely to meet your goals. However, if you can tolerate more market volatility or uncertainty, one of the charitable remainder unitrusts may best serve your needs.

THE TESTAMENTARY CRT

Cℛ *How does a testamentary CRT work?*

A *testamentary CRT* is established in a will or living trust and becomes effective when the testator or trust maker dies. It works the same as an *inter vivos* CRT in that the trust distributes an annuity or unitrust amount to one or more beneficiaries for either of their lifetimes or for a stated term of years, after which the remaining assets are distributed to charitable beneficiaries. In addition, the percentage limitations for testamentary CRTs are the same as for *inter vivos* CRTs.

Note that when you establish a testamentary CRT, it does not generate an income tax deduction and only the present value of the remainder to charity calculated at the time of death is eligible for a federal charitable estate tax deduction. The value of the interest given to the noncharitable beneficiaries will be subject to estate tax.

◌ *Can I change the benefits received by the beneficiaries?*

You can change the provisions of a testamentary CRT at any time up until your death or loss of capacity.

◌ *Why should I consider establishing a testamentary CRT?*

A testamentary CRT reduces federal estate tax and you retain total control over your property until your death.

POOLED INCOME FUNDS

◌ *What is a pooled income fund?*

A *pooled income fund* is another form of split-interest trust. Money or property contributed to the fund is split into two types of interests: an income interest paid to a noncharitable beneficiary and a remainder interest that passes to a charity when the noncharitable beneficiary dies.

◌ *How is the pooled income fund structured?*

A pooled income fund is a trust operated by a public charity—mostly large, nationally known organizations—to accept contributions from donors. Donors contribute cash or other property (but not tax-exempt bonds) to the trust, which is commingled with the property contributed by all other donors. In return for the contribution, the donor receives an income interest in the trust, payable to the donor and/or another beneficiary of the donor's choosing, for life. The trustees manage and invest the fund's assets and annually pay each trust beneficiary an amount based on the trust's rate of return for the year and the proportionate value of that beneficiary's contribution to the trust. When the donor (or the beneficiary chosen by the donor) dies, the income interest terminates, and the charity receives the remainder interest in the contributed property.

ᢙ *How does a pooled income fund differ from a charitable remainder trust?*

While the basic concepts behind pooled income funds and CRTs are the same, the two differ in these respects:

- With a CRT, the donor receives annuity or unitrust payments that are not tied to the trust's annual income (except for the NIOCRUT and NIMCRUT). A pooled income fund donor receives only a share of the trust's annual income, with no promise that the donor will receive a certain amount each year.

- A CRT holds only the assets contributed by the trust maker, who then serves as trustee (or selects the trustee) and manages the trust and invests the trust's assets. A pooled income fund donor has no voice in the management of the fund, which consists of not only his or her contribution but also the contributions of all other donors.

- CRTs provide more flexibility as to the length and value of the noncharitable interest. The only option for a pooled income fund donor is a lifetime income interest.

- A CRT trust maker can designate one or more qualified charities as the charitable beneficiary and reserve the right to change that designation. The remainder interest in a pooled income fund donation must go to the charity operating the fund.

- A CRT is a tax-exempt trust. A pooled income fund is not tax-exempt, although as a practical matter; it rarely pays any income taxes.

- The income tax treatment of distributions is different: the four-tier tax system for CRT distributions (described earlier in this chapter) does not apply to pooled income fund distributions. Rather, distributions from a pooled income fund will always be characterized as ordinary income in the hands of the donor.

- The 10 percent minimum-remainder rule does not apply to a pooled income fund.

❧ What are the benefits of a pooled income fund versus a CRT?

A charitable remainder trust can be expensive to establish and maintain. There are usually start-up fees, such as the cost of hiring an attorney. Also, there are continuing costs for administering the trust, such as the preparation of annual income tax returns and possibly investment fees. With a pooled income fund, there are no start-up fees and no need for an attorney to draft documents, although donors should seek tax advice prior to making a gift to a pooled income fund. While a pooled income fund has ongoing administrative costs just like a CRT, these costs should have only a nominal impact on the trust's income, due to economies of scale.

Also, donors contributing a highly appreciated asset to a pooled income fund get immediate investment diversification without recognizing capital gains because they receive an undivided interest in the fund's total portfolio in return for their contributions. While this result is possible with a CRT, pooled income fund donors are likely to receive greater diversification.

❧ Can I receive tax deductions for donations to a pooled income fund?

Yes. For income, estate, and gift tax purposes, the deduction equals the present value of the remainder interest in the property transferred to the fund. The present value of the remainder interest is determined by subtracting the present value of the noncharitable beneficiary's income interest from the fair market value of the property on the date of transfer. The present value of the noncharitable beneficiary's income interest depends upon two factors: (1) the actuarial life expectancy of the income beneficiary and (2) the fund's *deemed rate of return*. The deemed rate of return of a pooled income fund is the highest annual rate of the average yearly rate of return for the 3 taxable years immediately preceding the year in which the transfer of property to the fund is made.

❧ How do I know whether the CRT or the pooled income fund is better for me?

Generally, pooled income funds are appropriate when a charitable donor does not want to be bothered with administration. Typically, individual donations to pooled income funds can be smaller than those made to CRTs. CRTs are usually established by individuals who wish to make larger donations to charity and who want to retain some level of control over the investments.

CHARITABLE GIFT ANNUITIES

ᘓ *What is a charitable gift annuity?*

A *charitable gift annuity (CGA)* is an arrangement whereby a donor transfers cash or other property to a qualified charitable organization in exchange for a commitment by the organization to pay the donor an annuity—a specified amount each year for the remainder of the donor's life or for a term of years. The transfer is, in part, a charitable donation because the value of the donated property exceeds the value of the annuity. Put another way, the cost of obtaining a CGA is more than the cost of obtaining a similar commercial annuity from an insurance company. It is this excess that is the charitable contribution. Figure 8-2 depicts how a CGA works.

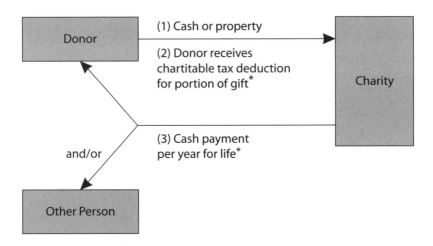

*Generally, the value of the charity's promise to pay is actuarially less in value than the cash or property given; therefore, the charitable deduction.

Figure 8-2   Charitable gift annuity

ᑕᖇ *Is a charitable gift annuity a trust?*

A CGA is not a trust. It is a contractual agreement between the donor and the charity. You give the charity an asset and the charity agrees to pay you *X* percent for the rest of your life or for a term of years. In short, it is a commitment on the part of the charity to pay you an annuity in exchange for the property you transfer.

ᑕᖇ *What are the main objectives for using charitable gift annuities?*

There are generally two reasons why people use charitable gift annuities:

1. the taxpayer wants an income stream for the annuity period or
2. the taxpayer wants to make a gift to a charity.

In achieving these two objectives, the transaction is treated partly as a purchase of an annuity and partly as a charitable contribution. As such, the annuity rate in a gift annuity will be lower than that paid on a commercial annuity.

ᑕᖇ *In a nutshell, how does a CGA work?*

Here's how a CGA works:

1. A donor transfers cash or other property to a charity in exchange for the charity's promise to pay a fixed amount (an annuity) to the donor or another annuitant for life or other specified time period.
2. The amount of the annuity is based upon the age of the annuitant at the time of the gift. It can be paid to one annuitant for life or two annuitants for both lives.
3. Part of each payment is a return of principal and is tax-free. Additionally, part of each payment is interest and is taxed as ordinary income.
4. The donor receives a charitable deduction for the difference between the value of the property given and the present value of the annuity received.
5. If the donor transfers appreciated property to the charity for the CGA, the transfer is treated as a bargain sale for tax purposes. Because the donor is receiving an annuity in return for the

contribution, the bargain-sale rules apply and part of the adjusted cost basis of the property given to the charity is treated as if it had been sold to the charity. As a result, part of the gain is allocated to the donor's cost basis and the donor must recognize some gain over the life of the annuity. Part of the gain will be allocated to the charitable gift amount and there will be no capital gain on that portion. (See chapters 4 and 15 for further discussions of bargain-sale rules.)

○R How is the annuity rate determined?

Most charities rely on annuity rates suggested by the American Council of Gift Annuities to determine your annuity payment. The older you are, the greater the annuity payment.

○R How does a charitable gift annuity differ from a charitable remainder trust?

The main difference centers around who is responsible for making the payments.

In a CRT, the donor-trust maker sets up a separate trust that pays the trust maker-income beneficiary an income stream and distributes the remainder interest to charity. The source of the income stream is the trust property.

With a CGA, the source of the annuity is the charity's promise to pay, unsupported by the donated property. The property given to the charity does not secure the charity's promise to pay. The charity's promise to pay is only as good as its credit rating.

○R What are the charitable income tax deductions for a CGA?

You receive a charitable income tax deduction when you make the gift. The amount of the deduction is the value of the property you contribute to the charity less the present value of the annuity payments. The deduction is available for the tax year when you establish the gift annuity. If you cannot use the deduction entirely in that year, you have up to 5 years to carry over the unused amount.

○R How will I be taxed on payments from a charitable gift annuity?

You will be taxed in the same manner as you would on a regular commercial annuity. A portion of each payment from an annuity is considered a return of principal and is, therefore, free from income tax. A portion of each payment will consist of interest taxed at ordinary income rates. A portion of each payment may qualify for capital gain treatment, if the asset contributed was eligible for long-term capital gain treatment prior to the transfer. These calculations are rather complex, so make sure your tax advisor provides you with the numbers before you proceed with a CGA.

ᙅᖇ Can you give me an example of how a charitable gift annuity might work?

Let's assume that Brad, age 75, purchased stock several years ago for $5,000. Today, that same stock is worth $50,000 and is only paying a 3 percent dividend of $1,500 per year. Let's also assume that Brad would like to increase his income but does not want to pay $9,000 in capital gain taxes ($45,000 × 20%) by selling his low dividend-paying stock. Finally, let's assume that Brad donates the stock to charity in exchange for a gift annuity. If he does, here is what happens:

1. Brad receives an annuity payment of $4,500 per year (300 percent more than the dividend he was receiving), of which 56 percent is a tax-free return of principal.
2. Brad's gift provides a charitable income tax deduction of approximately $20,000. In Brad's marginal tax bracket of 36 percent, the tax savings are $7,200.
3. Brad avoids capital gain taxes on a portion of the gain, saving approximately $3,600, and spreads out the balance of the capital gain taxes over the period of time that he is receiving the annuity.

ᙅᖇ What are some primary advantages of a charitable gift annuity?

CGAs offer these benefits:

- The donor can exchange appreciated assets for a gift annuity and reduce capital gain tax exposure.
- The donor is entitled to a charitable income tax deduction plus a 5-year carryover if he or she cannot use the entire deduction in 1 year.
- The donor receives a fixed annuity, typically for life, without the risk of market swings and interest rate changes.

- A gift annuity removes assets from the donor's estate for estate tax purposes.

- The CGA is shielded from the claims of creditors.

- Donated assets are insulated from mandatory Medicaid spend-down requirements.

TABLE 8-4   Comparison of Charitable Remainder Trust Annuity and Unitrust Payments*

Trust type	Required annual payment	Comments
CRAT	$100,000	• Annual distributions are fixed at $100,000 on creation of trust. • Year 1: Principal is reduced by $20,000 to make the required payment.
CRUT	100,000	• Distributions may vary annually because they are based on an annual value of trust. • Year 1: Principal is reduced by $20,000 to make the required payment. • Year 2: Distribution is 10% of reduced value of $980,000, plus growth.
NIMCRUT	80,000	• Principal remains at $1 million. • Annual distributions are the *lesser* of payout rate or what trust earned but makes up the difference in later years. • Year 1: pays $80,000 but owes $20,000, which it will pay when income exceeds 10%.

*Assumes $1 million contribution, 10 percent payout rate, and trust earned 8 percent income ($80,000) in year 1.

TABLE 8-5   Comparison of Charitable Remainder Trust Options

Requirements	CRAT	CRUT	NIMCRUT	FLIPCRUT
Payout rate requirements	5% minimum 50% maximum	5% minimum 50% maximum	5% minimum 50% maximum	5% minimum 50% maximum
Charitable remainder value must equal at least 10% of the initial value of property transferred to the trust	Yes	Yes	Yes	Yes
Additional contributions allowed	No	Yes	Yes	Yes
Payment amount based on annual value of property	No	Yes	Yes	Yes
Payout rate	Fixed when trust created	Fixed when trust created	Fixed when trust created	Fixed when trust created
Payment amounts calculated	Fixed amount (*annuity*) calculated originally on value of property when transferred to the trust	Calculated annually based on annual value of trust assets	Calculated annually based on annual value of trust assets	Calculated annually based on annual value of trust assets

Deficiency between required payment and trust income made up with trust principal	Yes	Yes	No; if trust earns less than payout rate, trust issues "IOU" to pay deficiency when it earns more than payout rate.	No; prior to triggering event, trust issues "IOU" to pay when it earns more than payout rate.
Comments	Payment amount never changes. If the trust earns more/less than payout rate, income beneficiary does not participate in increase/decrease. Principal is not preserved; decreases as well as increases in value are eventually passed on to charity.	Payment amount fluctuates based on growth/decline of trust assets: If trust earns less than payout rate, income beneficiary receives percentage of a smaller amount. If trust earns more than payout rate, income beneficiary receives percentage of a larger amount. Principal is preserved and income beneficiary benefits from appreciated value.	Payment amount fluctuates based on growth/decline of trust assets: If trust earns less than payout rate, income beneficiary receives percentage of a smaller amount. However, when trust income exceeds payout rate, trustee can pay excess earnings to make up shortages from prior years. Preserves principal and income beneficiary benefits from appreciated value.	Starts out as a NIMCRUT and "flips" to a CRUT at specific date or "triggering event." When trust does not earn the payout rate, shortfalls can be carried forward until the flip and then all payments are based on the fixed percentage rate of the CRUT.

chapter 9

Charitable Lead Trusts

INTER VIVOS CHARITABLE LEAD TRUSTS

Overview of *Inter Vivos* Charitable Lead Trusts

ca *What are charitable lead trusts?*

Charitable lead trusts (CLTs) are irrevocable split-interest trusts—a lead interest and a remainder interest. CLTs are the opposite of charitable remainder trusts in that the order of the beneficial interests is reversed: with a CLT, the charity receives the income interest and noncharitable beneficiaries receive the remainder interest. As we will see in this chapter, CLTs come in a variety of forms and are used by donors to accomplish a variety of charitable and personal planning goals.

ca *Can these also be* inter vivos *or testamentary?*

Yes. You can create a CLT to be effective during your life (*inter vivos* or *living* CLT) or you can create a CLT in your will or in your trust to take effect at your death (*testamentary* CLT).

⌘ *How does a charitable lead trust work?*

The donor-trust maker (or trust makers) creates the trust, naming the charitable and noncharitable beneficiaries and specifying the other trust terms, then transfers property to the trustee of the trust. The trustee administers the trust and is responsible for investment of its assets. The trustee pays the required amount to the charitable beneficiary for the specified period of time, then distributes the balance of the trust property to the remainder beneficiaries.

⌘ *Why would I want to use a CLT?*

Donors use charitable lead trusts to make annual, ongoing donations to charity. Beyond that, a CLT can be used as an estate planning tool to pass wealth to family members and to obtain a substantial income tax deduction in 1 year. Depending on the trust maker's objectives, one or both of these tax planning goals can be achieved through a CLT.

⌘ *When would I use the charitable lead trust?*

You should consider using a CLT when you

- own an income-producing asset but do not need the income that it produces,
- want to provide funds to charity for a period of years but want to keep the property in the family,
- might need a large income tax deduction to offset a high-income year.

⌘ *When is it* not *advisable to use a charitable lead trust?*

A CLT is not likely to fit your planning desires if you

- need all or most of the income you are currently earning to support your lifestyle or
- do not own appreciating, income-producing assets that you would like to pass to family members or other beneficiaries at little or no tax cost.

Beneficiaries

CR *Who can be the charitable beneficiaries of a charitable lead trust?*

The charity or charities receiving the income interest from the trust must be qualified charities. That includes both public charities and private foundations.

CR *Who can I name as the remainder beneficiaries of the CLT?*

You can name yourself, your spouse, other family members, or whomever you choose. Each choice produces different estate and gift tax consequences, as discussed later in this chapter.

CR *I can name myself as the noncharitable beneficiary and get the property back?*

Yes. When the donor has the right to receive the trust property back at some future date, it is known as a *reversionary interest*. In this scenario, the donor-trust maker specifies in the trust document that the trustee make distributions to the charity for a number of years and then return the balance of the trust property to him or her. If the donor is not alive at that time, the trust typically distributes the property to the donor's estate.

CR *Can I change the charities that are receiving the income payments?*

While it is possible for you to retain the power to change the charitable beneficiaries, in most instances that power will keep you from achieving your tax planning objectives.

However, you can build flexibility into the CLT document for a trustee, other than yourself, to choose the charitable beneficiaries or to change them. For example, you can name a primary charitable beneficiary and then include a list of contingent beneficiaries, giving the trustee the discretion to choose one of the charities on the list. Or, you can give the trustee general instructions as to the type of charity to benefit, such as charities that support medical research or animal welfare. So, even though you do not have the right to change the charitable beneficiaries, if you and your attorney draft the CLT document properly, it will have enough flexibility to allow a change.

Payment Options

CR *Are there different payment options for charitable lead trusts?*

There are basically two payment options for CLTs:

1. Charitable lead annuity trust (CLAT)
2. Charitable lead unitrust (CLUT)

These function similarly to the charitable remainder annuity trust (CRAT) and the charitable remainder unitrust (CRUT) in that the former is a fixed interest and the latter is an interest that varies with the underlying value of the principal amount.

Charitable Lead Annuity Trust

CR *What is a charitable lead annuity trust?*

With a *charitable lead annuity trust (CLAT),* the trust pays to one or more charities each year a fixed rate or fixed amount based on the value of the assets at the time they were originally contributed to the trust. At the end of the trust term, the remaining assets are returned to the donor-trust maker or distributed to other individuals whom the trust maker designated in the trust.

CR *How does a CLAT work?*

The charitable beneficiaries of a CLAT receive an amount that is fixed at the date the trust maker transfers the assets to the trust. This fixed amount may be expressed in dollars or as a percentage of the assets. For example, you can say "the annuity interest amount is equal to $10,000 per year," or say "the annuity interest amount is equal to 5 percent of my initial transfer of $200,000 to the trust." Both techniques produce identical results. In this example, regardless of how much the value of the CLAT assets fluctuates over the term of the trust, the payment going to charity will never be more or less than $10,000 per year. If the trust earns less in income than is needed to make the payment to charity, the trustee must use principal to make up the difference.

Charitable Lead Unitrust

CB *What is a charitable lead unitrust?*

A CLUT pays to charity each year a fixed percentage of the annual fair market value of the trust assets. This requires a valuation of the assets each year to determine the requisite payment amount. If the trust earns less income than is needed to make the payment to charity, the trustee must use principal to make up the difference.

CB *Can you provide an example of how a CLUT works?*

Yes. If a donor-trust maker transfers $1 million into a CLUT with a unitrust amount of 5 percent, the charitable beneficiary will receive $50,000 in the first year. Thereafter, the assets must be valued each year to determine the amount that, when multiplied by 5 percent, will yield the amount that must be paid to charity.

Let's say that at the beginning of the second year the assets' value has dramatically climbed to $2 million. The charitable beneficiary will receive $100,000, or 5 percent of the new $2 million value. A valuation in the third year will probably result in a different payment amount, depending on whether the value of the CLUT assets increased or decreased since the second year's valuation.

CB *Is the need to value CLUT assets annually a practical problem?*

If the trust holds only marketable securities, the annual valuation is not a burden. However, if the trust holds hard-to-value assets, such as real property or closely held business interests, a valuation is an annual expense that needs to be factored into the planning deliberations.

CLAT versus CLUT

CB *How does a unitrust differ from an annuity trust?*

Table 9-1 summarizes the differences between a CLAT and a CLUT. As you can see, the unitrust distributes a percentage of the trust assets annually to the charitable beneficiaries. As the trust principal fluctuates, so does the annual distribution to the charitable beneficiary.

TABLE 9-1   Comparison of CLT Payment Options

Requirements	CLAT	CLUT
Additional contributions of property allowed	IRC does not prohibit additional contributions, but additional gifts do not provide additional tax deductions.	Yes. Additional tax deduction for additional contributions
Payment amount based on annual value of property	No	Yes
Payout rate/amount requirements	Fixed amount each year (*annuity*) based on value of property when initially transferred to the trust	Fixed payout rate based on trust assets valued annually
Comment	<ul><li>Payment amount remains the same.</li><li>If the trust earns less than payout rate, principal is used to make the payment.</li><li>If the trust earns more than payout rate, charitable beneficiary does not receive the extra income.</li><li>Increases in value and excess income are eventually passed on to noncharitable beneficiaries.</li></ul>	<ul><li>Payment amount fluctuates based on the appreciation and depreciation of trust assets.</li><li>If trust income is insufficient to pay unitrust amount, principal is used to make payment.</li><li>Both charitable and noncharitable beneficiaries benefit from appreciation and excess income.</li></ul>

℞ *Are there any minimum or maximum payment requirements to the charity, or anything like the 10 percent rule, that the charitable remainder trusts require?*

No.

Permissible Payout Periods

℞ *When must the payments be made to the charity?*

The trustee must make the payments periodically, which may be semiannually, quarterly, monthly, or, at the very least, annually.

Term of the Trust

႙ *What are the possible terms of the CLT?*

The term can be for a specific number of years or for the life or life-times of a person or persons. When using lives of individuals to measure the CLT's term, the individuals must be alive on the date of the gift to the trust; in other words, a measuring life cannot be an unborn child.

႙ *Do most of your clients use the measuring lives of their family members or a term of years?*

Our clients usually select a term of years.

႙ *How do I determine the right number of years for my charitable lead trust?*

The decision as to the appropriate term in a given plan is usually based upon the following:

- How long the client wants to benefit the charity
- How soon the client wants the property back or wants other remainder beneficiaries to receive the trust assets
- How much, if any, estate or gift tax the client is willing to pay

Tax Consequences of *Inter Vivos* Charitable Lead Trusts

Income Taxes

႙ *Can a lead trust be set up so the trust maker gets an income tax deduction for the payments to charity?*

Yes. Depending on the terms of the trust, the donor may receive a charitable income tax deduction. The amount of the deduction is the present value of the stream of payments going to charity over the term of the trust. Needless to say, this amount could be substantial. Because the donation is "for the use of" a charity and not "to" a charity, your income tax deduction is limited to 30 percent for public charities and 20 percent for private foundations.

Not all CLTs provide their donors with an income tax deduction for the payments to charity. Whether the donor receives this deduction is largely based on the wishes of the donor and how the trust is drafted.

◌ֆ *Why wouldn't I want the income tax deduction?*

A CLT is not a tax-exempt trust like a CRT, so someone has to pay taxes on the trust income. To receive an income tax deduction for the payments going to charity, the trust maker must pay income taxes on the income generated by the trust assets while the trust is in effect, without the benefit of receiving additional deductions for the annual payments to charity after the initial deduction. The donor will add all the trust's income to his or her own when calculating federal income taxes. This tax liability could more than cancel out the benefits of the upfront income tax deduction.

◌ֆ *I anticipate needing a big deduction next year so I'm willing to pay the income taxes on trust income. How do I set up the trust so I can get the income tax deduction when I make the transfer?*

The most common method for getting the income tax deduction is to name yourself as the remainder beneficiary. By having the trust property return to you after a period of years, you will almost always be entitled to the income tax deduction in the year you transfer the asset to the trust. If you do *not* want the trust property returned to you, it is possible to construct the trust so the remainder passes to others (usually family members) and you still get the income tax deduction. Remember, however, you will pay income taxes on all of the trust's income during the period that the charity receives its annuity or unitrust payments.

◌ֆ *What if the charitable income tax deduction is more than I can use in the year that I make the contribution?*

Normally, you carry over unused charitable deductions for 5 years. The Internal Revenue Service has taken the position in the past that donations "for the use of" the charity (which the CLT donation is) cannot be carried forward. Most tax experts disagree with this position. As a practical matter, taxpayers are carrying forward the deduction without IRS objection.

ଔ I don't like the idea of paying the trust's income taxes. Is there another option?

Yes. It's quite common to structure a CLT so the trust maker does *not* pay income tax on the income that the trust generates, nor does he or she receive a charitable income tax deduction for the payments to charity either at the initial transfer or when the trust makes the payments. Under this arrangement, the trust pays the income taxes, after taking a charitable income tax deduction for the amount it paid to charity that year. If the trust recognizes income in excess of the required payment to charity, the trust will have to pay the tax on it.

This option is typically available only when someone other than the donor or the donor's spouse is the remainder beneficiary. Otherwise, as we previously indicated, if the donor maintains the reversion or names his or her spouse as the remainder beneficiary, he or she will usually receive an income tax deduction and then pay the trust's income taxes.

Estate and Gift Taxes

ଔ What are the gift tax consequences of a CLT?

A CLT trust maker makes one and, potentially, two gifts when he or she funds the trust. First, the trust maker makes a gift of the unitrust or annuity interest to the qualified charity. This gift does not generate gift tax because the trust maker receives an offsetting gift tax deduction for the value of the charity's interest. If the trust maker retains a reversion in the trust (is the remainder beneficiary), there is only the one gift to charity—you can't make a gift to yourself. If the trust maker names someone else as the remainder beneficiary, he or she makes a taxable gift to that person or persons.

ଔ Does the remainder interest qualify for the annual exclusion for gift tax?

No, it will not qualify for the annual exclusion because the gift of the remainder interest is a gift of a future interest, not of a present interest.

ଔ Does the amount the charity receives affect the gift tax that may be due?

Yes, it certainly does. There is an inverse relationship between the total amount that the charity receives and the value of the remainder interest that family members receive: The higher the payment amount and the longer the period of time that it is paid to charity, the lower the value will be of the remainder going to family members for gift tax purposes.

∝ What are the estate tax consequences of a CLT?

If the donor of the CLT is not the remainder beneficiary in the trust and has not kept any "strings" of control over the trust, the CLT property will not be included in his or her gross estate and thus will not be subject to federal estate taxes. If the donor is the remainder beneficiary, the trust property will be included in his or her gross estate and will be subject to estate taxes.

Generation-Skipping Transfer Taxes

∝ What are the generation-skipping transfer tax consequences of using a charitable lead trust?

Unless the grandchild's parent (your child) is deceased when you set up the trust, naming a grandchild as a remainder beneficiary of a CLT triggers the generation-skipping transfer (GST) tax (described in Chapter 6, Federal Estate and Gift Tax Deductions). The exact results depend on whether the trust is an annuity trust or a unitrust.

∝ What if I name my grandchild as the remainder beneficiary of a CLAT?

IRS regulations provide that a gift from a CLAT to a grandchild or other person more than one generation removed from the donor is valued at the termination of the trust, but the GST tax exemption must be allocated when the trust is established. Moreover, when the donor-trust maker allocates GST tax exemption to the trust, the amount allocated "grows" at a rate determined by the government.

This presents a significant planning problem. To achieve many of the donor's original goals for using the CLT, we hope and expect that the value of the remainder interest in the annuity trust at the end of the term is far greater than the original gift. With a CLAT, GST taxes are applied to this larger value. Because we won't know until the end of the annuity trust term the exact value of the remainder interest in the trust, we don't know exactly how much GST tax exemption to allocate to the trust. Invariably, the donor will either allocate too little and the GST tax will have to be paid when the grandchild receives the remainder or allocate more of his or her GST tax exemption than needed to offset the GST tax, in which case the donor is wasting some of this precious planning resource.

Are the results the same if I name my grandchild to receive the remainder interest of a CLUT?

The IRS regulations create a different result for a unitrust. Donors to a unitrust can calculate the GST tax impact on the original donations. The value of the gift and the GST tax consequences are known with certainty from the onset, because the GST tax on the gift is based on the present value of the grandchild's remainder interest. Thus, by allocating to the trust an amount of GST exemption equal to the present value of the grandchild's remainder interest, the GST tax is avoided completely.

A charitable lead unitrust can pass a substantial amount of assets to grandchildren or great grandchildren at very low gift tax costs while minimizing the amount of the generation-skipping transfer tax exemption that must be allocated to the gifts.

Calculating the Deductions

How are deductions calculated?

As a split-interest trust, the CLT has two interests: the lead interest that is a stream of payments to charity and the remainder interest that goes to the noncharitable beneficiaries.

To determine the income and gift taxes for the trust maker:

- The value of the gift to charity is the present value of the payment stream to charity over the term of the trust.
- The value of the gift to the remainder beneficiaries is the fair market value of the asset when it was transferred to the trust, less the present value of the payments to charity.

The gift to charity does not incur gift tax, but the donor does make a taxable gift of the remainder interest if he or she is not the remainder beneficiary. If the trust is structured in such a way that the trust maker is entitled to an income tax deduction, the value of the charitable gift for income tax purposes is the present value of the charitable interest. In other words, it's the same value for both income tax and gift tax purposes.

❦ How is present value determined?

The present value of a stream of payments such as an annuity or unitrust interest is based on four factors:

1. the *applicable federal rate (AFR)*, which is an assumed rate of return published monthly by the government;
2. the term of the trust—the number of years that the charity will receive the payments;
3. whether the charity's interest is an annuity or a unitrust; and
4. the payout rate.

❦ Can you give me an example of how these calculations work?

Yes. Let's assume that Jerry creates a charitable lead annuity trust that is to pay his favorite charity $50,000 each year for 15 years. The remainder beneficiaries of Jerry's CLAT are his three children. Jerry transfers an asset worth $500,000 to the trust. The AFR rate at the time of Jerry's transfer is 7.4 percent. Using the IRS tables for calculating the present value of the income payments to charity, Jerry's advisors determine that the present value of the gift to charity is $456,234. They subtract that amount from the original value of the asset, which results in $43,766. This is the value of the remainder interest passing to Jerry's three children and is the value of the gift that Jerry is making to his children. If the trust is structured so Jerry is entitled to an income tax deduction, the value of the charitable gift for income tax purposes is also $456,234.

❦ How does a charitable lead trust discount the value of a gift?

The key concept is the time value of money. If we compare a gift of $10,000 today with the promise to pay $10,000 5 years from now, it is clear that $10,000 today is more valuable than the promise of $10,000 5 years later. If we put the $10,000 in a trust and then pay $500, or 5 percent, per year to a charity, the trust will need to grow at least $500, or 5 percent, each year to stay even. Thus, if you make a $10,000 gift to a charitable lead trust, which will pay $500 per year to your favorite charity, and provide that, after 5 years, whatever is in the trust will go to your children, the *present dollar value* of what your children will receive *as valued today* is far less than $10,000.

More important, keep in mind that the actual growth of the asset value while the trust is in effect is irrelevant for purposes of calculating the value of the remainder interest. So, if the asset transferred to the CLT grows more than originally calculated to make the required payment to charity, the remainder beneficiaries will receive a substantial gift with minimal gift tax costs. Following the example in the previous answer, if the value of the property remaining in the trust after 15 years—after making all the payments to charity—has grown to $1 million, Jerry has transferred this significant sum to his children for a taxable gift tax of only $43,766.

Is it possible to "zero-out" the gift or estate tax?

We often do this for our clients. Using a charitable lead annuity trust with a sufficiently high payout rate and term, it is possible to obtain a mathematical value of the charitable interest equal to the value of the property contributed. The result is that for determining the gift or estate tax, the value of the remainder interest is zero. If there is any amount left in the CLT when the charitable interest expires, that amount passes to the remainder beneficiaries free of estate or gift taxes.

This technique only works with a CLAT. Moreover, depending on the AFR when the donor funds the trust, the charity's annuity interest must run for 17 years or more to reduce the value of the remainder to zero.

Trustees

Who can be my trustee?

If you have retained a reversion, you can usually serve as trustee without any adverse tax consequences. But if you have named someone else as the remainder beneficiary, our advice is *not to be your own trustee*. You jeopardize the favorable gift tax results if you do so and may be required to pay the income taxes on the trust's income (although you would receive an upfront charitable income tax deduction). For the same reasons, it is not advisable to name your spouse as trustee. Any other family member can serve as trustee without adverse tax results. Otherwise, the best choice for a CLT is a corporate, or institutional, trustee.

Planning Considerations for *Inter Vivos* Charitable Lead Trusts

ᘓ *Which payment arrangement is more commonly used, the annuity or the unitrust?*

Our clients tend to favor CLATs. A CLAT's investment performance does not affect the amount of the annual payment to charity but it will impact, usually favorably, the amount of the remainder interest going to its noncharitable family beneficiaries.

ᘓ *When should I use a CLAT and when should I use a CLUT? Can I use them in combination?*

You should use a CLAT to zero-out your federal estate tax. You should use a CLUT to maximize your opportunities to do generation-skipping transfer tax planning. They are often used together to accomplish both objectives in a trust maker's estate plan.

ᘓ *Do most of your clients go for the income tax deduction?*

In our experience, most clients take a pass on the income tax deduction because they do not want to pay the taxes on the trust's income for all those years. However, clients who will have a very high income in 1 year and less in future years often take the immediate charitable income tax deduction to lower their taxes in the year they fund their trusts.

For example, one of our clients was the recipient of her father's pension plan benefits. When her father died, the pension plan required that she take a lump-sum distribution of $200,000 from the plan. That entire distribution was taxable to her, so, to offset her larger-than-normal tax bill for that year, she created a CLAT, structured to provide her with a sizeable offsetting income tax deduction.

TESTAMENTARY CHARITABLE LEAD TRUSTS

Overview of Testamentary Charitable Lead Trusts

ભ *I like the concept of a charitable lead trust, but I am not con-templating making a significant gift during my lifetime. Can I wait and use one after my death?*

Yes. This is called a *testamentary charitable lead trust (T-CLT)*. A T-CLT is a very flexible and powerful wealth transfer strategy that you can place in your will or living trust to take effect at your death. It allows you to retain your property while you are alive; and then, after your death, to benefit charity for a period of years and to eventually pass that property to your family at little or no estate tax cost.

ભ *What is the primary reason for using testamentary charitable lead trusts?*

A T-CLT can achieve significant estate and generation-skipping transfer tax savings. An additional advantage is that the assets that go into the lead trust receive a step-up in basis to their fair market value at the death of the donor. This may be a significant advantage if the assets are low-basis assets. It also gives the trustee of the lead trust the opportunity to sell the assets at no taxable gain when diversifying the trust's portfolio.

Tax Consequences of Testamentary Charitable Lead Trusts

ભ *How does a testamentary charitable lead trust reduce my estate taxes?*

With a T-CLT, the donor's estate is entitled to a charitable estate tax deduction for the present value of the charitable annuity or unitrust interest. This tax deduction will lower the amount of estate taxes due.

୧ର *How does a testamentary charitable lead trust eliminate estate taxes?*

As we explained previously, it is possible to establish a charitable lead annuity trust in which the value of the charity's annuity is equal to the total value of the property passing to the trust. For example, if a donor dies owning assets valued at $1 million and those assets pass to a T-CLAT containing a "formula" clause that will fix the value of the annuity interest at $1 million, the estate receives a $1 million estate tax deduction, which eliminates the estate taxes on the assets even though the assets remaining in the trust will pass to family members when the trust terminates.

୧ର *My children might be in their 60s or 70s by the time my T-CLT terminates. Can I shorten the time period?*

The length of time that remainder beneficiaries must wait to receive their inheritance is certainly a downside to a T-CLT. To minimize the effects of the delay, most clients engage in other planning during their lifetimes to provide an inheritance to their children at their deaths.

୧ର *Won't inflation erode the buying power of the remainder given to the family?*

Not necessarily. If the trust assets are appreciating in value, that appreciation reduces the value of the fixed amount going to charity and passes increased wealth to your family members free of tax.

chapter 10

Issues Common to All Charitable Trusts

APPROPRIATE DONATIONS THROUGH CHARITABLE TRUSTS

Best Assets to Donate to Charitable Remainder Trusts

ᴄ℞ *What are the best types of assets to use with a charitable remainder trust?*

The best assets are high-value, low-cost-basis, non-income-producing assets, such as real estate or securities, that you would like to sell if it were not for the capital gain tax. By transferring highly appreciated assets to a CRT, the taxpayer avoids immediate capital gain recognition from the sale, improves cash flow, and makes a gift to his or her favorite charitable cause.

Best Assets to Donate to Charitable Lead Trusts

CR *What are the best assets to use with a charitable lead trust?*

If your goal is to transfer wealth to children or others through the CLT, the best assets are those that generate a high rate of total return.

The value of the noncharitable remainder interest is calculated using the length of the charitable term, the payout rate of the trust, and an assumed rate of return (known as the applicable federal rate) on the trust assets. These factors produce the value of the interest that will pass to the noncharitable beneficiaries at the end of the trust term, on a present-value basis.

If the trust assets earn less than the assumed rate of return, the actual value of the remainder will be less than projected. The goal of the CLT is to have the trust return on assets exceed the assumed rate of return so the remainder interest is larger than what was projected. Thus, income-producing assets that are also appreciating significantly make ideal CLT property.

Assets That Require Special Consideration

CR *Are there any assets that shouldn't be contributed to charitable remainder or charitable lead trusts?*

Assets that create problems are active businesses, professional corporation stock, subchapter S corporation stock, debt-encumbered property, and real property with environmental problems. Some of these assets are problems for tax reasons; others, like professional corporations, are problems because of state law requirements on ownership.

Stock of Closely Held Corporations

CR *Can we contribute the stock in our business to a charitable trust?*

Some of the best candidates for using charitable remainder trusts are the owners of closely held businesses. If your exit strategy is to sell your business some day, you would certainly have significant capital gain and estate tax issues that could be easily resolved with a CRT.

You can also use a charitable lead annuity trust to transfer all or part of your company stock to children, with little or no gift taxes. The only caveat is that the company *must* generate sufficient income to make the annuity payments because the trust maker cannot contribute cash to a CLAT to make up the deficiency.

⚮ *Can we contribute subchapter S stock to a charitable trust?*

You can transfer subchapter S stock to a CRT, but the transfer would require the corporation to terminate the S election and become a C, or regular, corporation. Terminating an S election could have significant tax consequences for the corporation and its shareholders.

Transferring the subchapter S stock to a CLT may or may not terminate the S election; and, depending on the terms of the trust, such a transfer could create additional tax consequences—a discussion of which is outside the scope of this book. Your advisors can explain these if you are considering donating subchapter S stock to a CLT.

⚮ *I'm a physician. Can I transfer the stock in my professional corporation to a CRT or a CLT?*

Under state corporate statutes, an individual who is a licensed professional must at all times own the stock of a professional corporation. Contributing your stock to a CRT or a CLT would be in violation of state statutes.

Debt-Encumbered Property

⚮ *What problems exist when we want to contribute debt-encumbered property to a CRT?*

Several problems could occur when you contribute real property that is subject to mortgage or other debt to a CRT. Some of the problems include:

- Property financed partially or totally by debt can generate unrelated-business taxable income (UBTI; discussed below). If a CRT realizes any amount of UBTI, the entire undistributed income, including capital gain for that trust year, is subject to income taxes at the trust level.
- If the debt is the donor's personal debt, payment of the obligation by the trust will result in the trust being treated as a grantor trust

(a trust that does not file a separate tax return but whose tax items appear on its maker's return), which disqualifies it as a CRT.

- When you contribute debt-encumbered real property to a CRT, it will be considered a bargain sale even though you receive no cash. (See chapters 4 and 15 for discussions on bargain sales.)

Do the same problems exist if we transfer debt-encumbered property to a CLT?

Yes and no. Because a charitable lead trust is not tax-exempt, the UBTI issue is not applicable. However, just as with the CRT, payment of the obligation by the trust will result in the CLT being treated as a grantor trust (its tax items appear on your tax return). Having the CLT treated as a grantor trust may or may not be in keeping with your original objective if that objective was to avoid paying income taxes on the trust income. Also, the bargain-sale rules may or may not apply. The major concern, however, is a practical one: Will the debt-encumbered property support both the mortgage payment and the payment to charity?

Annuities

Can we contribute an existing annuity contract to a charitable trust?

Yes, you can, but you may be required to personally recognize (as ordinary income) the amount of accumulated earnings inside the contract at the time you make the contribution.

Depending upon the amount of the accumulated earnings and the ages of the income beneficiaries, the amount of taxable income that you have to realize may be largely or entirely offset by the amount of the charitable income tax deduction available to you.

Retirement Plans

Can I give my individual retirement account to a charitable remainder or charitable lead trust during my lifetime?

Yes, you can. Unfortunately, if you do transfer assets from your IRA to a CRT or a CLT during your lifetime, the transfer is treated as a distribution to you and will be subject to income tax and possibly an early-withdrawal penalty. You would be contributing after-tax dollars to the charitable trust. The charitable deduction that you would receive for your cash contribution to the charitable trust is limited to 50 percent of your contribution base in any given year.

Currently, there is no way to transfer your IRA or other retirement account to a charitable remainder trust during your lifetime on a tax-free basis. However, at the time of writing this book, Congress is considering legislation that would allow a lifetime transfer of retirement assets to a charitable remainder trust on a tax-free basis for some individuals.

Can I leave my retirement plan proceeds to a charitable remainder or charitable lead trust at my death?

You can leave your retirement plan proceeds to a CRT at your death. This is highly recommended if your goals are to benefit charity and to reduce estate taxes on the plan proceeds.

Because a CLT is not a tax-exempt trust, funding a CLT with your retirement plan proceeds at death would likely result in excessive income taxes on the plan proceeds that the trust will have to pay.

Promissory Notes

We recently sold some appreciated real estate on installment terms in an effort to spread out the capital gain tax over the term of the note. Would the installment note be a good asset to transfer to a charitable trust?

Unfortunately, transferring an installment note to a CRT accelerates the recognition of the capital gain that you are trying to defer. In some cases, however, the capital gain that you have to realize may be offset by the charitable income tax deduction that you receive for the contribution.

It is unclear under the Internal Revenue Code whether transferring an installment note to a CLT will accelerate the gain recognition.

Unrelated-Business Taxable Income Property

CR *What is unrelated-business taxable income?*

Generally speaking, *unrelated-business taxable income (UBTI)* is income derived by a charity from any unrelated trade or business that it carries on and that is not specifically excluded by statute. Typically, investment income or capital gains are not UBTI (unless the asset is debt financed). Revenue from an active trade or business, however, is generally considered to be UBTI.

UBTI is a highly technical tax concept designed to prevent tax-exempt charities from operating businesses in competition with entities that have to pay taxes on their earnings. Even though charities normally do not pay income taxes on what they earn, they will be taxed just like any other business on any UBTI that they derive from business activities unrelated to their charitable purposes.

Because charitable lead trusts are not tax-exempt, UBTI rules do not apply to them. They are, however, especially important for charitable remainder trusts, as we discuss below.

CR *Can you give me an example of UBTI?*

The net income earned by a church from operating a bicycle repair shop would be a classic case of UBTI. This is a rather obvious example, but what is not so obvious, and trips up unsuspecting charitable organizations, is that certain investments, such as publicly traded master limited partnerships or real estate investment trusts, may throw off UBTI.

CR *I have an apartment building. In addition to the usual rental income, I rent some of the apartments furnished and provide cleaning services. In addition, the building has coin-operated washers and dryers. Can I put this property into a charitable remainder trust?*

You can put the apartment house into the CRT and the trust can continue to receive apartment rents. However, unless the amounts earned are "incidental" in comparison to the rent payments, a CRT cannot earn income from the rental of personal property—the furniture rentals and the washers and dryers—or from providing services without incurring serious consequences. Income from these sources is UBTI in most cases.

ℜ *Why is UBTI a major problem in charitable remainder trusts?*

If a charity earns UBTI in any year, it is taxed on *only* the UBTI that it earned that year. By contrast, if a CRT has UBTI in any year, the CRT is taxed on *all* of its undistributed income, irrespective of its source. This means that even if it has only $1 of UBTI and $50,000 of other income that year, it would be taxed on the entire $50,001.

This could be especially disastrous if it occurred in a year that the CRT realizes substantial capital gains upon the sale of the highly appreciated asset that the donor contributed. If a primary motivation for creating the charitable remainder trust was to defer immediate imposition of capital gain taxes on the sale of a highly appreciated asset, the donor's entire purpose could be frustrated by the receipt of any UBTI.

ℜ *Will debt-encumbered property generate UBTI?*

Yes, it will in most circumstances. The income earned from debt-financed property will, in almost all cases, constitute UBTI. There is an exception for debt-financed property received by the trust as a contribution, but qualifying for that exception can be difficult and the exception only lasts for 10 years.

PRIVATE FOUNDATION RULES

ℜ *Why do I have to be concerned about private foundation rules if I'm setting up a charitable trust?*

The 1969 Tax Reform Act was passed, in part, to regulate private foundations. This law directly addressed abuses in charitable giving and instituted rules to absolutely prohibit certain conduct by private foundations and disqualified persons. These rules apply equally to a number of other charitable entities, including charitable remainder trusts and some charitable lead trusts.

The *private foundation rules* relate to self-dealing, excess business holdings, various types of expenditures, mandatory payout requirements, investment practices, and other compliance-oriented issues. Failure to comply with these rules results in substantial penalties and disqualification of the underlying charitable entity.

Self-Dealing

ᢕ *I contributed an apartment building to a CRT. If my son is willing to pay fair-market-value rent, can he live in one of the units?*

CRTs and CLTs are subject to most of the private foundation rules. One rule prohibits self-dealing between your CRT (or a CLT) and a *disqualified person,* which includes you and members of your family. *Self-dealing* includes any sale or lease or other financial transaction between the trust and a disqualified person. Therefore, your son may not live in your CRT-owned rental property—even if he paid more than the fair market rental value of the property—without violating the prohibition on self-dealing.

ᢕ *Can I receive a trustee fee for being trustee of my own CRT or CLT?*

Yes. The IRS has held, in several private rulings, that a donor-trust maker who serves as trustee for his or her charitable trust may be paid a fee for those services, providing the payments are reasonable and consistent with amounts ordinarily paid under state law. Such fees, however, may not be paid from the amount due the income beneficiary of the trust.

Excess Business Holdings

ᢕ *What are excess business holdings?*

Another private foundation rule is known as the *excess business holdings* rule. This rule limits the percentage amount that a charitable trust can own in a commercial business. Under this rule, a charitable trust is limited to less than 20 percent of the voting stock in a corporation. This rule applies to all charitable remainder trusts and the majority of charitable lead trusts. There are exceptions to this rule, most notably a foundation can own what would otherwise be an excess business holding for up to 5 years if it received the holding as a contribution from a donor.

Taxable Expenditures

◌੨ What constitutes a taxable expenditure?

A *taxable expenditure* is defined as a payment for any of the following purposes:

1. Distributing propaganda or otherwise attempting to influence legislation
2. Influencing the outcome of any specific public election or carrying on, directly or indirectly, any voter registration drive, unless certain conditions are met
3. A grant to an individual for travel, study, or other similar purposes, unless the grant meets certain requirements
4. A grant to an organization other than a public charity, unless the granting foundation exercises "expenditure responsibility"
5. Any purpose that is not a charitable purpose

Payments for these purposes will result in substantial fines on the charitable remainder or charitable lead trust and their trustees.

TIMING OF THE TRANSFERS TO CHARITABLE REMAINDER TRUSTS

◌੨ Can I find a buyer for my highly appreciated real estate, make an agreement for the sale, and then transfer ownership of the property to a CRT just before the sale so that I can defer the capital gain tax?

No, you cannot. If you do so, the IRS will seek to collapse this transaction under the *step-transaction doctrine*. The IRS would view the sale as occurring prior to the transfer to the CRT. And, if the IRS succeeds in characterizing the transaction as a step transaction, you will lose all of the tax savings that you would ordinarily receive from a properly timed CRT transaction.

It is not uncommon for an owner of a nonmarketable or limited-market asset to enter into preliminary negotiations for a sale before funding a CRT with the asset. However, even preliminary negotiations can be enough to taint the tax-advantaged nature of transferring the asset into a CRT and then having the CRT sell it. If you have a written purchase agreement on the asset, it is definitely too late to consider placing it in a charitable remainder trust.

If you and your advisors are prudent, you will transfer any "for sale" asset into your CRT prior to offering it for sale so you can enjoy the tax advantages of a CRT without having to worry about the IRS.

◌ৎ How would the IRS even know about any of the specifics of my sale and transaction with the CRT?

When your charitable remainder trust sells an asset within 2 years after you have transferred the asset to the trust, the trustee of your CRT must notify the IRS of the sale. If the IRS determines thereafter that you, rather than the trustee of the trust, initiated the sale of the asset, you will incur the capital gain tax liability.

◌ৎ If I get caught in the step-transaction doctrine, who pays the tax?

You, not your CRT, will pay the capital gain tax. Since you already transferred the asset to the CRT, the proceeds from the sale would *not* be available to you to pay the tax. The charitable trust owns the asset *and* the proceeds from the sale of the asset—and the charitable trust is irrevocable.

◌ৎ Can I even list the property for sale prior to transferring it to a CRT?

Yes, but this can be a bit risky. You may offer the property for sale, but you cannot have entered into a binding agreement with a buyer prior to funding the property to the CRT. The CRT trustee cannot be under an express or implied obligation to sell the property when the trust receives it. As a general rule, the trustee must have the ability to negotiate the transaction, change the terms of the sale agreement, or walk away from the deal. Again, timing is crucial. If the trust maker contributes real estate or a closely held business to the CRT—assets that normally take some time to sell—and the trustee sells the property a few days later, the transaction is likely to be scrutinized by the IRS.

NAMING PRIVATE FOUNDATIONS AS CHARITABLE BENEFICIARIES

℃ *Can my private foundation be the charitable beneficiary of a lead or remainder trust?*

Yes. One of the most rewarding aspects of wealth strategies planning is helping families develop a comprehensive plan for wealth transfer and a family legacy of giving. By combining charitable trusts with a family foundation, a family can reduce taxes, leverage various exemptions, maintain control of family wealth, and perpetuate family values.

℃ *Are there any problems with making my private foundation the beneficiary of my lead trust?*

If the maker of the CLT is also a director or trustee of the private foundation to which the CLT is making payments and can participate in decisions on how the CLT payment should be distributed, the assets of the CLT will be includable in the maker's estate if the trust maker dies within the trust term. The solution to this problem is to include a provision in the foundation's documentation precluding the CLT maker from participating in decisions as to the funds received from the CLT.

PART FOUR

Uses for Charitable Planning

Beyond the immeasurable satisfaction of benefiting the charity of your choice, what can you achieve through charitable planning? That is the question we explore in Part Four. Our contributors integrate the concepts and strategies explained in the previous three parts of *Giving* with their clients' most common financial and estate planning goals to illustrate the tangible benefits that can come from planned giving.

The topic of chapter 11 is financial planning. As we wrote *Giving,* we were in the wake of declines in the stock market and the much-publicized losses of retirement funds by employees of Enron. Thus, more than ever before, financial planning is of concern and should be important to most Americans. Many people have also experienced serious setbacks with do-it-yourself financial planning and investing. Good advice is worth its weight in gold when your personal financial health is concerned.

What many people do not realize is that charitable planning can make their financial plans more successful. No one expects you to give away more than you can afford, and to do any planning, you first must know what happens to your money—in essence, you must determine your income and expenses to prepare a personal profit-and-loss statement—and then calculate all of your assets and liabilities to create a personal balance sheet. Only when you clearly understand how much comes in and how much you spend and the extent of your financial resources, can you determine what you need to sustain your lifestyle and what you can do charitably.

Incorporating charitable giving into your financial plan has many advantages. By using certain charitable strategies, you may be able to reduce your income taxes, to defer capital gain tax on sales of highly appreciated assets, or to diversify your investment portfolio. Other charitable strategies might provide you with a stream of income now, or to save more for significant life events, or to defer income for retirement. And you get to reap these benefits while supporting the charitable causes that are important to you. It is a true win–win situation.

Estate planning is a critical aspect of financial planning. Chapter 12 provides ideas on how charitable giving may assist you in preparing a flexible estate plan, which is important in light of the Economic Growth and Tax Relief Reconciliation Act of 2001. Lifetime and testamentary gifts to charity certainly reduce federal estate taxes. More important, the charitable strategies that we discuss in *Giving* may enable you to transfer wealth to your loved ones in a manner that will either reduce or eliminate federal estate taxes.

In this chapter you will learn how to create a zero estate tax plan using the charitable strategies you read about in *Giving*. Our contributing authors' clients also asked how to reduce gift taxes on wealth transfers, how to preserve the gift tax exemption when possible, and how to use that exemption effectively. One important strategy our contributors describe is the use of life insurance and an irrevocable life insurance trust, or wealth replacement trust, to replace amounts that donors give to charity. You can replace the assets that you transfer to charity with life insurance of an equal or greater value—and structure it so the life insurance proceeds will pass to your beneficiaries tax-free!

Business succession planning is a major concern for many small-business owners. In chapter 13, our contributors discuss how vital family participation is to the development of a solid succession plan for a business. Our contributors also explain the charitable bailout and the charitable employee stock ownership plan techniques as possible exit, or succession, strategies that allow business owners to benefit charity as they retire from an active role in operating their businesses. In this chapter our contributors advise that S corporations require special planning.

Charitable planning seems a logical accompaniment to both financial and estate planning, but most people would not guess that charitable planning can also benefit retirement planning. Our contributing authors demonstrate how to use charitable planning vehicles to create more income for your retirement years even if you're already participating in a traditional tax-deferred retirement plan.

Those who wish to donate real estate outright to charity or use it to fund a charitable trust face special issues. For example, real estate potentially carries many liabilities and hazards that some charities may be either unwilling or unable to accept. In chapter 15, *Giving* contributors analyze these issues in great detail. They also offer techniques that are specially suited for transferring real estate to charity, including the bargain-sale technique that clients frequently ask about.

Conservation easements are becoming a popular method for making charitable gifts of real estate. Our research further indicated that many people are interested in donating their residences to charity but retaining the right to live in the homes for the rest of their lives. In addition, our contributors discuss how nonproductive real estate can be converted into an income stream through a charitable gift annuity or charitable remainder trust.

As you will read in Part Four, you can use charitable planning to leverage almost any goal you have. It can expand the options for any type of planning you do for your future and that of your loved ones. The marvelous aspect of charitable planning is that you can do good for others while also achieving your noncharitable goals. The old adage "charity begins at home" misses the mark. You can be generous to yourself and to worthwhile causes at the same time. You can use charitable strategies in combination with one another and with other planning techniques to create a financial synergy that is exciting and impressive. Although the rules and regulations governing these techniques can be complex, our contributors have done an excellent job of explaining them so you can ask them or your own advisors if any of these techniques are suitable for your specific situation.

chapter 11

Financial Planning

GOALS

ᘓ *Giving to charity is one of our personal goals, but we are uncertain about what impact our giving may have on our lifestyle over the years. What can we do to determine the limits of how generous we can be?*

Understanding your money and your total financial picture is a critical step in sharing it. You won't know how much you can give to charity until you know what you have and what you need. A financial plan will include planning for your gifts to charity.

We suggest that you gather all documents that describe your wealth. These include items such as paycheck stubs; credit card and bank statements; checking account registers; mortgage and loan documents; stock, bond, and mutual fund statements; retirement account statements; trust documents; partnership agreements; tax returns; and insurance policies.

This documentation will give you the necessary information to prepare a financial statement of assets and liabilities and a profit-and-loss statement with your income, expenses, and investment capabilities.

At this stage, you may wish to retain the services of a financial planning professional. He or she can help you clarify your goals, budget your living and investment needs, and coordinate your own financial interests with your charitable aspirations.

◌ *What does a financial plan include?*

We discussed in chapter 2 how to create your charitable mission statement. A financial plan is a macro view of your financial goals and prospects within which your charitable plan must fit. A proper financial plan generally should include:

- *A Vision Statement:* This is a short but meaningful statement of your major financial goals and purposes, including your charitable goals. We encourage our clients to envision how they want their lives to be 5 years into the future.

- A *Mission Statement:* Next you have to determine what you must do in the intervening 5 years to get you to the successes you envisioned. In your mission statement, you should state as simply as you can what you must do to make your vision a reality.

- *Objectives:* From the mission statement, create a set of specific financial objectives that you will refer to continually in order to stay on your financial course. For example, two of your objectives might be to have, at the end of 5 years, at least 25 percent of your child's college tuition accumulated and a scholarship fund established in memory of your parents.

- *Strategies:* Your strategies will state, in general, all of the ways by which you will accomplish your objectives. For example, you will reduce expenses, defer more into your 401(k) plan, and put an additional amount of money into mutual funds every month.

- *Action Plans:* Action plans are the specific steps you have to take to carry out your objectives and when you will take them. For example, you will change your 401(k) deferred amount by X date; you will create a budget by X date, which reduces expenses by X dollars, 25 percent of which goes into your 401(k) plan and the rest to your investment account.

CR What are some financial goals that I can achieve by making gifts to charity?

In our experience in working with a number of clients in this regard, gifts to charity can:

- Reduce income taxes
- Defer and/or avoid capital gain taxes
- Increase income streams for donors
- Defer current income for later retirement
- Diversify investment portfolio to reduce risk
- Provide asset protection

REDUCE INCOME TAXES

In General

CR Why does the government encourage charitable giving?

One of the more popular benefits of charitable giving is that all or a part of the contribution is income-tax–deductible. Congress understands that the nation's charities provide a great many benefits for society that reduce our reliance upon the public treasury. Therefore, to encourage giving, it allows donors to deduct all or a portion of their contributions, which results in income tax reductions.

Outright Gifts to Charity

CR How can charitable giving result in major tax savings for me and my husband?

Let's assume that you and your husband have a gross income of $120,000, itemized deductions of $34,200, and personal exemptions of $5,800; and, therefore, a net taxable income of $80,000. Let's further assume that the 2002 tax on that $80,000 is $16,524 if you did not make a gift to charity.

Table 11-1 compares these tax results with those of making a

TABLE 11-1   Tax Results of No Gift Versus a Gift

	Without a gift	With a gift
Gross income	$120,000	$120,000
Itemized deductions	34,200	34,200
Personal exemptions	5,800	5,800
Charitable contribution	0	36,000
Net taxable income	80,000	44,000
Tax	16,524	6,600
After-tax income	$ 63,466	$ 37,400

$36,000 cash gift. Although your charitable gift is 45 percent of your contribution base, it results in more than a 60 percent decrease ($9,924) in your tax. Instead of paying the government the $9,924, you directed that amount to your choice of charity. Looked at another way, you were able to make a gift of $36,000, of which you paid $26,076 and the government paid $9,924.

Your financial planner will run calculations such as this to help you to determine how much tax savings you can realize and how such gifts to charity might help you achieve other financial goals.

Charitable Remainder Trusts and Pooled Income Funds

How does a charitable remainder trust reduce income taxes?

Donors to a CRT are entitled to an income tax deduction for the present value of the remainder interest passing to charity. To calculate the remainder interest, you first calculate the present value of the stream of income payments you expect to receive over the term of the trust, and subtract that value from the fair market value of the property on the date that you contributed it to the CRT. The resulting amount is the remainder interest going to charity. The present value of that amount is the amount of charitable contribution you use to reduce your income taxes.

How can gifts to a pooled income fund reduce payment of my taxes?

Pooled income funds work the same way as the charitable remainder trusts in that

- you contribute assets to a pooled income fund;
- the fund provides you with income for the rest of your life and, upon your death, passes the remainder interest to charity; and
- the present value of the remainder interest is the amount of your income tax deduction.

Charitable Lead Trusts

My company is being bought out and I will receive a large "golden parachute" payment, so I need an income tax deduction. I want to benefit charity but would prefer to keep the bulk of that money in the family. Do you have any suggestions?

You could set up a charitable lead trust structured to give you an immediate charitable deduction for the assets that you place in the trust. However, with this type of CLT, you will also pay the tax on all of the income that the trust earns over the term of the trust. Since you are likely to be in a lower income tax bracket in the future, the immediate tax deduction may be worth the trade-off of paying taxes on the trust's income. Also, you might invest the funds inside the CLT in a mixture of tax-exempt securities and long-term growth assets that do not produce taxable income in order to reduce the income tax implications to you.

I have a lot of vested stock options from my employer. Can I donate those to charity? What are the tax consequences for me?

Assuming that your vested stock options are nonqualified stock options (NSOs) and that your employer's plan allows transfers during your lifetime, you may contribute them to charity. Before you do so, however, you should consider the following federal gift and income tax issues peculiar to gifts of NSOs:

- You will not recognize income or gain upon the donation of your NSOs to charity. When the charity exercises the options, you will recognize ordinary income in the amount of the difference between the fair market value of the underlying stock at the date of exercise and the strike price of the NSOs. In other words, you will be taxed on this amount even though the charity receives all the benefits of exercising the options.

■ You will be entitled to a federal income tax deduction in the year that you make the transfer, if your gift of the NSOs to charity is unrestricted and you retain no control over when the charity can exercise the NSOs. If your NSOs have no readily ascertainable fair market value when you make the charitable gift, their value would presumably be quite low. This low value would result in a modest federal income tax deduction in the year of the gift. Moreover, because you are recognizing ordinary income, your charitable income tax deduction would be 50 percent of your contribution.

Because your recognition of compensation income would occur at some later time when the charity exercises the NSOs, you could be forced to recognize a substantial amount of ordinary income in a future year without the availability of any offsetting income tax deduction.

The Internal Revenue Service has allowed employees to retain some control over when and to what extent the charity can exercise the NSOs so employees can avoid this situation and match their charitable deductions with receipt of the income when the charity does exercise the options.

In view of the complexity of giving NSOs to charity, you should consult with experienced tax counsel before proceeding. If the amounts at issue are substantial, you should consider requesting a private letter ruling from the IRS before making a gift of your NSOs.

DEFER AND/OR AVOID
CAPITAL GAIN TAXES

Outright Gifts to Charity

℞ *I bought 500 shares of stock quite a few years ago for about $4 per share. Over the years, the stock has split and grown in value so that I now own 1,200 shares worth $60 per share. I want to* *sell the stock and give the money to my church. Is there a way I can avoid paying the capital gain tax?*

Yes. You can give the stock to your church, which allows you not only to avoid the capital gain tax on the stock's appreciation but also to receive an income tax deduction for its appreciated value. The church can sell the stock without paying tax and have the use of 100 percent of the proceeds.

CR *I have available cash to give to charity and would like to make a gift. I also own highly appreciated stock, but I'd like to keep that stock in my portfolio. What should I do?*

Give your appreciated stock to charity, and use the cash to purchase more of that same stock. By doing this, you will increase your basis (cost of the stock for income tax purposes) to its current value and avoid the capital gain tax on the stock you donated.

CR *Can you give me an example of this technique?*

Sure. Bob and Cindy want to make a $10,000 gift to the YWCA. They can afford to make the gift in cash, but they also have stock that they purchased several years ago for $1,000 that is now worth $10,000. After talking to their accountant, Bob and Cindy decide to contribute the appreciated stock instead of cash. They receive a $10,000 charitable income tax deduction and avoid the capital gain tax on the $9,000 appreciation. The YWCA doesn't pay the tax either because it is a tax-exempt charity, so it has the use of the full $10,000 after it sells the stock.

Bob and Cindy use the $10,000 in cash to buy stock in the same company. They now own the same stock with a $10,000 basis. If, in the future, the stock is worth $15,000, their gain on the sale will be only $5,000 rather than $14,000.

Charitable Gift Annuities

CR *If I give highly appreciated stock in exchange for a gift annuity, can I save capital gain tax?*

A portion of the appreciation escapes capital gain tax entirely, and you may spread out any reportable capital gains over your actuarial life expectancy.

Pooled Income Funds

℞ My spouse and I are in our mid-40s. Years ago we invested $5,000 in a stock, which is now valued at $35,000 and paying dividends. We like the idea of supporting a local charity and don't like the idea of paying capital gain taxes, but we don't want to give up the dividend income. What can we consider?

You can contact the charity to see if it has a pooled income fund. If so, you can donate the appreciated stock to the charity's pooled income fund, avoid the capital gain tax, and receive income payments for a term of years, in addition to receiving a charitable income tax deduction. The pooled income fund's earnings will fluctuate based on its holding, so the income you receive will reflect these fluctuations over the years.

Charitable Remainder Trusts

℞ I have several thousand shares of non-dividend-paying stock in a publicly traded company. My wife and I would like to turn this stock into some type of income-producing investment but can't stand the thought of paying more than $100,000 in capital gain taxes. Are there alternatives?

You could establish a charitable remainder trust. The trustee of the CRT can convert the non-dividend-paying stock to income-producing stock with no capital gain tax consequences. You defer your capital gain tax bill, create an income stream for the rest of your lives, and receive an income tax deduction for making a donation.

℞ I am ready to retire and want to sell a rental property to invest in something that will pay me an annual income of at least $140,000. I believe that I can sell the property for about $2 million cash. Unfortunately, I have a $200,000 adjusted

TABLE 11-2 Comparison of Sales and Donation

	Cash sale	Installment sale	Contribution to a CRUT
Annual payments*	$ 131,200 (for life)	$ 153,630 (15 years)	$ 160,000 (for life)
		142,544 (9 years)	
Total lifetime payments	3,148,800	3,587,346	3,840,000
Principal at death	1,640,000	1,781,807	0

*Assumes a 24-year life expectancy.

basis in the property and will incur a huge capital gain tax. Is there a better alternative than selling it?

A better solution than selling the property may be to place it in a charitable remainder trust. The CRT could sell the property without paying tax and pay you an income stream to meet your needs for the rest of your life. Keep in mind, however, that if you took depreciation deductions on the property, some of the gain on the sale may be subject to tax under the depreciation recapture rules.

℞ *Can you give me an example of this technique?*

Yes. You say that you own a building worth $2 million, your adjusted basis is $200,000, and you need an income of around $140,000 a year. Let's assume that you and your wife are ages 67 and 66, respectively. Let's further assume that your investments will earn an average 8 percent return; that your ordinary income tax rate is 35 percent; and that the federal capital gain tax rate is 20 percent. Let's compare three alternatives: a cash sale, an installment sale, and a charitable remainder unitrust. For the sake of simplicity, we have not included income taxes in our examples.

■ *Cash Sale*

If you receive $2 million cash, you will pay capital gain taxes of $360,000 on the $1.8 million gain, leaving you with $1.64 million to invest. If you invest that in a portfolio earning 8 percent, you will earn $131,200 each year. Over your joint-life expectancy (24 years) these earnings add up to $3,148,800 in income for you and your wife. Assuming you do not spend the $1.64 million of principal, that amount is included in your estate.

- *Installment Sale*

  If you sell the property for $2 million with a $685,000 down payment and the buyer pays you $153,630 per year for 15 years (at an 8 percent interest rate), you would pay approximately $123,300 in capital gain taxes on the down payment and could invest the remaining $561,700.

  You are receiving $153,630 a year from the buyer, so you would not have to touch the $561,700. Assuming that it earns the same 8 percent return, there would be approximately $1,781,807 in that investment account at the end of 15 years. You then live off the 8 percent return on that amount ($142,544) for the rest of your lives.

- *Charitable Remainder Unitrust*

  Another alternative is to place the property into a charitable remainder unitrust (CRUT) that pays you 8 percent annually. Based upon your ages and the current applicable federal rate of 5.6 percent, you would receive an immediate charitable income tax deduction of approximately $431,740, saving you an estimated $151,109 in federal income taxes.

  With an 8 percent CRUT, you would receive $160,000 per year in income and would avoid the immediate capital gain taxes because using any CRT allows you to recognize the capital gains over your life expectancy.

Table 11-2 compares the financial results of these three options. Each option has its advantages and disadvantages, depending on your particular goals. A charitable remainder trust, however, provides two benefits that the cash and installment sale options do not provide: (1) You have an opportunity to be philanthropic and support your favorite causes while receiving a charitable income tax deduction to do so; and (2) you removed the remaining principal from your estate for purposes of federal estate taxes. The downside is that you removed the remaining principal from your estate, so your heirs would not receive any inheritance out of this asset. But you could use the income tax savings or a portion of your income payments from the CRUT to purchase life insurance inside an irrevocable life insurance trust to replace the value that your heirs are losing.

CREATE AN
INCOME STREAM

Can I receive an income from assets I give away to charity?

Charitable remainder trusts, pooled income funds, and charitable gift annuities are all charitable giving instruments that will allow you to receive income during your lifetime. Depending on the assets you contribute, your age, and other factors, each of these vehicles can provide benefits in the appropriate situations.

Charitable Gift Annuities

My mother is 78 and living off the income from her $200,000 in certificates of deposit. My sister and I would like her to have more income, but she won't accept any help from us. What might we do to help?

You might have your mother consider a charitable gift annuity. A CGA is most often used by individuals who own assets that produce little or no income and need to generate more cash flow to help them meet their living expenses. The older the donor is, the higher is the annual payment. When a donor contributes an appreciated asset to a CGA, he or she usually is able to increase the return significantly. Your mother's annuity payments will remain the same every year for the rest of her life no matter what happens in the financial markets.

For example, if she established the CGA in February 2002, your mother would receive an annual annuity payment of $16,800 for life from the charity in return for her $200,000, a return of 8.4 percent. In addition, she would receive a charitable income tax deduction of $90,250, which would substantially reduce her income taxes for several years.

Charitable Remainder Trusts

Can a charitable remainder trust increase the amount of income I am receiving on my assets each month?

If you have a highly appreciated asset that produces little or no income, contributing it to a CRT can immediately increase your cash flow. Through a CRT you can easily convert the asset to income-paying investments without incurring an immediate capital gain tax in the process. This results from the fact that the CRT, being a tax-exempt entity, pays no income tax on the sale of its assets. It may sell a non-income-producing asset and reinvest all of the sale proceeds into assets that produce a higher income, which you will receive in the form of an annuity or unitrust payment.

We are in our 80s and are more concerned about having predictable cash flow than protection against inflation. What type of CRT would best meet our needs?

A charitable remainder annuity trust (CRAT) may be just what you are looking for. Older couples who desire a predictable cash flow, and who are not worried about an inflation-protected income, tend to be interested in a CRAT. A CRAT distributes a fixed percentage of income based upon its original value.

A CRAT will provide fixed payments throughout its term, regardless of the return on the trust's investments. However, if the rate of return continually falls far short of the annuity rate, the CRAT assets may be depleted to the point at which there would be no residual benefit to charity.

We want a continuous stream of income that goes up with inflation and a bull market. What sort of CRT would be best for us?

A charitable remainder unitrust would fit you perfectly. It pays a fixed percentage of the trust assets, valued annually. The trust value will obviously fluctuate, so you bear the risk of inflation and downturns in the market, as well as the benefits of market upswings.

Can a charitable remainder trust provide income to beneficiaries other than my husband and me?

Yes. You can name your parents, children, grandchildren, or anyone else to receive the payments from a CRT. You can also have the income paid to you for life and, then at your death, to other family members.

Keep in mind, though, that whenever you name layers of beneficiaries, you are reducing the value of the charitable remainder interest and, therefore, reducing the value of your income tax deduction.

∝ *I have two daughters in their mid-40s. I would like to provide a steady cash flow of $4,000 to $5,000 per month to each of them for the remainder of their lives. I would also like to make a gift to charity. Is there a structure that would achieve these seemingly divergent objectives?*

A charitable remainder trust would work very well for this fact situation. You could contribute assets into a CRT, which would pay a steady stream of income payments to each of your daughters for their lifetimes, and then distribute the remainder of those assets to your charitable beneficiaries.

∝ *Is it better to have one trust for both daughters or one trust for each daughter?*

Since your daughters are in their mid-40s and based on your desire that your daughters receive approximately $50,000 per year, it would probably be more efficient to set up a remainder trust for each daughter. This is due to the tax law requirement that the present value of a CRT remainder interest be equal to 10 percent of your contribution to the trust. A single beneficiary is actuarially far more likely to die sooner than two beneficiaries, thereby ensuring that each trust will meet the 10 percent test.

∝ *I am gay, and my life partner is also my business partner. We each own a one-half interest in a shopping mall. We want to retire and sell the shopping mall. Can we create a joint charitable remainder trust and transfer our shopping mall to it?*

Probably not. While legally married couples can create a joint charitable remainder trust and contribute jointly owned assets to it, it is unclear whether unmarried couples can. The IRS might view a joint charitable remainder trust in your situation as a business association rather than a CRT. As a result, you would not enjoy the tax benefits of a CRT.

In addition, when you and your partner fund a joint CRT, one of you will likely be making a taxable gift to the other. The fact that the two of you must file separate income tax returns also complicates this plan.

Instead, each of you should create your own CRT and contribute your respective interest in the shopping mall to your trust. This should still accomplish most of your estate and charitable planning goals.

ᘒ *My spouse and I are well-to-do and want to teach our young adult children how to handle money before they receive their inheritance. We are very interested in charity and would like to combine our charitable interests with our desire to help our children. Do you have any suggestions?*

Talk to your advisors about creating a charitable remainder trust and a charitable lead trust in tandem. You could create a 15-year charitable remainder trust, which would provide your children with a series of income distributions to manage.

At the same time that you create the CRT, you also create a charitable lead trust that terminates at the end of 15 years. At the end of the 15-year CLT term, these "mature" adults receive a lump-sum distribution of the trust principal to invest and manage over their remaining lifetimes.

This is a terrific financial and estate plan for parents with your specific goals. The adult children receive income from the charitable remainder trust for the 15 years (we'll call it the "training years"). Perhaps they spend the first few checks before considering investing, but by the end of the 15-year term, when they receive the principal from the CLT, they hopefully have learned sound investment principles.

This also provides mom and dad a wonderful discount on their federal estate taxes while helping their children, grandchildren, and community.

DIVERSIFY INVESTMENT PORTFOLIO

ᘒ *How can charitable giving help me to diversify my portfolio?*

Imagine that you've worked for the same company for your entire career and, because of its generous stock option plans, you have accumulated a sizable portfolio of that company's stock. A financial advisor most certainly would tell you the following:

- To reduce your investment risk and to improve investment results, you need to be diversified among various asset classes.
- To diversify, you must sell a great deal of your stock—probably paying capital gain tax—and reinvest the balance.

- But by utilizing any of a number of charitable strategies, you can accomplish diversification without incurring the immediate capital gain tax, which actually leaves you with more funds to invest and diversify.

℞ *I have a concentrated position in my company's stock and would like to diversify my portfolio. Would a charitable trust work for me?*

One of the major reasons investors cite for not wanting to diversify their concentrated holdings is having to pay capital gain tax. Many of these investments have been acquired through incentive stock options, employee stock purchase plans, gifts, or inheritances, and have a very low cost basis. Many people are hesitant to sell these investments even though they realize that they need to reduce the risk levels of their portfolios.

A charitable remainder trust gives people a means to sell the investments and reinvest the proceeds in a more risk-prudent allocation without adverse capital gain tax consequences. You could also use a pooled income fund or a gift annuity if you do not want to administer the trust or the investments.

℞ *I have worked 25 years with a company that has gone public. Seventy-five percent of my wealth is highly appreciated, low-basis stock in this public company. How can I diversify with little or no loss in taxes to create an income stream when I want it rather than immediately?*

If you are not ready to retire, you might consider establishing a charitable remainder unitrust with flip provisions and transferring the stock to the trust. The trustee will sell the stock with no capital gain tax consequences and can reinvest 100 percent of the proceeds in a diversified portfolio that fits your goals of minimizing current income while you are still working. For you to accomplish this planning, your attorney must draft the trust so the trust will convert to a standard unitrust when you reach the age that you want to retire.

℞ *My husband worked for General Electric for years and the company contributed a lot of its stock to his retirement plan. He's retired now, and we would like to find a way to diversify the GE holdings. Is there anything we can do?*

Yes. You can withdraw the stock from the plan (incurring some income tax liability), transfer the stock to a CRT, and then sell it without incurring capital gain tax. Normally, withdrawing funds from a retirement plan to fund charitable planning is a bad idea, but you should take advantage of the special rules for employer stock, which we discuss in Chapter 14, Retirement Planning.

PROVIDE ASSET PROTECTION

○ℛ *What is asset protection planning?*

Asset protection planning is legally permissible planning that clients carry out, when they are *not* facing lawsuits, that allows them to legitimately protect their assets from future legal attacks by creditors.

○ℛ *Can I use charitable planning to protect my assets from potential creditor claims?*

Although asset protection planning is usually not the primary reason for charitable trusts, they do offer asset protection benefits. Charitable trusts are irrevocable trusts. When you transfer an asset to a charitable trust, the trust takes ownership of that asset. From the standpoint of asset protection and as long as your original transfer to the trust does not constitute a fraudulent conveyance, the asset that you transfer to the trust cannot be acquired by your creditor because you do not own that asset anymore; the trust does. But creditors may be able to reach the rights you retain in the trust, such as the income payments you receive. In general terms, a transfer could be considered a *fraudulent conveyance* if you contribute assets to the trust when you know that creditors are or will be seeking those assets or filing claims against you.

○ℛ *My father's health is failing and he is going into a nursing home. He has some highly appreciated land and we would like to be able to use the proceeds from that land to pay for his nursing home costs. However, if his medical bills become exorbitant, we would like to protect some of those proceeds for the benefit of my mother and my brother and me. Can we do so with charitable trust planning?*

You may want to consider establishing a CRT, which would pay income first to your father and mother for their lifetimes, and, upon the death of both of them, to your brother and you. Depending on your ages, this trust may be limited to a 20-year term instead of a joint-life expectancy term. By implementing this plan, you could use your parents' payments from the trust to pay nursing home and other costs for your father, an income to your mother if she survives your father, and later you and your brother will benefit from the trust.

CR *What happens if I get sued during the term of a lead trust? Can a creditor get to the assets of my CLT?*

If the remainder of the CLT is going to any beneficiary other than you at the end of the term of the trust, the trust assets remain protected from creditors.

chapter 12

Charitable Estate Planning

OVERVIEW

◌ Should I rely on repeal of the federal estate tax and not worry about estate planning?

You cannot rely on political possibilities when planning for your loved ones. You must design your estate plan with sufficient flexibility to incorporate your hopes, fears, dreams, and aspirations under the certainty that you do not know when you may die or become disabled; and within the context of the law as it is today. There are several possible scenarios, all of which you and your advisors must consider in estate and wealth strategies planning:

1. If you die prior to 2010, your estate is subject to federal estate taxes in an amount that will gradually decrease between now and 2010.

2. If you die in the year 2010, there is no federal estate tax.

3. If you die in 2011 or beyond, there are three possible scenarios:
    a. The Economic Growth and Tax Relief Reconciliation Act of 2001 (EGTRRA, or 2001 tax act) might have expired;

meaning, among other things, that the old law is in effect and decedents' estates are subject to a maximum 55 percent estate tax with a $1 million applicable exclusion amount.

b. Prior to 2011, Congress might have affirmatively voted to make the 2001 tax act permanent and there are no estate or generation-skipping transfer taxes, only gift taxes; more important, heirs may not receive a step-up in basis to fair market value for all the assets they inherit.

c. Congress might have passed entirely new legislation imposing estate and gift taxes with a new rate structure and a new applicable exclusion amount.

If you were to know that you would die in 2010, planning would be easy; you wouldn't have to take any action to reduce your potential federal estate tax, although you might face gift tax issues. If you die before 2010, without planning, your heirs may pay far more in federal estate taxes than you expected. If you become disabled before you do any planning and are not legally competent to do it, you will be in trouble before and after 2010. These scenarios are not unrealistic, and they show just how flexible your planning must be.

Does the lingering death and likely resurrection of the estate tax mean that charitable estate planning is still viable?

It means that charitable and other forms of estate planning are more relevant, necessary, and, in some instances, more complicated then ever before.

How do I go about deciding how much to leave to charity and how much to leave for my children?

To answer those questions, you may first need to start with, How much is enough for your children? What do you want for your children? Who are they and where are they in their lives? Are they responsible with their money, or do they throw it away? Are they hardworking and motivated, or are they uncertain of their own goals? How did you get your wealth? Did you inherit it, or did you create it yourself? Do you want the same for your children?

Many parents struggle with these questions—which have no right answers. You must find the answers that work for your family. By incorporating a charitable element into your planning, you may be able to give your children just the "right amount" to satisfy your goals for your family.

Can I create charitable gifts that take effect only after my death?

Yes. They are called *testamentary* charitable gifts because they take effect only at your death. You can set up these types of gifts through a will or a living trust or beneficiary designations for some assets such as retirement plan accounts and life insurance policies. The trust, will, or beneficiary designation form should specify the charitable beneficiary and the object and purpose of the charitable gift.

LIFETIME GIFTS VERSUS TESTAMENTARY GIFTS

Should I make gifts during my lifetime or at my death under the new tax law?

Because of the lack of certainty as to which direction the federal estate and gift tax laws will go, you should always consider making lifetime gifts. If you have more money than you need to live comfortably, you should consider gifts.

If the federal estate tax is *not* repealed, the gifts that you make now and in the future will reduce the value of your estate. Once again, you have helped your family by potentially reducing your federal estate taxes. If the federal estate tax *is* repealed, tax-free gifts that you make now and in the future will do no harm. You helped others with no adverse effect on you.

Making gifts, no matter what the federal estate and gift tax laws are or may be, is a winning strategy as long as you observe two cautions:

1. Do not give away more than you can afford. It is much better to be less generous and pay federal estate taxes to ensure that you have the funds to live comfortably during your life.

2. Do not make taxable gifts over the $1 million gift tax exemption amount. Unless and until the federal estate and gift tax confusion has been eliminated, paying gift tax is probably not wise.

The key to making solid planning decisions is good advice from experts. The fees you pay for planning with knowledgeable advisors will likely save a great deal of time, money, and distress for you and your family.

Are the tax consequences the same for charitable gifts that I make now or at my death?

Not entirely. If you make the bequests at your death, your estate taxes will be reduced by the charitable estate tax deduction.

If you make the gift during your lifetime, you will receive both a charitable income tax deduction and a gift tax deduction for your gift. Depending on the nature of your gift, you will also reduce the value of your taxable estate either because the donated property is not included in your gross estate or your estate is entitled to a charitable estate tax deduction.

I have decided to wait and make gifts to charity at my death. How do I know which assets to give to charity and which property to leave to my children?

In determining the best assets to give and when to give, there are two major considerations:

1. *Step-up in basis:* When beneficiaries receive assets upon the death of the owner, a basis step-up occurs. This means that the basis of an asset left on death is adjusted or stepped-up to its fair market value at death.

    Therefore, if you leave your son highly appreciated IBM stock through your will or living trust, his basis in the stock is its date-of-death value instead of your cost basis. If your son later sells the stock, he pays tax only on the gain from the date he inherited it rather than on your original cost basis. Because your heirs receive a step-up in basis on inherited appreciated assets, we suggest that you leave such property to them at death and, if possible, leave other assets to charity.

2. *Income in respect of a decedent:* Some classes of property have a large income tax liability that does not go away at their owner's death. These classes of property are known as *income in respect of a decedent (IRD)* assets. They are assets that were never taxed

for income tax purposes when their owner was alive. IRD assets include, among others, annuities, individual retirement accounts or other retirement accounts, and promissory notes. The value of these assets is subject to the estate tax *and* the beneficiaries have to pay the income tax on these assets when they receive them just as the decedent would have if he or she had survived. For instance, your IRA may be subject to estate tax at your death, and your children will be subject to federal and state income tax liabilities. The combined effect of these taxes means that your children might receive less than one-quarter of the account after all taxes are paid.

IRAs, annuities, or other IRD assets may be the ideal assets to leave to charity. At your death, they will be included in your estate but this value will be offset with a charitable estate tax deduction. Because the charities do not pay income tax, the built-in income taxes will also go away.

REDUCE ESTATE TAXES THROUGH LIFETIME GIFTS TO CHARITY

Outright Gifts to Charity

ભ *My children's school wants to build a new middle-school building. If I give the school the land on which to build it, will any of the value of the land be included in my estate when I pass away?*

The value of the land will not be included in your estate at your death if you make the gift during your lifetime and don't retain an interest in the land. That's called making a gift of a present interest with "no strings," or no restrictions, attached. If, however, you retain any interest in the land for any period of time, you are making the gift "with strings" attached, and a portion of the value of the land might be included in your estate at your death—depending on what type of strings you attach to the gift.

Charitable Gift Annuities

☞ *Are there estate tax consequences of a gift annuity?*

If you are the only annuitant, the assets you transfer to the charity in return for the annuity are not counted as part of your estate for estate tax purposes.

☞ *If I arrange for a CGA to pay out for my life and the life of another beneficiary, are there any tax implications?*

Annuity arrangements involving a beneficiary other than you, the donor, will have estate and gift tax consequences. If the other annuitant is your spouse, the gift qualifies for the estate and gift tax marital deduction. If you name someone other than your spouse, you make a taxable gift to that person based on the present value of the annuity interest that he or she receives. If you name an annuitant who is two or more generations younger than your generation, the transaction may also have generation-skipping transfer tax implications.

Inter Vivos Charitable Remainder Trusts

☞ *What are the estate and gift tax consequences of transferring property to an* inter vivos *CRT when my wife and I are the only noncharitable income beneficiaries?*

You have made a gift of the remainder interest to a charitable beneficiary. That gift qualifies for a deduction for estate and gift tax purposes. You have also made a gift to your wife, but that gift is shielded from transfer taxes by the marital deduction.

☞ *If my wife and I create a trust for our lives and then for the life of our adult daughter, will we also avoid estate tax on this gift to charity?*

Not entirely. In fact, there may be a substantial tax to pay. Assuming you were to die first, upon your death the gift is not a gift to your wife alone; it is a gift to your spouse and daughter. This means that the gift is not protected by the unlimited marital deduction. The value of all of the property in the trust will be included in your estate. The charitable estate tax deduction will have to be calculated as of the date of your death. If your daughter is fairly young, the present value of the CRT income stream going to her over her life expectancy could be substantial. The younger she is, the less will be the value of the gift passing to charity and the less your charitable estate tax deduction will be.

Your estate will have to pay tax on the difference between the value of the assets in the trust and the value of the remainder interest that eventually passes to charity.

Inter Vivos Charitable Lead Trusts

ରୁ *Will you describe the role of a charitable lead annuity trust in planning my estate?*

There are many possible uses for charitable lead annuity trusts (CLATs) in an estate plan. As a general rule, however, a CLAT is often used to leverage the donor's gift tax exemption to make a large gift at a small gift tax cost.

Gift taxes are based on the present value of the future gift. Present value can be calculated with great specificity using formulas and rates provided for in the Internal Revenue Service regulations. Generally, the longer the term of the trust and the more it pays to charity annually, the lower the present value of the remainder interest for the noncharitable remainder beneficiaries and the lower the gift tax that is due.

ରୁ *Can you give me an example of how I can use a CLAT to transfer wealth to my family?*

Let's say that your annual charitable gifts amount to $50,000 and that you anticipate making these gifts to charity for at least the next 15 years. You could set up a CLAT for 15 years, paying $50,000 in annual payments to your charities, with the remainder going to your children. You then fund the trust with $500,000.

Depending on the applicable federal rate (AFR) at the time, the gift tax value of the remainder to your children could be quite small, or even zero. For example, if the AFR is 5.4 percent, the present value of the remainder is zero, meaning that for gift tax purposes, you have not made a gift to your children.

But, remember that the actual growth of the asset value while the trust is in effect is irrelevant for purposes of calculating the value of the remainder interest. So, if the $500,000 you contribute to the CLAT earns approximately 10 percent per year, your beneficiaries will receive the $500,000 tax-free at the end of the term. If the trust earns an average of 15 percent per year during that period, your children will receive $1.7 million tax-free at the end of the 15 years.

℞ *What happens if I die within a short time of creating the lead trust? Can the IRS pull the asset back into my estate and tax it?*

As long as you do not retain any interest in or power over the CLT, the trust property will not be included in your estate, no matter when you die.

REDUCE ESTATE TAXES THROUGH TESTAMENTARY GIFTS TO CHARITY

Bequests

℞ *How do I name a charity as the beneficiary of a gift at my death?*

You name the charities and the amounts of the bequests that you are leaving them. The bequest would be in one of the following forms:

- *You can designate the gift as a percentage of your estate:*

  I give, devise, and bequeath to Westminster Grade School, located at 123 Main Street, Tucson, Arizona, five percent (5%) of the residue of my estate.

- *You can designate the gift as a dollar amount:*

  I give, devise, and bequeath to Lee High School, located at 456 Main Street, Tucson, Arizona, the sum of ten thousand dollars ($10,000.00).

- *You can make a gift of specific property:*

  I give, devise, and bequeath to Community Hospital, located at 789 Center Street, Chicago, Illinois, all of my right, title, and interest in the real property located at 201 Second Street, Chicago, Illinois. The legal description of the property is Lot 15 of Tract 921, as recorded in book 22, pages 1–4, of the county recorder of said county.

A cautionary note about percentage gifts to charity: While it may be easy to draft a percentage gift to charity, administering the gift at death may be cumbersome and contentious. As a beneficiary of a percentage of the estate, a charity is entitled to an accounting and to reasonable access to the books and records of the estate. In addition, with a percentage gift, the charity has an interest in maximizing the value of the estate, but maximizing the value of the estate is generally contrary to the decedent's wishes for estate tax purposes. A better alternative, in most cases, is either to make a gift of a specific asset or, simply, a specific dollar amount.

Testamentary Charitable Remainder Trusts

଼ *My children are successful and do not need an inheritance from me. I would like my children to receive a nominal inheritance upon my death, but I would eventually like to have my charities receive the bulk of my estate. Is there a way for me to achieve my goals?*

You should consider establishing a testamentary charitable remainder trust for the benefit of your children. Under this plan, you include provisions in your will or trust to establish a CRT at your death. You could design the T-CRT to pay your children the annuity or unitrust amount for a specific term of years and then to distribute the balance of the trust property to your charities when the term expires.

Testamentary Charitable Lead Trusts

଼ *Are testamentary charitable lead trusts good planning vehicles for reducing generation-skipping transfer taxes?*

If a donor desires to provide for his or her grandchildren with the remainder from a testamentary lead trust, he or she will likely be advised to use a testamentary charitable lead unitrust (T-CLUT).

The T-CLUT allows the donor to apply his or her generation-skipping transfer (GST) tax exemption to the present value of the gift (determined as of the donor's death). This will allow the donor to take maximum leverage of the tax laws and pass huge sums of wealth tax-free to successor generations.

 ◊ *Can you give me an example of a testamentary charitable lead unitrust?*

Yes. Sophia would like to leave a substantial sum for her young grandchildren at her death. Figure 12-1 depicts this example.

Let's assume that Sophia dies in 2002, leaving her $3 million estate to a T-CLUT with a 15-year term that pays 7.5 percent of its annual value to charity. If the applicable federal rate at her death is 5.6 percent, the present value of her gift to the grandchildren for both estate and GST taxes is only $993,735. Her federal estate tax applicable exclusion ($1 million in 2002) and GST tax exemption ($1.1 million in 2002) are more than sufficient to exempt the bequest from taxes. If the trust earns 10 percent during the term, at the end of the term the trust may have more than $4 million (depending on the trust's income taxes) to distribute to her grandchildren, totally free of taxes. In addition, her favorite charities receive more than $4 million.

In contrast, if Sophia had simply left her estate to her grandchildren, the net amount they would receive, after estate and GST taxes, is only slightly over $1 million—federal transfer taxes consume two-thirds of her estate—and her charitable causes would receive nothing.

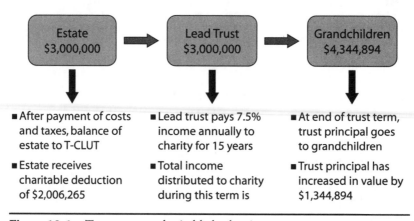

Figure 12-1   Testamentary charitable lead unitrust

SPECIAL USES FOR LIFE INSURANCE IN CHARITABLE GIVING

Is it possible to make a charitable gift of life insurance?

You can use life insurance for charitable giving in a number of ways. You can give it outright to charity. You can buy life insurance to protect a pledge made to a specific charity. You can use it to replace a bequest to charity. And you can use life insurance to replace for your family the value of an asset that you donated to charity.

Outright Gifts to Charity

I give an annual sum of money to my favorite charity. Is there a more efficient way to make these gifts that will give the charity more money?

You can make an outright gift of life insurance. Giving life insurance to charity allows you to make substantial gifts at a relatively small cost. And as long as you name the charity as the owner of the policy, the premiums are fully deductible for income tax purposes and the proceeds of the policy are not included in your estate for purposes of calculating estate tax. Here's how you can do it:

1. Contact your insurance agent, who will then arrange a physical to determine if you are insurable, and will give you preliminary cost estimates based upon his or her shopping for different carriers.

2. Name your qualified charity as the owner and beneficiary of the policy.

3. Pay the premiums directly to the carrier or write the check to the charity and let it pay the premiums.

4. Increase the amount of the coverage as your ability to pay larger premiums increases, as long as your agent crafts the policy to allow that.

If you are uninsurable, you can insure the life or lives of family members to accomplish the same results.

CR *What if I don't want to give up ownership of my life insurance policy but I do want to make a charity my beneficiary?*

If you continue to own the policy, your premium payments will not provide you with an income tax deduction but you will receive a charitable estate tax deduction for the insurance proceeds that pass to the charity upon your death.

CR *What are the overall benefits of giving life insurance as a charitable gift?*

Making a gift of life insurance is generally considered making a gift on the "installment plan" through the annual premiums, so you can donate a substantial sum to charity through a number of smaller, and therefore more affordable, payments, made over your lifetime. This is also known as "leveraging" your gifts to charity.

CR *If I do not have a taxable estate and want to benefit my children and my favorite charities upon my death, should I leave my life insurance to my children or to my charities?*

You may have a taxable estate and not realize it. If you own a life insurance policy on your life, the death benefit of the policy will be part of your taxable estate.

Life Insurance to Protect a Pledge

CR *How do I use life insurance to protect a pledge?*

Let's assume that you have pledged a charitable gift of $20,000 a year for 5 years to your local animal shelter. If you were to die before you were able to pay the full pledge, the animal shelter might assert a claim against your estate for the balance of your pledge. If you were to buy a 5-year term policy equal to the value of your pledge, you would cover this outstanding obligation at a nominal cost.

Life Insurance in Place of a Bequest

CR *How is life insurance used in place of a bequest?*

Let's say you want to leave $500,000 to a charity at your death.

Instead of making a charitable bequest of that sum in your will or trust, you can purchase a life insurance policy for $500,000, naming the charity as owner and beneficiary of the policy. Your premium payments will entitle you to an income tax deduction each year that you pay the premium. In this way, Uncle Sam will participate in your premium payments. The total premium outlay, taking into account the tax deductions, likely will be much less than the $500,000 you want the charity to receive. In the end, the charity will receive the $500,000 and your heirs will receive more of your wealth at your death.

Life Insurance to Replace Donated Assets

ᑳ *I very much like the benefits of a charitable reminder trust but do not want to disinherit my children. Is there a way to do the former without disinheriting my children?*

Yes. You can match the value of the amount you give to charity with a life insurance policy for your children and grandchildren through a wealth replacement trust.

ᑳ *What does it mean to match the value of the gift with a life insurance policy?*

Although you can implement this strategy to replace any gift that you make to charity, it is used most often in conjunction with CRTs or pooled income funds. When you donate to charity through one of these methods, you effectively disinherit your family.

Life insurance and a wealth replacement trust allow you to replace the value of the gifts so you can benefit both charity and your heirs.

ᑳ *Where will I get the money to pay the premiums?*

When you use a CRT or pooled income fund, you normally pay the premiums for this policy with the increased income stream and the tax savings provided by the CRT or pooled income fund.

ᑳ *Should I purchase an insurance policy on my life, on my wife's life, or on our joint lives?*

If your children are going to receive their inheritance upon the death of the survivor of you and your wife, you would purchase a *last-to-die*, or *second-to-die, insurance policy* that will pay its death benefit at the time you wish your children to receive their inheritance.

A last-to-die policy pays its proceeds on the death of the survivor of you and your wife, and is significantly less expensive than a policy on a single life. If, however, you wish your children to receive a portion of your estate at your death only, you would insure your life.

◯ *Can you tell me, in a nutshell, how a wealth replacement trust works?*

You create an irrevocable trust, referred to as a *wealth replacement trust* or an *irrevocable life insurance trust (ILIT),* that is the owner of the policy. You, or you and your spouse, are the trust maker of the trust and your children are the beneficiaries of the trust. Within the trust document, you include your specific instructions for how the trustee is to distribute the proceeds.

You give the premiums (usually the tax savings that you realized by setting up your CRT) to the trust and the trust pays the premiums on the policy. At your death, the life insurance proceeds pass federal estate tax–free to the trust because the trust, not you, owned the policy; and the trustee distributes the proceeds to your children per your trust instructions.

◯ *Can my wealth replacement trust provide liquidity to my estate in case it has to pay estate taxes or settlement costs?*

Yes. If your trust document provides for doing so, it may either loan money to your estate or purchase assets from your estate that will give your estate the necessary liquidity to pay its expenses and taxes.

◯ *May I use an existing life insurance policy for my ILIT, or do I have to purchase new insurance?*

You may place an existing life insurance policy inside your trust; however, you need to be aware that a gift of an existing life insurance policy to your trust will be included in your taxable estate if you die within a 3-year period following its transfer. On the other hand, a new policy purchased by your trust is immediately exempt from estate taxes.

CR *Is there a gift tax in any of the wealth replacement trust transactions?*

Each year when you give money to the trust to cover the annual premium payments, you make a gift to the trust beneficiaries. With careful planning, however, you can avoid a gift tax on these gifts.

Anyone can give $11,000 annually (indexed for inflation) to whomever he or she wishes, without gift tax consequences. If the premium payments are less than $11,000 per beneficiary, you will avoid gift tax on that transfer from you to the trust. This technique requires that the trustee give each of your beneficiaries a limited right to withdraw the gift and your lawyer must draft the trust agreement with special language for this.

CR *How do I plan for gift taxes if the amount of the annual insurance premium exceeds $11,000 per beneficiary?*

You could consider adding beneficiaries, such as grandchildren, to the trust to increase your annual exclusions. It is acceptable for you to name some beneficiaries to receive only the amount you give to them through the trust in annual exclusion gifts and to name other beneficiaries to receive the annual exclusion gifts plus the insurance proceeds at your death. This requires special drafting in the trust document but, by adding beneficiaries and properly structuring the trust, you can utilize additional annual gift exclusions while preserving the death benefit for a select few beneficiaries.

You could also consider utilizing all or a portion of your $1 million lifetime gift tax exemption to cover premium contributions in excess of the aggregate of your annual exclusion amounts.

CR *If the beneficiaries are entitled to take the money that I'm giving to the trust to pay the premiums, how does this help me to pay the premiums?*

To avoid gift taxes, the law requires that the gift must be a present-interest gift, which means that your beneficiaries must have the right to withdraw the gift from the trust within a period of time (usually 30 to 60 days). Your trustee must notify the trust beneficiaries that they are allowed to take distributions from the cash you give the trust for this limited time. In our experience, once the beneficiaries understand that they will ultimately benefit more by not withdrawing the money, they do not exercise their power of withdrawal.

℞ *Can you give me a quick summary of the benefits of a wealth replacement trust?*

The benefits include

- *Flexibility:* You can choose almost any policy amount and increase or decrease the coverage any time you want—subject to your health and age.
- *Inheritance for your children endowed by government:* Your children will receive policy proceeds paid for by a federal income tax deduction generated by your CRT or pooled income fund.
- *Avoidance of estate tax:* Properly structured, the life insurance proceeds will be entirely tax-free to children and grandchildren.

℞ *Do I need to be aware of any other issues if I want to use a wealth replacement trust?*

To avoid gift taxes and to keep the policy proceeds out of your estate so they are not subject to estate taxes, you should follow these steps in this order:

1. In conjunction with your planning team, you will decide on the type and amount of the coverage to purchase. Your life insurance professional will provide you with quotes on the cost of the insurance.
2. You will undergo a medical examination to determine your insurability, and whether you will pay a standard premium or a higher premium based upon health risks.
3. You will meet with your attorney to design the wealth replacement trust, including the distribution provisions you want for your beneficiaries. Your attorney will draft the trust document.
4. Your attorney will review with you, and you will sign, the trust documentation.
5. Your trustee will apply for the life insurance by signing and submitting the application.
6. Your trustee will set up a checking account for the trust to receive your contribution and to pay the policy premium.

7. You will transfer to the trustee of the trust a cash contribution equal to or greater than the life insurance premium.

8. Your trustee will deliver a notice to the trust beneficiaries that they are allowed to take distributions within a specified time from the cash you have given to the trust.

9. Your beneficiaries do *not* remove the funds within the allotted time.

10. Your trustee will pay the premium.

11. The insurance company will issue the policy naming the trustee as owner and beneficiary and will deliver it to your trustee.

12. Repeat annually steps 6 through 10, with regard to funding and notice to beneficiaries prior to premium payment.

13. Upon the death of the insured(s), the trustee will collect the policy's death proceeds and place them into the trust federal estate tax–free.

14. Your trustee will make distributions to your beneficiaries in accordance with your instructions in the trust document.

ZERO ESTATE TAX STRATEGIES

Inter Vivos Charitable Remainder Trusts

ଓ *What is a zero estate tax plan?*

One zero estate tax planning strategy involves combining a CRT with a wealth replacement trust. To achieve zero estate taxes, you transfer the taxable portion of your estate (typically, appreciated assets in excess of your estate tax applicable exemption; e.g., $1 million in 2002) to a CRT. You receive a charitable income tax deduction that you can spread out over the year of transfer plus 5 additional years and the CRT provides you and your spouse with an income stream for your lives. You use the tax savings from the deduction and a portion of the CRT payments to fund the gifts to your wealth replacement trust, which the trustee uses to pay the premiums on a life insurance policy insuring your life or your and your spouse's lives.

With this strategy, no estate tax will be due at your death because the estate size is at or below your applicable exemption amount. Your CRT property passes automatically to charity, free of federal estate tax. Your heirs inherit your estate federal estate tax–free because it equals the exemption amount, and they receive the insurance proceeds tax-free because they were in your wealth replacement trust.

Usually you purchase at least enough insurance to replace the amount your heirs would have inherited but for your gift to the CRT. However, if the value of your estate still exceeds the applicable exclusion amount after using the above strategies, you may wish to purchase enough additional insurance to pay the estate tax on the rest of your estate. By doing so, you effectively reduce your estate taxes to zero.

Testamentary Charitable Lead Trusts

ભ *I have been fortunate enough over my career to build up signifi-cant assets. If something happens to my wife and me, our assets would be subject to estate taxes and my children would receive much less than what we leave. Is there a way for me to avoid the estate taxes in favor of my children and provide benefits to charity, too?*

You could design your will or trust to establish a testamentary charitable lead annuity trust (T-CLAT) to receive a testamentary distribution of your assets over and above the amount of your estate tax exemption. A charity would be the beneficiary of the trust for a period of years, and your children would be the beneficiaries of the remainder interest. There would be a calculation of the present value of those interests. The calculation would determine the number of years your children would have to wait to receive those assets effectively estate tax–free. Said another way, the value of the remainder interest going to children and grandchildren is reduced for each year that they must wait before receiving the distribution.

For example, if a couple has an estate of $3 million in 2002 or thereafter and has done proper estate planning to preserve the $1 million estate tax applicable exclusions for both spouses for a total of $2 million, they would still have $1 million subject to estate taxes. By putting that $1 million into a T-CLAT for a period of years, they can avoid estate taxes on that amount and still provide additional funds to their children down the road.

☙ *How long do my children have to wait to receive their inheritance with a T-CLAT?*

To zero-out the asset remainder interest going to your children or grandchildren for tax purposes, it may be necessary to maintain the charitable trust for as long as 20 years.

☙ *If my goal is to zero-out the federal estate taxes upon my death, which form of T-CLT should I use?*

The T-CLAT, or testamentary charitable lead annuity trust, is used for children because an annuity interest allows the present value of the charitable income interest to equal the value of the assets donated to the trust. This is not possible with a unitrust because of the way the charity's annual payments are determined. A formula clause in a T-CLAT creates a determinable amount, ascertainable as of the date of the maker's death.

☙ *Who is a good candidate for a T-CLAT?*

T-CLATs are excellent tools for people who cannot utilize other planning techniques because of age or poor health. Otherwise, almost anyone can benefit from a T-CLAT. We most often see these trusts used in conjunction with other estate planning techniques that reduce the client's estate tax liability as much as possible. Then the rest of the client's estate passes to a T-CLAT at his or her death to eliminate the rest of the estate taxes.

☙ *What if I want my children to receive money before the T-CLAT's charitable period runs its course?*

Again, the T-CLAT is used most often in conjunction with other planning techniques so that the children receive an inheritance from other planning vehicles, such as a wealth replacement trust, at your death.

☙ *Does the size of the estate determine whether a T-CLAT can be used to zero-out my federal estate tax?*

This zero-out technique can be applied to any size of taxable estate.

SPECIAL PLANNING FOR
RETIREMENT ACCOUNTS

○⽴ *Can I give my IRA to a charity?*

If you give your IRA to charity by any method while you are alive, you will get a deduction for the amount you give to charity. But you will also have to include that value as part of your income in the year of the gift. As a result, it is rarely advantageous for clients to give their IRA accounts to charity during their lifetimes.

○⽴ *A lot of my pension plan is tied up in the stock of my employer. I would like to use this stock now for charitable planning. Are there any options?*

Yes. You can withdraw the stock from the plan (incurring some income tax liability) and transfer the stock to a CRT, pooled income fund, charitable gift annuity, or you can simply make a gift of the stock to your favorite charity. Normally, withdrawing funds from a retirement plan to fund charitable planning is a bad idea, but there are special rules for employer stock that you should take advantage of. We discuss this technique more in chapter 14.

○⽴ *I'm thinking about leaving cash and my IRA to my son and to charity in my will. Are there any tax consequences of which asset I leave to whom?*

It is prudent to leave taxable assets to charity because of the tax-exempt status of a charity. Because of the tax-deferred nature of an IRA, it is an income in respect of a decedent (IRD) asset—someone eventually has to pay the income taxes on those funds. When money is disbursed from an IRA, the beneficiary is considered to have realized the deferred income in the IRA. Your son would have to pay income tax on the funds, while the charity does not. Therefore, if you have the choice of leaving an IRA to either your son or to a charity, you will want to leave the IRA to charity.

○⽴ *Can I leave my IRA to my private foundation upon my death and avoid estate taxes in the process?*

Yes. When you designate a charity, including your own qualified private foundation, as beneficiary of an IRA on your death, the value of your IRA is included in your gross estate; however, there is an offsetting charitable estate tax deduction, so there is no net estate tax. In addition, although the distribution to your foundation is considered IRD, which ordinarily would require payment of income tax, it, too, will not be assessed because the charity-foundation is tax-exempt.

❧ *May I give only part of my IRA to charity?*

As of 2001, the answer to that question seems to be yes. The new regulations on distributions require that the beneficiary be determined by December 31 of the year following the year in which the IRA owner passes away. This will allow you to split the distribution between your family and a favorite charity.

❧ *Can I use a testamentary charitable remainder trust as the beneficiary of my IRA to avoid income tax?*

If you designate a T-CRT as the beneficiary of your IRA, the entire proceeds would pass to it free of income tax. By doing this, the trust can use the entire principal balance of the IRA to generate income. Of course, the distributions to your beneficiaries will still be subject to income taxes.

❧ *If I designate a testamentary charitable remainder trust as the beneficiary of my IRA, won't that adversely affect my required minimum distributions?*

No. Under regulations proposed in 2001 governing IRA minimum distributions, you may name a T-CRT as the beneficiary of your IRA without affecting the distribution requirements.

❧ *Are there any disadvantages to leaving my IRA to a testamentary charitable remainder trust with my wife as the noncharitable beneficiary?*

Yes. One disadvantage is that if your wife needs more money than the trust is designed to give her in the way of the annuity or unitrust payout, the trustee of the T-CRT is restricted from making any additional distributions to your wife.

ᘓ *I have named my children as the beneficiaries of my IRA. I'm concerned that they, or their creditors, will drain the IRA immediately after my death. Can you recommend a plan that would prevent this?*

Your will or trust could establish one or more testamentary charitable remainder trusts as the beneficiaries of your IRA. Your children would be the beneficiaries of the T-CRTs.

For example, if you have a $1 million IRA and two children, you could split the IRA into two $500,000 IRAs and name a T-CRT as the beneficiary of each IRA. When you die, the balance of each IRA will go into a T-CRT for the benefit of each child. Your children will receive money out of their T-CRTs for the rest of their lives. Your named charitable remaindermen would receive any remaining funds at the deaths of your children.

ᘓ *Are there any downsides to using this technique for my children?*

It is possible to leave qualified retirement plan and IRA funds to a T-CRT but this requires some careful planning and it has several possible pitfalls. It is important to understand that, while there may be some relief from taxes, there is a lot of uncertainty with this strategy. When you leave your qualified retirement plan or IRA to a T-CRT for the benefit of someone other than your spouse (which is what you are doing), the present value of the income stream from the T-CRT will be includable in your estate and the deduction for the contribution to the T-CRT may offset only a small portion of the IRA.

The main problem with doing this is that it is impossible to calculate exactly what that value will be until you die. Therefore, you may be creating additional taxes for your estate. While it is possible to make some intelligent "guesses" about the proper structure and terms of the T-CRT, it is often better to consider other techniques for qualified retirement and IRA accounts or to leave them outright to charity.

chapter 13

Business Succession Planning

BUSINESS + FAMILY + PHILANTHROPY

🙟 *How can a charitable solution possibly help me to pass on my family business to my children and grandchildren?*

Creative application of the charitable giving rules affords advisors yet another arena to explore with business owners, saving a lifetime of emotional and economic effort for themselves and their families.

Charitable remainder trusts (CRTs) and employee stock ownership plans (ESOPs) provide succession opportunities and exit strategies. In particular for family-owned businesses, the rules relating to private foundations give families another way to preserve, control, and benefit from their wealth. We'll discuss this last option in Chapter 16, Private Foundations.

🙟 *How important are our particular family dynamics to the succession plan, and should we seek professional advisors to help?*

A great deal—and yes. An important consideration in family planning, and especially in family business succession planning, is the family itself: its makeup, the number of individuals involved and not involved in the family business, and personal as well as business issues with which family members may be grappling. Often, multiple agendas—hidden as well as direct—and significant interpersonal roadblocks must be identified and addressed in planning for the succession of family businesses.

◌ *When and how should we begin our succession planning?*

If you think you'd like to retire some day, you should begin planning as soon as possible, and start by discussing the matter with your family. A family that actively discusses business planning and succession issues fares better and is generally healthier than one that is reluctant to do this. When these conversations take place in family meetings in an appropriate way, the potential for successful planning greatly increases. Ideally, all family members will be present, will engage in candid conversation, and will listen actively and respectfully. When family members are involved in this manner, consideration of succession planning issues and, particularly, "hands-on philanthropy" can have a positive effect on the continuation of the family business.

STRATEGIES TO EXIT THE BUSINESS

Charitable Remainder Trust

◌ *I own a small business and my son and daughter work in the business. Each of them is equally important and I would like to transfer ownership to them. I also believe that I have a significant responsibility to help my community. My business is structured as a C corporation that currently has a significant amount of excess cash. Is there some way to contribute this cash to my community and still receive some benefits from it?*

Yes, you can use what is known as a *charitable bailout* strategy to accomplish your goals. Here are the steps you would take to make your desired results happen:

1. Transfer a small amount of stock equally to your children by using your annual exclusion and, if necessary, a part of your gift tax exemption.

2. Contribute the balance of your stock to a charitable remainder trust of which you will be the noncharitable income beneficiary.

3. Following the transfer, the corporation will make a general offer to all shareholders to redeem its outstanding stock at a specified price. The independent special trustee of your CRT agrees to sell the stock to the company for the offered price. The corporation, using loans or retained earnings, or other methods, purchases the stock, which then becomes "treasury stock."

Benefits of the charitable bailout are that

- your children are the only remaining stockholders in the corporation and are in full control;
- your CRT will have cash in it that your trustee can invest in a diversified pool of assets to provide a lifetime of annuity or unitrust payments to you and your spouse;
- there will be no immediate capital gain tax on the sale because the CRT sold the stock;
- after you and your spouse are deceased, the remaining funds in the CRT will pass to your family foundation or any other qualified charity that you choose to support; and
- on top of all that, you get a charitable income tax deduction for a portion of the value of the stock that you gave to your CRT.

℺ *Can you give me an example of this strategy using some figures?*

Certainly. Marvin Smart owns 100 percent of the shares of XYZ, Inc. The current value of the company is $1.8 million and Marvin's cost basis is $170,000. As he phases himself into retirement, Marvin wants to transfer the business to his son, Tracy. But Marvin is faced with the following problems:

- If Marvin gives his stock to Tracy, he will pay gift tax of more than $300,000 and Tracy will own the stock with his father's cost basis.
- If Marvin sells the stock to Tracy, Marvin will be forced to pay capital gain taxes at 20 percent (approximately $326,000) and

Tracy will have to come up with the money to purchase the stock.

- If Marvin retains ownership of the stock until he dies and transfers it to Tracy via his will, the full value of the stock will be included in his estate for estate tax purposes.

- And while Tracy will receive a step-up in the basis of the stock he receives from Marvin's estate, a large percent of the stock value will be lost to estate taxes.

To solve these problems, Marvin could take the following steps:

1. Give Tracy a small number of XYZ shares.
2. Create a charitable remainder unitrust (CRUT) and transfer his XYZ stock to it. The CRUT pays Marvin and his wife, Marlene, income for their lives.
3. Create an irrevocable life insurance trust (ILIT), or wealth replacement trust, to replace the value of the stock transferred to the CRUT and to provide for a balanced inheritance for all of their children. The Smarts will fund the ILIT with the tax savings the CRUT generates and, in part, through the unitrust payments. The trustee of the ILIT will use the cash to purchase a survivorship, or second-to-die, life insurance policy on the lives of Marvin and Marlene.
4. The CRUT's independent trustee will sell the XYZ stock in the trust back to XYZ, Inc., for a cash payment at its then fair market value.
5. The CRUT's trustee will reinvest the cash received from the sale into a diversified portfolio of investments and pay the Smarts the unitrust amount each year based on the value of the trust's assets.

The benefits that the Smarts receive from using this strategy are that

- Marvin defers capital gain taxes when the CRUT sells the stock back to the company;
- Marvin's son, Tracy, ends up owning the company;
- Marvin and Marlene receive a substantial retirement income for the rest of their lives;
- the value of the family company is removed from their estate;
- the Smarts create a charitable legacy for the causes they support;

- their other children receive the value of the company in cash via the wealth replacement trust—free of all tax; and
- the Smarts receive a charitable income tax deduction, giving them more cash to fund their wealth replacement trust for the benefit of their family.

ભ *I am considering selling my business in conjunction with a charitable remainder trust. Is there anything I should be concerned about?*

Yes. It is important that you set up and fund your CRT well in advance of any bona fide offers to sell your business. If you have a deal in place prior to transferring the business to the CRT, the Internal Revenue Service may argue that, in substance, you sold the business prior to funding, and may insist that you pay tax on the gain from the sale.

ભ *I own my own business as a C corporation and am getting ready to retire. My business broker tells me I am unlikely to find anyone to buy the stock so this will be an asset sale. My accountant has informed me that if we do an asset sale and liquidate the corporation, the corporation will pay capital gain tax on the gain in the assets, and that I will pay capital gain tax on the gain in the value of my stock. Consequently, she believes a charitable remainder trust is not an option. Is that true?*

Not necessarily. You could place some or all of the stock in a CRT and complete the asset sale/liquidation inside the CRT. Although the corporation would still pay the first level of tax for the gain on the sale of the assets, the CRT would defer the second level of tax on the capital gain of the stock upon liquidation.

ભ *What are the benefits to me if I create a CRT and make a gift of my company's stock to it?*

Among the ways the CRT will benefit you are that

- you avoid estate tax on the value of the stock;
- you do not incur an immediate capital gain tax upon the sale of the business;

- you receive a current income tax deduction based on the amount that eventually passes to qualified charities; and
- the CRT provides you with periodic payments: monthly, quarterly, semiannually, or annually.

℞ *In your experience, what type of CRT is most commonly used for business succession purposes?*

In our experience, the charitable remainder unitrust, because it pays a specified percentage of the trust corpus based on the *current value* of the trust, valued on an annual basis.

Charitable Employee Stock Ownership Plan

℞ *I own a successful private company valued at $10 million. My son currently works in the company and shows an interest in the business but is not ready to take over now. I would like to develop a strategy for business succession that would allow me to keep control of the company while I train and mentor my son. At the same time, I would like to keep my options open in the event that he loses interest or is unable to take over the reins from me. I'm also interested in developing an estate planning strategy that minimizes estate taxes in favor of charitable gifts. What sort of plan might work for me?*

You could combine an *employee stock ownership plan (ESOP)* with a charitable remainder trust to accomplish all of your objectives. An ESOP is a type of qualified retirement plan that primarily owns stock of the employer.

The two devices work together like this:

1. You create a CRT and contribute some portion of your stock to it.
2. Your company establishes an ESOP to purchase your stock from the CRT.

Your company funds the ESOP by making contributions to the ESOP trust. Because the ESOP is a type of qualified retirement plan, these contributions are limited by law, but within those limits they are fully tax-deductible to the company.

By using the ESOP, you maintain family control of the business and buy yourself time to determine if your son will be ready to take over the company some day or whether you need to find a new owner for the company. An ESOP also gives you the option to sell additional stock and still remain in full control.

Using the CRT gives you a current income tax deduction for the charitable contribution, allows you to sell company stock without any immediate capital gain tax, and removes the value of the stock placed into the CRT from your taxable estate. Finally, by using this combined ESOP and CRT strategy, you will have implemented a flexible business succession plan that provides for family ownership and control in the future.

SPECIAL CONSIDERATIONS FOR S CORPORATIONS

ℭℛ *Can I transfer my subchapter S corporation stock to a CRT?*

Most people automatically rule out a CRT because, under the federal income tax law, a CRT is not a qualified stockholder and any transfer to a charitable trust will automatically terminate the S election. When the S election terminates, the company automatically becomes a C corporation subject to "double taxation," meaning that the corporation will pay income taxes on its profits and the shareholders will pay taxes on the same profits when they receive them as dividends.

Termination of the corporation's S election may have additional negative tax impacts on the company. Whether the tax costs of termination present too great a problem depends upon the specific situation.

ℭℛ *It is essential that I maintain the subchapter S status. Is there another option available to create a CRT with business assets?*

Yes. The S corporation itself could create the CRT and transfer assets (e.g., appreciated real estate that the company owns) to the trust. Because a nonperson is creating the CRT, the term is limited to 20 years.

CR *How would this operate, and would I receive an income tax deduction for this plan?*

The CRT pays the unitrust amount to the corporation, and the corporation, in turn, distributes the payment pro rata to its shareholders. The income tax deduction for establishing the trust flows through to the shareholders on a pro-rata basis.

chapter 14

Retirement Planning

CHARITABLE REMAINDER TRUSTS

CR *I am in the peak of my earning years and want to maximize the opportunities for increased income when I retire. Can charitable planning help?*

Yes. You can use a charitable remainder unitrust with net income makeup provisions (NIMCRUT) or a charitable remainder unitrust with "flip" provisions (FLIPCRUT) during your peak earning years. The key reason for using a NIMCRUT or a FLIPCRUT as a retirement plan is that they allow you to defer payments, much like a qualified pension or individual retirement account:

1. You make contributions to your trust.
2. The trustee invests the trust's assets for long-term growth rather than income—such as in mutual funds, growth stocks, or a variable annuity.

3. You let the CRT assets grow in value and do not take income from it during the early years.

4. At the specified time, typically retirement, the trustee converts the investments to income-producing investments and the CRT can begin making payments to you. These payments can include makeup amounts for any shortfalls in income that you did not receive earlier.

ᑕᖇ *What are the advantages of using a NIMCRUT or a FLIPCRUT over traditional IRAs, company 401(k) plans, and other retirement plans?*

There are many advantages for using a NIMCRUT or a FLIPCRUT as a retirement planning tool over tax-deferred retirement plans:

- *Unlimited contributions:* There is no limit to the amount of money that the donor-trust maker can contribute to a NIMCRUT or a FLIPCRUT in any year as there is with the tax-deferred retirement plans, although the income tax deduction may be limited.
- *Penalty-free withdrawals:* There are no penalties for early withdrawal prior to age 59½.
- *Control:* The donor-trust maker and/or a spouse may be the trustee. There is no need for plan administrators—although there may be a need for a special independent trustee, depending upon the trust assets and the planned transactions.
- *Payment flexibility:* The donor-trust maker may contribute cash, stock, or other property to the trust and, regardless of the type of property, always receive a deduction, and always defer capital gain tax on the sale of the assets in the trust.
- *Tax-advantaged payments:* The income payments can be designed to produce capital gains, which will reduce income taxes in the future.

ᑕᖇ *Can you give me an example of how a NIMCRUT works like a private pension plan?*

Suppose a married couple, both age 40, wish to save $10,000 annually toward retirement and they also wish to support charitable causes. Their attorney helps them establish a joint NIMCRUT with a 5 percent payout, and they contribute $10,000 to the trust each year for 25 years until they retire.

They receive approximately $54,000 in charitable income tax deductions over the 25 years. Assuming an average growth rate of 10 percent and no distributions over 25 years, and assuming that they convert the trust assets at retirement to 6 percent income-producing and 2 percent growth investments, the couple would receive a unitrust payment of approximately $64,000 the first year, and the payments could possibly be even higher in future years as the trust makes up for payments not made in earlier years. After both of their deaths, the charity that the couple selected receives approximately $1.7 million.

CR I am a 40-year-old software engineer currently earning more than $100,000 per year. I would like to retire when I am 55. I have maxed out all of my IRA and qualified plan contributions. Are there any options to set money aside for retirement that would limit the current income taxation of those funds as they grow and allow me access to the funds before I reach age 59½ without paying a penalty?

Using a charitable remainder unitrust with net income makeup and flip provisions may be appropriate. A FLIPCRUT starts out as a NIMCRUT for a certain term of years or until the occurrence of a certain event, such as age 55, paying you the lesser of the trust net income or a certain percentage of the value of the trust property, valued each year. Upon the triggering event, the trust flips to a standard charitable remainder unitrust (CRUT) and begins making regular unitrust payments to you based on the value of the trust property as it is valued each year.

If you invest all of the funds in non-income-producing vehicles, funds grow on a tax-deferred basis without the trust making any distributions until it flips to a standard unitrust.

CR Can I control the date that it changes?

Not entirely. You must fix the triggering event—the time or event when the trust flips—when you create the trust. This is required to ensure that a donor-trust maker is not overexerting control for his or her personal benefit. When you create the trust, you should set a triggering event, such as 10 years after the date of creation of the trust or upon reaching age 65. Either way, the goal is to have the trust flip when you plan to retire, without actually saying in the document that the triggering event is "when I retire," because that is an event under your control.

When creating FLIPCRUTs, many of our clients specify a triggering event such as "upon the earlier to occur of my death or 10 years from the creation of this trust." This allows the trust to flip upon the trust maker's untimely death (to provide for the surviving spouse) or to flip 10 years after the creation of the trust, when the trust maker plans to retire.

✧ Can I establish a CRT where income can be turned off and on at the trustee's behest?

Yes, you can create a charitable remainder unitrust with net income makeup provisions such that, if the assets in the trust do not generate current income—that is, interest or dividends—the shortfall is tracked in a makeup account.

If the trustee invests the trust assets in a deferred annuity that the trustee has not annuitized, the trustee can request distributions from the annuity periodically as warranted. Distributions from the annuity are deemed ordinary income.

Using this mechanism allows the trust assets to accumulate and grow inside the CRT and then commence the payments years down the road at a time when the trust maker has retired or is in a lower tax bracket. Once the "spigot is opened," the trust can potentially pay the entire amount owed in the makeup account in addition to the payment due for the current year.

✧ I just retired, and my retirement account at work has a lot of my former employer's stock in it. I'm thinking about rolling over the account to an IRA because I do need some income from it, but I wish I could use the plan proceeds to fund a CRT. Is there a way to do this?

As we explained before, the normal rule is that it's not possible to transfer retirement plan money to a charity or to a CRT without paying income taxes on the full amount withdrawn. As with any rule, however, there's an exception. Employer stock held in your retirement plan is subject to special rules. As an example, let's say you have $200,000 in employer stock in your retirement account. When your employer contributed the stock to the plan, it was worth $50,000. You can withdraw the stock from the plan now and pay income taxes only on the value of the stock when your employer contributed it ($50,000), not on its current value of $200,000. The $150,000 difference (known as *net unrealized appreciation*, or *NUA*) is not taxed until you sell the stock, and is taxed at capital gain rates, which are lower than ordinary income rates.

You can contribute the stock to a charitable remainder trust without triggering the taxes on the NUA. Your trustee can then sell the stock, without paying capital gain taxes, and invest the proceeds in a diversified portfolio. You and the charity that you select get all the benefits of a CRT described in this chapter. The value of the stock for purposes of calculating your income tax deduction is its current value.

On the other hand, if you roll over the employer stock into your IRA, you can still sell the stock tax-free inside the IRA, but the proceeds will be treated as ordinary income when they are distributed to you. As such, if you are charitably motivated, using the employer securities to fund a CRT is an extraordinary opportunity for you.

CHARITABLE EMPLOYEE STOCK OWNERSHIP PLANS

ભ *I am interested in retiring from my own business. I owe my success to my employees and would like them to own the company; yet, I would like to avoid as much tax as possible and ensure myself a steady cash flow. What would achieve these objectives?*

You could create an employee stock ownership plan (ESOP) in conjunction with a CRT. The ESOP allows your employees to buy the company from you at a fair price through the plan.

If you invest the sale proceeds in the stock market, you do not recognize a capital gain when you sell your company to the ESOP. Your cost basis in the investment portfolio will be your original basis in your company, so your subsequent sale of portfolio assets would create capital gain tax. To avoid this tax, you contribute the newly acquired investments to a CRT designed to make distributions to you and your spouse for your lifetimes while ensuring a steady cash flow.

Under this plan, you've sold the business to your employees, you will avoid capital gain taxes for as long as possible, and you will receive a steady stream of cash for your lifetime. In addition to achieving your original goals, you will achieve the benefits of helping charity and receiving a charitable income tax deduction.

CHARITABLE GIFT ANNUITIES

_Cℛ_ _I have heard a lot of advertisements on the radio about gifts to charity where I can receive money back from the charity for the rest of my life. Does this work?_

Yes, it works just fine. You can achieve this objective in several different ways, but the advertisements that you heard are likely promoting a certain charitable device known as a charitable gift annuity (CGA).

A CGA is a wonderful tool if you are satisfied with the deductions that you would receive when making the gift of principal and are satisfied with the amount of the distributions that you would receive each year. Generally speaking, charitable gift annuities are used for smaller gifts to charities.

_Cℛ_ _How does a charitable gift annuity work?_

With a CGA, you can transfer money or property to a qualifying charity in exchange for the charity's promise to pay you a fixed income amount annually for the rest of your life. Your transfer of assets is considered part gift and part purchase of an annuity.

_Cℛ_ _Can I delay the start for receiving income from a CGA?_

Yes. In fact, that may be a wise decision for some donors. Not only will it increase the amount of your charitable deduction, but it also could allow you to defer payments to a time when you need that income, such as retirement and/or when you are in a lower marginal tax bracket.

In addition, the longer the delay, the greater will be the amount of income available to distribute to you.

୧ *I am a 45-year-old high-income executive who needs a current income tax deduction. I am already contributing the maximum allowable amount to my 401(k) and IRA plans. Is there a way that a gift annuity could benefit me?*

Yes, a deferred-payment gift annuity could be beneficial to you, both to provide you with a current income tax deduction and to increase your retirement income on a tax-sheltered basis.

Here's how it would work for you. You make annual contributions to your charity in exchange for a deferred-payment gift annuity. Payments to you will begin upon your retirement at age 65 and continue for the rest of your life and, if you choose, for your spouse's lifetime. Each year that you make the annual contribution, you will receive a charitable income tax deduction that will generate an annual tax savings to you. When you start receiving your annuity payments, a portion of each annuity payment will be tax-free. And, for more good news, there are no limits on your annual contributions as there are with qualified retirement plans.

POOLED INCOME FUNDS

୧ *How does a pooled income fund provide retirement income?*

Public charities create pooled income funds and appoint the trustees to manage them. When you make a gift to the fund, the charity will pay you a portion of the income each year for your life or for the lives of joint beneficiaries. At the death of the income beneficiaries, the principal passes outright to the charity. You receive an immediate income tax deduction for, and will not pay capital gain taxes on, the contribution of the appreciated assets to the charity. What differentiates them from a charitable gift annuity is that the income interest paid back to the donor is a true income interest, not an annuity interest.

Pooled income funds allow you to diversify assets, leading to potential growth that generates larger income distributions for retirement years. They provide these benefits without expensive set-up or annual costs.

chapter 15

Planning for Real Estate

DIRECT GIFTS TO CHARITY

Bargain-Sale Transactions

ᘒ *I had been told that if I sell my real estate to a charity, I may be able to make a gift, avoid taxation, and get paid at the same time. Is this true?*

Yes, it is true. It is what the Internal Revenue Code calls a *bargain sale*. In a bargain sale, a donor sells property to a charity for less than what the property is worth. The difference between the fair market value and the amount the donor receives is the "bargain" element and is treated as a charitable contribution.

Suppose you own real estate for which you paid $100,000 and that is now appraised at $200,000. Further assume that you would like to donate the property to charity, but you need to recover at least your original purchase price. To accomplish your objectives, you enter into an agreement with the charity whereby it would pay you $100,000 for the land.

ᏚᏒ *How is my charitable deduction calculated in a bargain sale?*

The treasury regulations define a bargain sale as a transfer of property that is partly a sale or exchange of the property and partly a charitable contribution. The amount of your contribution is the difference between the property's fair market value and the sales price. The amount of your charitable deduction for bargain sales to public charities is limited to 30 percent of your adjusted gross income.

ᏚᏒ *Can you give me an example of how the bargain sale works?*

Sure. Bob decides to sell a parcel of land to the YMCA at a bargain price equal to his cost basis of $300,000. He has owned the parcel for more than 5 years, and it has appreciated to a fair market value of $500,000. The YMCA agrees to purchase the land for Bob's cost basis of $300,000, so the transaction consists of a sale portion of $300,000 and a contribution portion of $200,000.

The rules require that Bob's cost basis in the property be divided *pro rata* between the portion he gives to the charity and the portion he sells. Once the cost basis is allocated between these portions, Bob determines if there is any gain on the sale portion. Here's how Bob's bargain sale looks:

$$\frac{\$200,000}{500,000} = \text{a ratio of 40\% contribution portion : FMV}$$

$$\frac{\$300,000}{500,000} = \text{a ratio of 60\% sale portion : FMV}$$

$$\begin{array}{r} \$300,000 \\ \times\ 60\% \\ \hline \end{array} = \$180,000 \text{ of cost basis allocated to sale portion}$$

$$\begin{array}{r} \$300,000 \\ -180,000 \\ \hline \end{array} = \$120,000 \text{ capital gain on the sale}$$

$$\begin{array}{r} \$120,000 \\ \times\ 20\% \\ \hline \end{array} = \$24,000 \text{ capital gain tax}$$

Bob's contribution represents 40 percent of the fair market value (FMV), and the sale price is 60 percent of the FMV, so 60 percent of the $300,000 basis is allocated to the sale portion. Bob's resulting capital gain is $120,000. The maximum federal capital gain rate is 20 percent, so Bob's capital gain tax is $24,000.

Bob uses the $200,000 contribution portion to calculate his charitable income tax deduction. He can offset only 30 percent of his contribution base with this type of gift, so if his contribution base is $200,000, he can deduct only $60,000 in that year. He can carry forward the remaining deduction for up to 5 years.

Is there such thing as a "bargain installment" sale?

Yes. If it is properly structured, property may be sold to a charity for less than its FMV in exchange for an installment note. And the gain attributable to the bargain sale can be reported using the installment method.

Can the capital gain that is realized by virtue of a bargain sale of a personal residence be excluded from income because of the $500,000 capital gain exclusion?

The IRS has stated in a private ruling that the gain resulting from the bargain sale of a principal residence qualifies for the $500,000 capital gain exclusion on a personal residence.

Conservation Easements

What is a conservation easement?

First, let's explain in general what an easement is. An easement is a "nonpossessory" interest in land. When you own property, you enjoy a certain "bundle of rights": You can fence it in, dig holes on it, subdivide it, keep others off, build houses on it, cut the trees growing on it, grow crops on it, sell it, give it away, or leave it to others at your death. An easement carves out one of those rights and gives it to someone else. The owner still has physical possession of the property, but someone else owns the particular right that the owner gave away.

Common easements are the right to develop the land, where the easement holder has the right to build an office building or apartments or houses; and the right of access, where the easement holder has the right to go across the owner's property to reach someone else's land. The rights that the owner gives up are recorded in the registry of deeds so future owners and the world will know they exist.

With *conservation easements,* the landowner gives to charity some right in the land but retains the remaining rights in the land, and can do anything not specifically given to charity through the conservation easement. The right that a donor gives up has a value, and this value constitutes the amount of the charitable deduction—if the right is being given to a qualifying charity.

The qualifying charity that receives the conservation easement is responsible for enforcing the terms of the easement. This is why only certain charities—usually local land or conservation trust entities—can accept conservation easements as gifts.

☞ *What are the requirements for making a gift of a conservation easement?*

The requirements are:

- The conservation easement must last forever
- The charity to whom the interest is given must be qualified to accept it
- The donation must be made for a permitted conservation purpose that includes preservation of land for the outdoor recreation of the general public; protection of areas for natural habitat of animals, birds, or fish; and protection of open space, farm land, or forest land for the scenic enjoyment of the general public
- The gift must be made exclusively for conservation purposes

This latter requirement means that the donor may not receive anything other than incidental benefits from the donation of the interest. The donor may not use the property in any way that is inconsistent with the conservation interest. As a general rule, the public at large must benefit from the charitable gift. This frequently means that public access to the land must be allowed (but not necessarily, as in the case of a scenic interest).

By giving an interest in this land to charity now, you have

removed the value of that interest from your estate, which will likely reduce the estate tax burden on your death.

◌ð *How is the income tax deduction figured?*

The property is first valued at its highest and best use. The value of the conservation easement is calculated by a qualified appraiser recognized by the IRS. The value of the conservation easement is subtracted from the property's valuation. If, however, the conservation easement adds value in any way, that added value is subtracted from the value of the easement to get the value of the deduction.

◌ð *Can you give me an example of a conservation easement calculation?*

Yes. The fair market value of the property, taking into account its highest and best use, is $1 million. The landowner places a conservation easement on it that makes it worth $500,000 as a ranch property. The value of the conservation easement is $500,000.

◌ð *I own a family farm and want to protect its character. I also want to make a charitable contribution and to provide for my children. Is a conservation easement an option for me?*

Yes. You could make a charitable contribution of the development rights in the farm as a conservation easement. The easement restricting the property's use to farming stays with the land, even though a burgeoning metropolitan area may spread subdivisions around it. This would satisfy your charitable goals, as well as protect the character of your family farm. It would also reduce the value of your estate for death tax purposes.

You could then leave the farm to your children upon your death, and they could farm it in perpetuity or dispose of it as they wish, subject to the conservation easement. The conservation easement would remain with the land forever, preserving its character for the benefit of future generations.

Prior to donating the easement, you might subdivide a few lots, exclude those lots from the easement, and leave them to your children to build on. Or you could exclude the homestead and surrounding grounds from the easement and leave it to your children.

☙ *Can my executor or living trust trustee donate a conservation easement to charity after my death so as to reduce the taxable estate?*

Yes, if you instruct him or her to do so in your will or living trust. Such a gift is called a testamentary gift. The result will be a charitable deduction for your estate.

Special Considerations for Residences

☙ *Can I give my home to my favorite charity, yet live in it for the rest of my life?*

You can enter into a "life estate" agreement with a charity whereby a charity gets your home at your death but you retain the right to enjoy the property for life. You will be responsible for all maintenance, repairs, insurance, and taxes while you are living in the home.

You receive a charitable income tax deduction now for the present value of the interest passing to charity (the value of the home, less your retained life estate, using government actuarial tables). You also remove the value of the property from your taxable estate.

☙ *Are we the right ages to accomplish this type of charitable planning?*

In our experience, this type of gift tends to be most attractive to clients who are in their mid-to-late 60s and older.

☙ *What if we decide to move out of our house?*

If you decide to move, you can rent the house or give your life interest to the charity and obtain an additional charitable deduction.

☙ *Why is this type of gift popular?*

This gift is attractive because it allows individuals and couples to make substantial gifts and to generate meaningful income tax deductions without having to change their lifestyles.

Can you give me an example of giving my home to charity?

Certainly. Let's assume Mary Ross, age 72, is a widow with six children who live in other areas of the country and are doing quite well financially.

Mary plans to leave the majority of her estate to her children but would also like to make a charitable gift as part of her estate plan.

Because none of Mary's children live in the area and are not interested in the home, Mary decides to make a gift of her home now to her favorite charity.

In doing so, she will retain the right to live in it for the rest of her life and will also retain the responsibility for maintaining it.

Because Mary has made a qualifying gift to a recognized charity, she is entitled to a charitable income tax deduction for the present value of the future interest going to the charity. If the home were worth $200,000, Mary would receive an income tax deduction of approximately $80,000.

Debt-Encumbered Property

Can I donate encumbered real estate to a charity?

This is usually not a good idea, as a charitable contribution of debt-encumbered property made during your life may result in adverse income tax consequences to you, as the donor. When you transfer debt-encumbered property to charity, the bargain-sale rules apply. You must realize consideration equal to the amount of the debt, even though you received no cash.

Also, whether you transfer mortgaged property to charity or a charitable remainder trust, the debt on the property should be at least 5 years old and you should have owned the property for at least 5 years—called the *5 and 5 test*. If this test is not met, a gift of encumbered property subjects the charity or CRT to unrelated-business taxable income (UBTI), which can have adverse consequences for the charity. The Internal Revenue Code provides an exception for debt-encumbered property received by a charity, as long as the owner passes the 5 and 5 test, allowing the charity to sell the property within 10 years without having a UBTI problem.

How do my deductions work if I give mortgaged property to charity?

Here's how it works. Suppose Terry owns land with a value of $100,000, a basis of $30,000, and a mortgage of $25,000. Terry gives the property to charity, and the charity agrees to pay the mortgage. Since Terry does not have to pay the debt, forgiveness of the debt is treated as an "amount realized" for purposes of the transaction.

In other words, the transaction is treated like a bargain sale, with the proceeds equal to the amount of the forgiven debt. Terry receives a charitable deduction in the amount of $75,000 ($100,000 FMV, less $25,000 indebtedness—the gift element) and Terry recognizes gain in the amount of $17,500 ($25,000 of debt that is forgiven, less the allocated basis of $7,500).

What are some potential ways to avoid the tax problems of making gifts of debt-encumbered real estate to charity?

There are several alternatives for you to consider if you wish to donate debt-encumbered property to charity:

1. *Remove the debt:* This is the easiest option. Once you pay the debt, you can easily make your charitable gift.
2. *Transfer the debt to other property:* If the lender will agree to this, it will remove the debt and allow you to transfer the property to the charity.
3. *Obtain a short-term loan:* You can obtain a "swing loan" secured by another asset. You use the loan proceeds to pay off the debt on the charitable asset. You then contribute an undivided interest in the property to a charity and retain an interest approximately equivalent to the amount of the loan. Thereafter, you and the charity sell the property and you use your share of the proceeds to pay off the swing loan.

Charity's Reluctance to Accept Real Property

Why would charities be reluctant to accept gifts of real property?

Charitable organizations might be reluctant to receive gifts of real property for several reasons:

1. *Lack of understanding:* Not all charities have board members or advisors who know and are comfortable with real property, and most people don't want to deal with something they don't understand.

2. *Marketability:* Charities must also consider how quickly they can sell the property and the terms under which they will sell it. Until properties sell, charities must cover the costs of real estate taxes, insurance, and all other expenses to maintain the property.

3. *Reluctance to manage:* Real property typically requires management and ongoing care. This management can bring associated liabilities with it, and the charity has to be comfortable with these responsibilities before accepting the gift.

4. *Worries about debt:* To the extent that charities receive property encumbered by debt, they worry about how they will discharge it.

5. *Environmental concerns:* Charities may not wish to assume the risk of extraordinary hazards that attach to real estate, such as earthquakes, environmental liability, hurricanes, tornadoes, and floods.

❧ How do charities handle gifts of real estate?

Most charities establish a real estate committee or gift acceptance committee that will consider, at a minimum, these questions:

- Is the property useful for purposes of the charity?
- Is the property marketable?
- Are there any restrictions, easements, or other reservations over the property?
- What are the costs of holding and maintaining the property?
- Is there environmental liability exposure?
- Is the property mortgaged?
- Is it a home or a commercial property?

❧ Is there a way to give the property to charity without giving the charity the responsibility to manage it?

You can give property to charity without the management responsibility in two ways:

1. The easiest way to do this is to give the charity an option to

receive the property as a gift or to buy it at a bargain-sale price. The charity can then arrange for the sale and simultaneous exercise of the option and can do so while the donor continues to own the property.

2. The second way, appropriate for complex situations, is for the donor to form a supporting organization whose purpose is to hold and manage the property while awaiting its sale. In this case, the charity can name representatives of its choosing to handle the property management without fear of incurring any liability from the property. This supporting organization strategy is especially useful when donating commercial or industrial property.

⌘ *Why use an option?*

The purpose of giving the charity an option to receive the property or to purchase it in a bargain sale is to provide the charity with an enforceable contract right that the charity can, in turn, sell to a third party, allowing the third party to take title. In our experience, many charities are reluctant to appear in the chain of title on property that might carry liabilities with it, and this option technique allows a charity to accept a gift without accepting legal responsibility. With this technique, the donor most likely is not entitled to an income tax deduction until the charity exercises the option, because that's when the donor gives up the property and the charity receives the benefit of the option.

Environmental Issues

⌘ *I wanted to give a commercial property to a local charity. Its board said it was concerned about environmental problems and declined to accept my gift. I'm sure the property is worth more than it would cost to clean up. What can I tell them?*

You need to do thorough research before you make this assumption. One of our clients bought a lot for $250,000 several years before seeking our help, and he spent $320,000 removing its environmental problems—after which he had a lot worth $250,000. The transaction was a dead loss before he had built anything on it.

Valuation Issues

℃ *How are real estate gifts valued for purposes of the charitable deduction?*

For purposes of taking an income tax deduction for real estate worth more than $5,000, the Internal Revenue Code requires that a qualified appraiser perform an appraisal. The appraisal must occur no later than 60 days prior to the gift, as the IRS considers anything older as stale. In addition, a number of rules define who may not serve as a qualified appraiser and what the appraisal must contain. The rules are quite extensive.

There are no equivalent rules for valuation under the federal estate and gift tax provisions of the Internal Revenue Code. But to reduce the likelihood of controversy, it is wise to follow the income tax regulations for valuation of any charitable gift of property, especially if it is worth a substantial amount.

℃ *How do I find a qualified appraiser?*

You can find appraisers for real estate in most urban areas. Be sure your appraiser is licensed or certified by your state. In addition, check for the designation "SRA" (Society of Real Estate Appraisers) or "AIA" (Association of Independent Appraisers).

If your proposed gift is commercial property, you must use an appraiser who specializes in commercial property, and some states require special certifications for those appraisers. Where there is land with timber, a registered forester must determine the value of the standing timber. Finally, for land in which conservation or preservation easements are being considered, you should seek appraisers with experience in this unique area.

CHARITABLE GIFT
ANNUITIES

℃ *How does a gift annuity work if we donate real property?*

A donor gives real estate to a charity in exchange for a fixed income stream for life. The charity applies a discount upfront to cover expenses associated with the property, and the annuity is calculated on the discounted value. Thereafter, the charity pays a guaranteed annuity amount to the annuitant for life.

 My wife and I are considering establishing a charitable gift annuity. We have an appreciated parcel of undeveloped real estate that we are considering using for our gift. Would this transfer be considered a nontaxable event?

You may exchange appreciated assets for a charitable gift annuity without immediate taxation of the capital gain. Rather, the gain is spread out over your life expectancy. Even if there is another income beneficiary, the capital gain on the gifted property will be taxable to you over your life expectancy, and the other annuitant will pay the capital gain tax only if you die before your life expectancy.

CHARITABLE REMAINDER TRUSTS

 I own several highly appreciated rental properties, which are debt-free. I am tired of all of the headaches that go with property management. Now my accountant tells me that I will owe substantial taxes if I sell the properties. Can a charitable giving strategy work for me?

Absolutely. You should work with a qualified advisor who can "crunch the numbers" to provide you with the tax and investment benefits of a charitable remainder trust.

 With proper planning, you can sell the rentals and not pay any immediate capital gain tax. In addition, you and your spouse may receive a lifetime income stream from a more diversified portfolio of income-producing assets. You can create the trust to pay you a fixed annuity or a unitrust amount that fluctuates annually with the value of the trust assets.

 Can you compare the options of selling our real estate outright and giving it to a charitable trust?

Certainly. Mr. and Mrs. Jones, both 70, invested $50,000 in a rental

TABLE 15-1 Jones's Comparison

	Outright sale	10% CRUT
Net sales price	$250,000	$250,000
Less: capital gain tax (20% × $200,000)	40,000	0
Net proceeds	210,000	250,000
10% Annual payment	$ 21,000	$ 25,000

property years ago. The property is now worth $250,000. They're ready to get out of the property management and maintenance business so they can travel and enjoy their life. Their accountant tells them they'll have to pay tax on the $200,000 gain. Their "wish list" is to dispose of the property, minimize or eliminate the tax bite, and receive more income for their retirement years. Table 15-1 compares the results of selling the property and giving the property to a charitable remainder unitrust with a 10 percent payout rate.

On top of the additional income, the Joneses get a sizable income tax deduction for their gift to the CRT.

ᚻ *I would like to set up a charitable remainder unitrust (CRUT) and fund that trust with undeveloped land, but I have no idea how long it will take to sell the land, and the trust obviously will have no money to make the unitrust payment to me until it sells the land. Is a CRUT a good option for me?*

Yes, but you should consider using a FLIPCRUT so payment of the unitrust amount is a nonissue until the trust sells the property, and then it can flip to a standard CRUT.

ᚻ *Can I use the same FLIPCRUT to make a subsequent donation of another parcel of currently unsaleable bare ground?*

Once you flip the trust to a standard CRUT, you give up the makeup provision. So if you later place an unmarketable asset into the trust, you want it to be saleable so it can be quickly converted to income-producing property.

℞ *I like the idea of using a charitable trust to dispose of my appreciated property; however, I need a lump sum upfront to purchase our retirement home. Is it possible to structure a partial gift so I can get cash out of the transaction immediately?*

Yes, a partial gift is possible. You contribute a partial interest to the CRT and retain an undivided interest. The basis, capital gain, and all costs associated with selling the property are allocated proportionately between you and the CRT. The portion that you retain will generate a capital gain tax; however, the charitable income tax deduction you receive for your contributed portion will generally offset the capital gain tax liability.

℞ *Can you give me an example of how this works?*

Sure. Steve and Cheryl own a rental property valued at $1 million for which they paid $100,000. Nearing retirement, they want to sell the property, minimize the capital gain tax, receive income, and keep approximately $280,000 of the sale proceeds to purchase a mountain cabin and a motor home.

They meet with their financial planner who presents the following analysis:

- Donate a 70 percent interest ($700,000) in the property to a CRT and retain the 30 percent interest ($300,000).
- Steve and Cheryl and the CRT sell the property for $1 million.

Their proportional basis was	$ 30,000
Capital gains	$270,000
Capital gain tax (at 20 percent)	$ 54,000
CRT portion	$700,000
Capital gain tax	$ 0

The bottom-line results are that Steve and Cheryl receive $246,000 ($300,000 − $54,000) after-tax cash from the sale of the portion of the property they kept. However, the tax deduction for the gift to the CRT should more than offset the tax liability on the sale, essentially allowing them to sell their interest in the property tax-free.

This is a powerful planning technique that can work with almost any capital asset. But when disposing of real estate with this technique, you must consider that

- you cannot arrange the sale prior to the transfer into the CRT; and
- an independent special trustee must negotiate the sale of the CRT property separately from your negotiations with the buyer.

For tax deduction purposes, the value of the undivided interest in real estate will be less than its pro-rata share of the property's total value. In other words, a 70 percent interest in a $1 million property is not worth $700,000, but likely is worth somewhere between $500,000 and $600,000. This decrease in value, known as a "fractional interest discount," applies to any undivided interest in property. So even though the trust may later sell its interest for $700,000 (which probably would happen only if you and the CRT sell your interests to the same buyer at the same time), your tax deductions will be based on a lower value.

PART
FIVE

Controlling Your
Charitable Gifts

Several charitable strategies will allow you to establish a legacy while giving you control over the charitable vehicle itself. We explore these strategies in Part Five. They can be extremely complex techniques—you may well find the rules governing them incomprehensible. Given some harrowing experiences that clients of the contributors to *Giving* have had with these more complex techniques, we cannot stress too strongly the importance of getting the best advice available for your planned giving program. It is always an invaluable investment.

One of the most effective methods for donors to control their charitable gifts is to establish a private foundation. For most of us, the idea of a private foundation conjures up an image of a wealthy family creating a massively funded organization that supports a self-serving agenda. This image is far from reality. Chapter 16 does much to uncover the truth and dispel misconceptions regarding private foundations.

Our contributing authors submitted a great number of questions and answers dealing with all facets of private foundations. From their responses, their clients clearly are extremely interested in private foundations—how they are used, the technical nature of their creation and operation, and how they differ from other charitable techniques. Equally clear is that the people who are interested in private foundations are not necessarily wealthy scions bent on self-aggrandizement. Rather, they are families, or heads of families, who want to ensure that their charitable funds are used to support important causes. They also seem to consider private foundations as mechanisms to create a family culture of giving and to bring families closer.

In the past, the perceived disadvantages of private foundations were the incredible amount of scrutiny and the numerous regulations surrounding these specialized charitable organizations. This chapter will *not* dispel that view, but our contributors display a wealth of professional experience with private foundations and provide excellent answers to the tough questions that clients ask about foundations, including the technical aspects.

If you don't know very much about private foundations, chapter 16 will provide an overview of the rules governing private foundations. More important, it will give you some insights as to how to reduce the complexities. Private foundations have been subject to abuses in the past. The rules now in place are designed to prevent those abuses. Yes, they are complicated. But when one understands that the rules are designed to ensure that the funds placed in private foundations go to legitimate charitable endeavors, the rules become much less intimidating.

Chapter 17 covers the supporting organization (SO). Only in the last 5 years or so have practitioners begun to recognize the supporting organization as a charitable organization worthy of use—and it has blossomed. The reason for this considerable oversight by most tax practitioners is the sheer complexity of the Internal Revenue Code (IRC) provisions governing SOs and the regulations interpreting those provisions. The IRC recognizes three types of supporting organizations, only one of which is applicable to private donors. This Type III SO is a viable alternative to private foundations. Many philanthropic individuals and families have adopted SOs as an efficient method of distributing their charitable dollars and controlling their gifts.

This chapter deals primarily with the technical requirements of creating a Type III supporting organization, although it touches on

Types I and II to give perspective to Type III SOs. Because the Type III SO is a product of a complicated statutory scheme, the clients of our contributing authors asked questions that required technical answers. These answers are most helpful for those who want to understand the concept of SOs.

In our experience, clients have a difficult time grasping the significance of supporting organizations and the role they can play in charitable planning. The questions and answers in this chapter go to the heart of what supporting organizations are, what steps donors must take to establish an effective Type III SO, and how a Type III SO must function to continue to fall within the IRC restrictions.

You will find some repetition in the questions and answers in this chapter. We did this deliberately for two reasons. First, without the repetition, a reader who reads only one section may not have the background to understand the answer. Second, the rules are so complex that even a person who reads through the chapter will likely lose track of the technical requirements of Type III SOs. In either case, the questions and answers in this chapter will certainly help you if you are confused about an area that is already a breeding ground for confusion.

The charitable giving provisions of the IRC offer tremendous variety in charitable giving opportunities. No matter what a person's charitable interest may be or how great that person's resources, he or she has an opportunity to make a charitable contribution. Endowment funds and donor-advised funds (DAFs)—one of the more interesting of the charitable giving methods for allowing donors to control their gifts—are discussed in chapter 18. We had a number of excellent questions and answers on endowment funds and DAFs. This chapter, however, is not a long one, mostly because the rules for these strategies are not as extensive as those for private foundations and supporting organizations.

Endowment funds and DAFs allow philanthropically motivated individuals and families the opportunity to use the resources and supervision of an established charity. Without creating its own organization, a family can donate money or property to a charity in a segregated fund—in the name of the family or certain family members. In an endowment fund, assets are permanently set aside at the charity and only the income or growth in the fund is made available to further the charity's mission and goals. Under a DAF, the donor can direct how that fund is distributed to charitable causes, as long as the supervising charity reviews and approves those charitable causes. Charities often give a great deal of latitude to individuals and families who create DAFs.

In this chapter, the rules for donor-advised funds are set forth in a direct and concise manner. You will come to understand how to set up and operate a DAF and also how DAFs compare with private nonoperating foundations and supporting organizations. From a charitable planning perspective, this chapter offers a summary of these three methods of controlling gifts and how each can be used, depending on the resources and objectives of a donor and his or her family.

One of the most overlooked topics in charitable giving is charitable investing. In our experience, neither clients nor their nonfinancial advisors give a great deal of consideration to the investment principles that must be followed. Therefore, many charitable planning techniques require an organization or a trust to invest and distribute money, but little time may be spent on understanding what is involved in investing that money. Chapter 19 includes those questions and answers submitted by our contributors on charitable investing.

Most of this chapter is devoted to charitable organizations, such as supporting organizations and private foundations. Information about the charitable investment rules for charitable remainder trusts and charitable lead trusts are found in the chapters dealing with those planned giving techniques.

Two major issues face the trustees and boards of charitable organizations. The first is the duty of trustees and board members to the charitable organizations and the causes they support. This duty is extremely high and must be taken seriously by those who serve on charitable boards and by those who volunteer or work for charities. The second issue is the importance of developing an investment policy statement. An investment policy statement is, we believe, an absolute necessity in developing a successful charitable endeavor.

A whole book could be written about charitable investing. The purpose of this chapter is to give you a basic understanding about charitable investing and some of the rules that govern it. From there, board members, trustees, volunteers, and employees can seek expert advice on how to put into practice the ideas that our contributing authors offer.

Because of the complex nature of these charitable strategies, we may have repeated rules and regulations more frequently in this section than in any other part of *Giving*. We encourage you to read the questions and answers that are relevant to you. We also encourage you to seek the best advice to plan your charitable giving program. We hope that proper planning will enable you, and the charities that are important to you, to receive all of the benefits and rewards that charitable giving can provide.

chapter 16

Private Foundations

OVERVIEW OF PRIVATE FOUNDATIONS

ᏅᏱ *What is a private foundation?*

In *The Ford Foundation: The Men and the Millions* (Reynal and Company, 1956, p. 3), Dwight MacDonald humorously states, "[A private foundation is] a large body of money completely surrounded by people who want some." Although this definition may reflect the reality of how some people view private foundations, in reality a *private foundation* meets four basic criteria:

1. A private foundation is a charitable organization.
2. A private foundation is formed from one source.
3. A private foundation receives funding from investment income on an ongoing basis.
4. A private foundation either makes grants to others for charitable purposes or conducts its own charitable programs.

A basic explanation of each component is important to help you understand what a private foundation really is.

- *First, a private foundation is a charitable organization:* This means that it must be organized and operated exclusively for religious, charitable, scientific, literary, or educational purposes or for the prevention of cruelty to children or to animals. The term *charitable* is quite broad and encompasses the arts, youth programs, senior programs, health care, historic preservation, and multiple social causes.

- *Second, a private foundation is formed from one source:* In other words, the foundation is formed and funded by an individual, a family, or one corporation. A private foundation differs significantly from a public charity in this regard because a public charity generally receives funding from multiple sources—the general public.

- *Third, a private foundation receives ongoing funding from investment income:* For example, John and Mary Smith contribute $1 million to the John and Mary Smith Foundation during 2001. The foundation invests this contribution—the endowment—and receives investment income on an annual basis. John Smith, Mary Smith, and other members of the Smith family may or may not make additional contributions to the foundation during their lives or at death.

- *Fourth, the private foundation will either make grants for charitable purposes to others or will conduct its own charitable programs:* Most private foundations are established as grant-making organizations and are often referred to as private nonoperating foundations. Private nonoperating foundations receive their funding from investment income on an ongoing basis and make grants to others for charitable purposes. Private foundations that conduct their own programs are private operating foundations.

⋆ What is the difference between a family foundation and a private foundation?

Technically speaking, there is no difference, and we use the two terms interchangeably in this chapter. Many people prefer to use the term *family foundation* because it reflects the involvement of the donor's family in operating the foundation. To the extent that there is a distinction, people rarely refer to a private foundation formed by a corporation as a family foundation.

⌘ *Can my family-owned business form a foundation?*

Yes. These types of foundations are known as "company founda-tions," but they are essentially identical in all respects to the other foundations we have described. If your family-owned business is a C corporation, its charitable income tax deduction for contributions to the company foundation cannot exceed 10 percent of the company's adjusted taxable income.

Although the company foundation is a separate entity, it is closely tied to the family business because the business provides the funding. The company's officials typically operate the company foundation.

One advantage of a company foundation is that it can build an endowment that will enable it to continue its charitable giving in years when company profits are low. The company builds the com-pany foundation with significant funding in profitable years to build an endowment so it can support charitable causes regardless of the future profitability of the company.

⌘ *What are the primary advantages of forming my own private foundation?*

There is a growing trend for philanthropic individuals, families, and companies to create their own private foundations. While you will have your own reasons for creating a private foundation, those who have created their own foundations tell us that a private foundation

- allows the family to have more control over how charitable con-tributions are used;
- carries out the founder's charitable intent for years to come;
- brings family members together as trustees or directors and teaches them the founder's charitable views;
- allows family members to receive trustee or director fees;
- provides family members with considerable influence in the community;
- replaces *ad hoc* and sporadic charitable efforts with an organized and systematic vehicle for charitable giving;
- provides a way to keep a family's name alive for generations; and
- provides the family an opportunity to support foreign charitable organizations.

◌ℛ *Why do people establish private foundations?*

Individuals and families throughout America have established private foundations for a variety of reasons, some of which are:

- As a way to give something back to society
- To teach future generations the importance of supporting community hospitals, libraries, youth and senior programs, education, fine arts, and social services
- As a memorial to a loved one
- To obtain income and estate tax benefits
- to have an organized method for giving to charity
- To create jobs for family members

◌ℛ *If our family establishes a private foundation, are contributions to the foundation deductible?*

Yes. Contributions to a private foundation are income, estate, and gift tax–deductible, but the amount of your deduction for contributions to a nonoperating foundation will generally be lower than a comparable gift to a public charity. These rules are discussed in detail in Chapter 5, Federal Charitable Income Tax Deductions.

◌ℛ *Can I use a family foundation to help my family stay a close-knit unit?*

A family foundation helps family members maintain close ties with one another and may even go beyond that, helping to mend some emotional wounds. In our experience, a family meeting associated with a family foundation can be a powerful tool for building warm, lasting relationships. When a family comes together to talk about doing good—giving money to deserving causes in the community or around the world—its members no longer focus on the individuals and their personal issues and instead ask, What can we do for other people? Working together to provide benefits and rewards for other people often makes inter-family squabbles to go away.

◌ℛ *Can I be a trustee or director of my own private foundation?*

Yes. This is one of the most attractive features of a private foundation.

You can retain control of the assets donated to your foundation, subject, of course, to the self-dealing and other rules imposed on operating a private foundation. You can serve alone or as one of several trustees, directors, or officers. The private foundation rules impose no restrictions on who can be a trustee or act as a director. Typically, the person establishing the foundation names his or her family members as directors or trustees.

ભ *I like the idea of setting up a private foundation that will allow my family to leave a lasting impact on the world. How much money do we need to start a foundation?*

No specific amount of money is required, but a number of factors come into play in determining the practical amount you need to establish a private foundation. In reality, $25,000 could be an effective start for a private foundation, provided that you intend to make additional gifts to build the private foundation's investment base (endowment).

The Internal Revenue Service estimates that there are at least 14,000 private foundations with less than $100,000. The Council on Foundations suggests that a permanent foundation with volunteer board members should have a minimum of $1 million in endowment funds. The council suggests that if the average return on investments is 9.5 percent annually, $1 million would provide $50,000 to $55,000 a year for grants and expenses while maintaining purchasing power through the years. In this scenario, expenses are estimated in the $5,000-to-$15,000 range, leaving the balance for grants.

The Council on Foundations also suggests a minimum size of $10 million if there is to be a full-time director and the salary and expenses are likely to reach $80,000 to $100,000 per year. A foundation of this size should yield $500,000 to $550,000 per year as its annual budget.

In the end, your objectives will play a significant part in determining the amount of funds needed to establish the private foundation. The more ambitious your goals and the scope of the foundation, the more funds it will need. On the other hand, foundations with highly focused objectives that require little management may not require huge sums to be effective. Creating a business plan for a proposed private foundation will help you and your family to understand the financial backing required for a successful endeavor.

❦ I want to leave much of my wealth to my foundation at my death, but I'm not interested in funding one now. Must I create the foundation now? If I create it later, I want to make sure it will be named after my deceased wife. She was heavily involved in church-related charities and I would like my foundation to benefit those charities.

You do not have to create your private foundation while you are living. You may instruct the trustee of your living trust or the personal representative of your will to create the foundation at your death. The trustee or personal representative creates the foundation under the terms and conditions you put in your trust or will. The trustee or personal representative has the fiduciary duty to carry out your instructions.

Your trust or will should provide specific direction as to the purposes of your foundation. You may have strong feelings about your local church and its many ministries now, but you should consider that your private foundation may have a perpetual existence. Churches change pastors, denominational ties, and even foundational doctrine.

Because your faith is important to you and you want to support causes consistent with your objectives, you should give the foundation managers the power to choose the charitable organizations to which your foundation may make distributions. Make the charitable purpose as clear as possible, as the charitable purpose is what you wish to support, not necessarily a specific organization.

❦ Can my charitable remainder trust be used to fund my foundation at my death?

Absolutely. You can name the charity of your choice as the charitable beneficiary of your charitable remainder trust (CRT), including your foundation. As we explained above, there is no need to set up the foundation while you are living; your personal representative or trustee can establish it according to your instructions after you die.

Putting together a plan such as this requires the advice and expertise of specialized advisors. Done properly, a CRT coupled with a private foundation can save a great deal in taxes, allow diversification of highly appreciated assets, create an income stream for life, and accomplish your charitable goals.

❦ I want to create a foundation that my children will manage after my death. I would also like to give as much as I can to my

children without paying estate tax, and give the rest to my foun-dation. Can I do this without reviewing my estate plan every time the tax law changes?

First of all, you and your advisors should review your estate plan, at a minimum, every 3 years and certainly whenever there is a change in the law. Many planning professionals have annual meetings with their clients, providing them the opportunity to keep all of their estate planning documents current based on changes in the tax law. Changing your plans because of new or changed laws is, unfortunately, a reality of planning in our society; but keep in mind that changes can offer new opportunities as well as challenges.

It is certainly possible to draft your estate plan so the maximum amount that may pass free of estate taxes will pass to your children, with the remainder distributed to your private foundation. If done properly, as the estate tax applicable exclusion amount increases through 2009, so will the amount that passes to your children.

Your planning should also allocate some of your assets to your children and some to your private foundation if the estate tax is eventually repealed; otherwise there is a chance that all of your assets would pass to your children. Your plan should clearly state your preferences under any and all possibilities.

TYPES OF PRIVATE FOUNDATIONS

ଔ *Is there more than one type of private foundation?*

Yes. There are four types of private foundations:

1. Nonoperating foundations
2. Operating foundations
3. Pass-through foundations
4. Common-fund foundations

Nonoperating Foundations

ଔ *What is a private nonoperating foundation?*

The *nonoperating foundation* is the most common type of private foundation. A nonoperating foundation does not actively conduct charitable programs. It receives contributions from a family, an individual, or a company, which it then invests. Generally, the foundation makes grants to qualified charitable organizations from its investment income, although a private nonoperating foundation can make charitable grants from principal. In other words, these foundations act as conduits, passing the income, and sometimes principal, from the donor's gifts to other qualified charities, called *operating charities.* Operating charities actually do the charitable work, such as housing the homeless, training the unemployed, and operating soup kitchens. Nonoperating foundations often provide the operating capital for many different operating charities.

℘ *Is the money I give to my private nonoperating foundation tax-deductible?*

Yes. For federal income tax purposes, cash gifts to a private nonoperating foundation are deductible up to 30 percent of your contribution base, which usually is your adjusted gross income. If you donate appreciated publicly traded stock to your private nonoperating foundation, it is deductible at fair market value, up to 20 percent of your contribution base. Other appreciated property is deductible at your cost basis, up to 20 percent of your contribution base. If your contributions in any 1 year exceed the annual deduction limitation, you may carry over the deduction for up to 5 years. If you live in a state that has an income tax, its rules may vary considerably from these federal rules.

Operating Foundations

℘ *How does a private operating foundation differ from a private nonoperating foundation?*

A private *operating foundation* actually conducts charitable programs and usually does not make grants to other charitable organizations. Charitable activities that private operating foundations commonly support include museums, libraries, historic preservation programs, and research institutes.

A private operating foundation is classified as a private foundation for tax purposes because it is formed from one source. Private operating foundations are required to spend at least 85 percent of net investment income directly on their charitable activities.

☃ *What are the advantages to a donor if a foundation is classified as a private operating foundation?*

The percentage limitations for charitable income tax deductions are higher for private operating foundations than for private nonoperating foundations. The charitable contribution limitation is 50 percent of the donor's contribution base for cash contributions to private operating foundations and 30 percent of the donor's contribution base for contributions of appreciated long-term capital gain property. As a general rule, the deduction is based on the fair market value of the property contributed.

☃ *Does the classification of a foundation as a private operating foundation have any disadvantages?*

Yes. A private nonoperating foundation can have a 1-year delay in the payout of its 5 percent minimum distribution amount. This delay allows a nonoperating foundation to hold onto funds longer, allowing them to grow. A private operating foundation must satisfy the payout test immediately, which means its funds will not grow as quickly.

Pass-through Foundations

☃ *What is a pass-through foundation?*

A *pass-through foundation* must distribute all of the contributions it receives during the year directly to operating charities. In addition, it must distribute any income earned on those contributions. Because it pays to other charities all of the contributions and income it receives, it does not build up an endowment. There is an exception for bequests, legacies, and devises; these may be kept in the pass-through foundation.

The primary reason that a donor establishes a pass-through foundation is to get the foundation up and running so it will be ready to accept a much larger gift at the death of the donor. A pass-through foundation is treated as a public charity for purposes of the charitable income tax deduction. A pass-through foundation can elect annually whether it will be a conduit foundation that year. If it does not elect to be a pass-through foundation, it will be either a private operating foundation or a private nonoperating foundation, depending on its activities and purposes.

Common-Fund Foundations

ल्R Isn't there a special kind of private foundation called a "common-fund foundation"?

Yes, there is such a private foundation. A *common-fund foundation* is a private foundation that pools all of the contributions made to it into a common fund. The income from any part of the common fund that is contributed by a substantial contributor must be paid annually to a public charity. In addition, all of the principal accredited to a substantial contributor must be paid to charity within 1 year after the substantial donor's death. A substantial contributor is a person who gives more than $5,000 to the foundation in any year and that donation is greater than 2 percent of all donations made to the foundation during the year.

A common-fund foundation has a number of other rules dealing with distributions. It is treated as a public charity for purposes of contributions made to it. Common-fund foundations are rarely used, but, when they are, they are a convenient method to make planned gifts to selected charities and, at the same time, qualify donations for the higher percentage limitations offered to public charities.

ORGANIZATIONAL REQUIREMENTS

Establishing a Foundation

ल्R How would I go about forming a private foundation?

Forming a private foundation involves two steps. First you must form the foundation itself by creating a charitable trust or a nonprofit public-benefit corporation. Each requires a legal document commonly known as "articles of organization." For a nonprofit corporation, the articles of organization are called "articles of incorporation." For a trust, the articles of organization are contained in a charitable trust document. The second step is to apply to the IRS, and the related state tax agency if appropriate, for tax-exempt status as a charitable organization.

⊂℞ Which should I use, a corporation or a trust?

In the past, private foundations were created as trusts. Although private foundations still are organized as trusts, it has become more common to establish them as nonprofit corporations. This trend has arisen because states have changed nonprofit corporation laws to limit the personal liability of directors, trustees, and officers.

Attorneys often recommend establishing a private foundation as a nonprofit corporation because the articles of incorporation are fairly easy to amend. A nonprofit corporation also has bylaws that set forth the corporation's operational rules. If a private foundation is established as a trust, the trust document may be difficult to amend, and it may even be necessary to have a court reform the governing trust document.

Nevertheless, a trust does offer some advantages over the corporate form because a trust

- is easier to set up;
- has fewer formalities in regard to meetings and reporting; and
- provides the most control—your wishes are included in the irrevocable trust document and it is difficult to change, sometimes requiring court intervention to do so.

State law governs drafting and filing of the private foundation's governing instruments, whether they are corporate documents or a trust. In addition to meeting the requirements of state law, the governing instruments must also contain certain provisions to secure tax-exempt status under the Internal Revenue Code (IRC).

Obtaining Tax-Exempt Status

⊂℞ How does a private foundation qualify as a tax-exempt organization?

To become a tax-exempt charitable organization, the newly established entity must file Form 1023, Application for Recognition of Exemption, with the IRS within 15 months after the month the foundation was formed. Many states have a comparable filing, and this state exemption application must also be filed for the foundation to become exempt from state income taxes. The timing for state applications varies from state to state.

The federal and state filings can take some time to prepare, as they require a comprehensive description of activities of the foundation; financial projections; director, officer, and trustee information; details about any scholarship procedures; and similar information. As a general rule, the IRS takes 100 days to review a Form 1023 and to respond to the organization's request for tax-exempt status. It is essential to retain a seasoned professional advisor to complete and submit the application. Typically, a representative of the IRS or the state asks for more information and clarification.

OPERATING REQUIREMENTS

Annual Distribution Requirements

Minimum Distribution Requirements for Private Nonoperating Foundations

QR *How much must a private nonoperating foundation distribute each year?*

Federal tax law requires that private foundations must distribute a minimum of 5 percent annually, and there are penalties for not meeting this requirement.

QR *How is the 5 percent payout amount determined?*

A private nonoperating foundation is required to distribute 5 percent of the value of its assets each year. The minimum payout amount in a given year is determined by the average monthly value of the preceding year. For example, for the year ending December 31, 2002, the distribution is based on the average monthly value for the year 2002, and the foundation must make the distribution by December 31, 2003.

QR *What distributions count toward this 5 percent?*

The law requires that the 5 percent be for a qualifying distribution. *Qualifying distributions* include

- grants to charities and to noncharitable organizations for charitable purposes;
- all administrative expenses for the conduct of the charitable activities of the foundation;
- costs of all charitable activities;
- amounts paid to acquire assets used to carry out charitable purposes (such as furniture and furnishings);
- certain set-asides; and
- program-related investments.

℘ *If my foundation distributes more than 5 percent, can the excess be carried over?*

Yes. The amount in excess of the qualifying minimum distribution amount of 5 percent may be carried over for up to 5 years. The foundation completes Form 990–PF each year showing the amount it is carrying over.

℘ *What happens if the foundation doesn't distribute all that it's supposed to?*

The penalty imposed for failing to meet the 5 percent payout is 15 percent of the amount that the private nonoperating foundation failed to distribute (the unpaid minimum payout amount). If the foundation does not promptly correct an underpayment, the penalty for failure to meet the 5 percent payout is equal to 100 percent of the remaining amount that the private foundation failed to distribute.

℘ *Are the minimum distribution rules applicable only to private nonoperating foundations?*

Yes. Private operating foundations have a different set of distribution rules. They are discussed in detail in the next section.

Annual Distribution Requirements for Private Operating Foundations

℘ *Our family is interested in a foundation, and our oldest daughter has expressed an interest in running the foundation's charitable programs. What are the requirements to qualify as a private operating foundation?*

A private operating foundation must satisfy an income test and one of three other tests regarding its assets and sources of revenue. The income test requires the foundation to use substantially all of its income to sponsor and manage its own programs. This test requires the foundation to spend the lesser of

- 85 percent of its adjusted gross income or
- 4.25 percent of its net investment assets each year.

In addition to the income test, a private operating foundation must satisfy one of three alternative tests each year: an assets test, an endowment test, or a support test. These three alternative tests are highly technical and are also designed to ensure that foundations devote their assets to charitable programs.

ᘓ *What will happen if my foundation doesn't meet these tests?*

If the foundation fails to qualify as an operating foundation for a given year, it is treated as a nonoperating foundation for that year. It can return to private operating foundation classification as soon as it satisfies the income test and one of the three other tests mentioned above.

Newly established organizations must meet the tests in their first year. If the application for recognition of exemption is filed before the end of the foundation's first fiscal year, the IRS will accept the organization's representations that it plans to qualify as a private operating foundation. Failure to qualify in the first year can be corrected if the foundation does qualify in its second, third, and fourth years of operations.

ᘓ *What will happen if my foundation makes an improper expenditure?*

The IRC imposes a 10 percent tax on the foundation and a 2½ percent tax on the directors or trustees on certain expenditures that foundations are restricted from making. These include expenditures for

- grants to nonqualified organizations;
- election campaigns or voter registration;

- grants to individuals (other than scholarships, prizes, or similar endowments awarded under an objective, nondiscriminatory set of procedures); and

- propaganda, lobbying, or legislation.

Taxation of Private Foundations

Although private foundations are supposed to be tax-exempt, I am told that this is not always true. Are private foundations subject to tax?

All private foundations are subject to taxation. These taxes come in two forms. One is an excise tax on some types of income. Although this is not an income tax in name, for all intents and purposes it is a tax on income.

Private foundations must file an annual tax return and pay a 2 percent excise tax on net investment income. A reduced tax rate of 1 percent is applicable if foundation distributions exceed a certain payout rate, which is generally based on the value of the foundation's assets and the income those assets produced. As we wrote this book, Congress was considering legislation to reduce the tax to 1 percent on all investment income.

The second type of private foundation tax is a penalty tax, imposed when a private foundation violates certain rules found in the IRC. These penalty taxes can be quite stiff.

Also, understand that private foundations are granted an exemption only from income taxes. This exemption is not a blanket immunity from all federal and state taxes. All private foundations are subject to state sales and use taxes, property taxes, and federal and state taxes of a similar nature, unless there is a specific statutory exemption from the tax.

Tax on Investment Income

How is net investment income calculated?

Interest, dividends, rents, royalties, and realized capital gains are investment income. The aggregate of all these investments is then reduced by ordinary and necessary expenses paid or incurred in the production or collection of such income. The result is net investment income.

Investment income also includes the gain realized on the sale of appreciated property contributed to the foundation. For lifetime contributions, the taxpayer's cost basis carries over with the property. When the foundation sells the property, it realizes the gain as investment income. The rules are more favorable when the gift comes to the foundation through a will or a trust at the donor's death. In those cases, the tax basis is stepped-up to the date-of-death value. If the 2001 tax act remains unchanged and the estate tax is repealed in 2010, this benefit will be lost.

Disclosure Requirements

℘ *Is our family's private foundation "open" to the public?*

The tax return of a private foundation is open to public inspection and must be available for inspection by a member of the public at the foundation's offices during normal business hours. A private foundation is required to make its annual tax return available for 3 years after the last date on which the return is required to be filed, including extensions. After the 3-year public inspection period, the private foundation is not required to permit public inspection of that return.

A private foundation must also make available for public inspection during normal business hours a complete copy of its Form 1023, Application for Recognition of Exemption. Upon request, a private foundation must make copies available.

Investment Options

℘ *Is a private foundation restricted in its investment options?*

Although the limitations on a private foundation's investment options are not strict, they do exist. *Jeopardizing investments*—investments that jeopardize the foundation's principal, or *corpus*—are not permitted, and a substantial penalty is imposed for owning such investments. No particular type of investment constitutes a jeopardizing investment, but the IRS has indicated that it will closely scrutinize transactions or investments that involve

- trading on margin;
- trading in commodity futures;

- investments in working interests in oil and gas wells;
- purchase of puts, calls, and straddles;
- purchase of warrants;
- selling short.

In evaluating a proposed investment for jeopardy, managers of a private foundation's investments should look to the "prudent investor rules" and a private foundation should have a written investment policy statement that follows the prudent investment standards. We discuss these investment principles in more detail in Chapter 19, Investing Charitable Donations.

Unrelated-Business Taxable Income and Excess Business Holdings

Can a private foundation engage in activities that are not directly related to its charitable purposes?

Yes, but only to a limited extent. Private foundations must be organized and operated primarily for charitable purposes. Because private foundations (and other tax-exempt organizations) are granted favorable tax status under the Internal Revenue Code, Congress concluded that such entities should not compete with taxable organizations. Accordingly, Congress imposed a tax on unrelated-business income as a reasonable compromise between allowing such competition and denying tax-exempt status to private foundations that derive some income from business activities that are not directly related to their exempt function.

What is unrelated-business income?

Any tax-exempt organization described within Section 501(c)(3) of the Internal Revenue Code, including a private foundation, is subject to income tax on its unrelated-business income. *Unrelated-business taxable income (UBTI)* is defined as net income from any unrelated trade or business regularly carried on by the organization. UBTI is subject to tax at the ordinary rates applicable to a comparable nonexempt entity. Thus, UBTI of a nonprofit corporation will be taxed at corporate tax rates, and UBTI of a nonprofit trust will be taxed at ordinary trust tax rates.

It sounds like the UBTI rules eliminate many sources of income. Are there any exceptions?

Plenty of them. Most passive investments do not generate UBTI. Income that is not UBTI includes

- dividends from C corporations,
- interest payments,
- rents from real estate,
- royalties.

By and large, the key here is whether the foundation is actively carrying on a trade or business or is merely a passive investor. Some investments—for example, certain real estate investment trusts—are passive investments but nonetheless throw off UBTI. In choosing an investment advisor for your foundation, make sure that he or she is familiar with these rules.

Can a private foundation use debt to purchase investments?

The UBTI rules also extend to income derived from debt-financed property. The public policy behind this is to discourage tax-exempt organizations from trading on their tax-exempt status.

Debt-financed property is defined as any income-producing property that the tax-exempt entity acquired through indebtedness and is *not* property that the foundation uses to fulfill its tax-exempt function. There is a limited exception for mortgaged property that donors contribute to a tax-exempt organization.

Can a private foundation own the stock of a closely held corporation?

The answer to this question is yes, subject to application of the rules governing excess business holdings. Congress enacted these rules to limit a private foundation's control of a business. The excess business holdings provisions generally limit a private foundation, and all disqualified persons combined, to 20 percent ownership of a corporation's voting stock or other interest in a business enterprise. In some circumstances, the 20 percent limitation is increased to 35 percent.

A foundation must dispose of excess business holdings within 90 days from the date that the foundation knows, or has reason to know, of the event giving rise to the excess holding. If the foundation fails to do this, the foundation will pay excise taxes on the excess holding, subject to certain exceptions. The primary exception to this rule applies to excess business holdings received by a private foundation by gift, and increases in business holdings resulting from business readjustments. In these instances, to avoid the penalties, the foundation must dispose of the excess business holdings or reduce them to acceptable levels of holdings within 5 years of receipt.

The penalty for owning an excess business holding is 5 percent of the value of the holding. The penalty tax increases to 200 percent if the excess business holding is not eliminated within the taxable period.

℞ *Can you give me an example of how the excess business holdings rules would apply if stock of a closely held business were given to a private foundation?*

Yes. Let's say that on December 30, 1999, John Smith made a charitable contribution of 2,000 shares of Smith Corporation to the John and Mary Smith Foundation, a private foundation. The company issued only 6,000 shares—all to John—so the two shareholders of the company are John and the foundation. The gift of the Smith Corporation stock is classified as an excess business holding for the foundation. Because the contribution of stock is a gift and not a purchase, the rules treat the stock of Smith Corporation as being owned by John Smith, a disqualified person, and not by the foundation, for the 5-year period ending December 29, 2004. During this period, the foundation must sell all or a portion of the Smith Corporation stock to avoid the excess business holdings tax.

Federal tax law permits a 5-year extension to dispose of the excess business holdings if the private foundation submits a request, explains why it needs an extension, and presents a realistic plan for how it intends to dispose of the excess business holdings within the 5-year extension period.

Restrictions on Self-Dealing

℞ *I'm told that private foundations are not allowed to engage in "self-dealing." What does that mean?*

Any direct or indirect financial transaction between the private foundation and the people who created it or the people who run it—known as *self-dealing*—is prohibited. The people who control and fund the foundation are referred to as *disqualified persons*. Whether the transaction between a disqualified person and the foundation is beneficial or detrimental to the foundation is irrelevant.

℺ *Who, specifically, are disqualified persons for purposes of the self-dealing rules?*

Disqualified persons include substantial contributors to the private foundation; and foundation managers, directors, officers, family members of these persons, and certain related entities. For purposes of the disqualified person rules, a *substantial contributor* is defined as any person who contributed or bequeathed an aggregate amount of more than $5,000 to the foundation if that amount is more than 2 percent of the total bequests and contributions received by the foundation that year. The term *family member* includes an individual's spouse, ancestors, lineal descendants, and spouses of lineal descendants.

℺ *What types of transactions are considered to be self-dealing?*

Self-dealing transactions include all of the following transactions—whether direct or indirect—between a private foundation and a disqualified person:

- Sale, exchange, or leasing of property to or by a foundation
- Lending of money or other extension of credit to or by a foundation
- Furnishing of goods, services, or facilities to or by a foundation
- Payment of excessive compensation and expenses by a private foundation to a disqualified person
- Transfer of the income or assets of a private foundation to, or use by or for the benefit of, a disqualified person
- Agreement by a private foundation to make any payment of money or other property to a government official, other than an agreement to employ such individual for any period after the termination of his or her government service if such individual is terminating his or her government service within a 90-day period.

ᛞ *What is the penalty for self-dealing?*

The self-dealing penalty is in the form of an excise tax, which is 5 percent of the amount involved in the act of self-dealing. The disqualified person who participated in the transaction must pay the tax. If the foundation manager knowingly participated in the act of self-dealing, an additional tax of 2.5 percent is imposed on the foundation manager. If the self-dealing is not corrected in a timely fashion, the IRS will levy an additional tax, equal to 200 percent of the amount involved, on the disqualified person and a 50 percent tax on the foundation manager. Repeated acts of self-dealing may result in termination of the foundation's tax-exempt status.

These penalties are not designed to discourage people from considering the use of a private foundation to meet their charitable goals. Rather, the penalties exist to discourage abuses of private foundations by insiders.

ᛞ *What if the act of self-dealing occurs innocently?*

Even if the disqualified person did not know that the transaction amounted to an act of self-dealing, the disqualified person is subject to the penalties. For the foundation manager, there is a requirement that the act of self-dealing be done with knowledge and willfulness.

ᛞ *I run a business and my corporate headquarters are in a large commercial building that I own. Does this self-dealing prohibition mean that I can't rent office space in my building to my private foundation, even if I charge them only one-half of what I would charge a normal tenant?*

Yes, the self-dealing rules prohibit this sort of transaction, regardless of the economic advantage to the foundation. However, if you don't charge the foundation anything, it will not be considered self-dealing. The private foundation could pay for utilities, maintenance costs, and janitorial services, as long as it makes the payment to the provider of the services and not directly or indirectly to a disqualified person.

ᛞ *Can a family member use private foundation funds to purchase tickets to charitable events?*

No. Family members cannot purchase tickets for charitable events—such as golf tournaments, musical events, dinners, balls, or any other special events sponsored by another charity—with the family foundation's funds. A private foundation is not, on the other hand, precluded from contributing money to the charity for an event if the contribution made by the foundation is unrelated to the family member's ability to attend.

ℭ *From time to time, charities that receive grants from my private foundation give my foundation tickets to fundraising events or performances. Do the self-dealing rules apply in this instance?*

Often, a charitable grantee will give the private foundation tickets to fundraising or cultural events. The IRS has not given clear guidance on this point. Caution is advised. An act of self-dealing can occur if those tickets are made available to disqualified persons. But the IRS has indicated no self-dealing when the ticket is used by a foundation manager who has the responsibility for evaluating the activities of the grantee. However, if the manager took his or her spouse along, the spouse's use of the ticket possibly would be self-dealing.

ℭ *Can a family member use the family foundation's funds to honor a pledge that he or she made to a charity?*

No. The regulations specifically prohibit a family member from paying pledges to charities with foundation funds unless that family member was making the pledge on behalf of the foundation.

ℭ *Can family members receive a salary or other compensation for serving as an officer or employee of the private foundation?*

Yes. A family member can receive a salary or a director's fee and be reimbursed for expenses as a director or employee of a private foundation provided that

- the salary is paid for services performed,
- the services are reasonable and necessary for the tax-exempt purpose of the foundation, and
- the payment is not excessive.

The reasonableness of the compensation depends on the financial size of the foundation, the amount of responsibility undertaken, the liability involved, the time required, the number of board members or number of trustees, and the tasks the family member performs for the foundation. Comparable salaries for services will help in determining what is reasonable. Surveys of salaries for services to foundations are available from the Council on Foundations. A foundation can pay a family member for legal services, investment services, and banking services, provided that the services are related to the tax-exempt purpose of the foundation and that the amounts paid are reasonable.

MANAGEMENT AND CONTROL BY DONOR AND FAMILY

Managers of the Foundation

◌ℛ My family is just starting a private foundation. Who should be on the board, and what are the responsibilities of the board?

The trustees or board of directors of a private foundation must operate effectively and efficiently so they can achieve the goals set out in the organizing documents. The responsibility of a trustee or board member is often underestimated. The responsibilities include

- securing a manager and the necessary staff, if appropriate, to operate the foundation;
- preparing and approving budgets and managing the finances and assets of the foundation in accordance with the budget;
- knowing and following the rules and the regulations governing family foundations;
- reporting to government agencies (IRS and state authorities) and the public about the foundation's activities;
- establishing a policy for making grants;
- reviewing and making grants;
- overseeing and auditing the grants to ensure not only compliance with the law but also that the funds are being used for their intended purpose;
- training new trustees or board members.

℞ I have been told that each board member or trustee of a foundation should sign a conflict-of-interest statement. Do you agree?

Yes. Because of the self-dealing rules, each board member or trustee must understand and agree not to engage in conduct that could create a conflict of interest.

℞ Should my private foundation keep a management book?

Yes. Keeping good books and records is essential to a foundation's well-being. Your management book should contain

- organizational documents of the foundation:
  - articles of incorporation or trust agreement
  - bylaws
  - amendments to organizational documents,
- tax determination letter,
- policies and procedures,
- forms and grant-distribution rules,
- tax returns,
- budgets,
- minutes of meetings, and
- grant requests.

℞ A private foundation is a perpetual entity. How can I create a foundation that will be meaningful and important forever?

You, as the founder, can retain the authority to change the organizational documents during your lifetime, and you can pass this authority to successors. You can have a committee of family members whose job is to focus on the purposes and uses of the foundation and adjust the organizational documents appropriately over time. For example, at some date, it may be appropriate for a foundation to shift its focus from medical research to delivery systems, or from nonoperating to operating status, and back again.

There is a double-edged sword in this flexibility to make changes. If you give your successors the freedom to change the organizational documents, they might change the character of the foundation so drastically that you wouldn't recognize it. Your successors might have beliefs or goals different from yours. Careful, frank, honest discussions should precede turning over the foundation to your successors. You should also consider requiring a "super majority" vote before major changes can be made.

One effective technique is to allow your successors to operate the foundation during your lifetime. In that way, you can see how they handle the decision-making process. You can be there to guide and teach; you may find that your first choice of successors is unsuitable; and you may learn a tremendous amount about yourself.

Liability Protection for Trustees and Board Members

ભ *What kind of insurance should the family foundation and the trustees and board members consider?*

The type of insurance coverage that you need will depend upon what kind of activities the foundation engages in, the value of the assets, the character of the property, and the extent to which the foundation funds programs. To protect the trustees and board members, you should consider the types of insurance shown in Table 16-1.

ભ *In addition to insurance, does any federal law protect a board member, officer, director, trustee, or other volunteer?*

Yes. In 1997, the federal Volunteer Protection Act was enacted to protect uncompensated board members, directors, trustees, officers, and other volunteers. Volunteers are individuals who receive less than $500 of compensation annually.

The protection is limited to volunteers who are acting within the scope of their duties. Any volunteer who is required to be licensed, certified, or in some way authorized to perform an activity has to maintain his or her license, certification, or authorization in order to avail himself or herself of the exemption as a volunteer under the act. The protection from lawsuits provided by this law encourages volunteerism. One important exception to the federal Volunteer Protection Act is that it does not protect a volunteer while operating a motor vehicle.

Foundation Intent and Operating Guidelines

ભ *How will the foundation know what types of charities to benefit?*

When founders form a private foundation, they set out in the organizational document its charitable purposes. Founders of a private

TABLE 16-1   Types of Insurance Coverage for Foundations

Type of insurance	Coverage provided
General liability	Protects board members and trustees against liability for • defamation of character • libel or slander • bodily injury • damage to property.
Casualty	Protects board members and trustees against claims for bodily injury and/or damage to property of another not in the care, custody, or control of insured.
Property	Protects against loss from fire, theft, etc., or injuries that occur on foundation property.
Workers' compensation	Protects foundation for injuries incurred by foundation employees while working.
Auto casualty	Protects foundation for property damage or bodily injury that occurs to others caused by vehicles owned by foundation.
Environmental liability	Protects foundation's real estate against environmental claims, covering clean-up and restoration costs.
Directors and officers	Defends directors and officers for activities within the scope of their duties.
Indemnification	Where foundation provides legal defense for trustees and board members; indemnifies the costs.

foundation often want the foundation to focus on specific charities or causes. The bylaws of a nonprofit corporation often address these specific charitable goals. A trust agreement for a foundation includes the detailed provisions that address the foundation's charitable goals.

⊂℞ *Should my private foundation have a mission statement?*

You should consider a mission statement, especially if you are involving other people to help you develop the detailed charitable purposes of the foundation. A mission statement is a great help to maintain the focus of board members or trustees now and in the future.

ℭ How do I develop a mission statement?

The founder of the foundation can prepare a mission statement, or it can be a product of the initial trustees or board. Typically, the trustees or board members meet and identify areas of common ground, as well as areas in which they do not necessarily agree. To prepare for such a meeting, the founder could circulate a questionnaire prior to the session. The questionnaire might ask the individual trustees or board members

- to list the specific goals and objectives that he or she would like the foundation to accomplish,
- to identify the organizations that the foundation might benefit,
- how much money he or she anticipates the foundation will distribute annually, and
- how much he or she expects the foundation's assets to grow over time.

After the trustees or board members reach a consensus on these items, they can develop a mission statement that will reflect the goals they want to achieve and also an underlying philosophy that should govern the operation of the foundation over time.

ℭ How do we, as a board, choose the charitable institutions we should support?

This presents both a problem and an important opportunity for your private foundation. No one wants to waste time or money supporting charities that are ineffective. Few people are experts about all of the things that they are passionate about. Many people care very much about continued cancer research, for example, but do not know much, if anything, about cellular medicine. How can a layperson know if a research project is a boondoggle or a cutting-edge idea?

Some foundations set up subcommittees to investigate projects and charities before committing resources. Subcommittees can also monitor the charity's use of funds, its operating efficiency, propensity to waste, and progress of results. Subcommittees can bring in

TABLE 16-2   Questionnaire for Evaluating Requests for Funds

☐ What is the problem the organization seeks to address?

☐ Does it fall within the charitable purpose(s) of our family charitable philosophy?

☐ Can the problem be ameliorated by our participation?

☐ What approaches might be used to improve or alleviate the situation?

☐ Specifically, what is needed to alleviate the problem or to facilitate the work?

☐ Can our family charity make a meaningful donation to assist this organization?

☐ Will the donation be enough?

☐ Does the gift have to extend for more than 1 year?

☐ Is the organization efficient?

☐ Is it worthy of receiving the funds?

☐ Are there any public charities that address the same need and are worthier?

☐ Does the organization have a current tax-exempt status?

☐ Is it run by experienced people with a track record for getting things done?

☐ Does the organization spend most of its money on the problem at hand rather than on administration, promotion, or collection of funds?

☐ Can our gift be monitored?

☐ Will our family have the ability to follow through to see that funds committed to a project are used as promised?

---

experts to help analyze projects, conduct audits, provide background information to decision makers, interview potential recipients, and serve other functions to inform donors as to the efficacy of a gift or series of gifts.

Can you suggest an easier way to determine whether a request for funds is worthy or appropriate for a contribution from our family charity?

After considerable preparation, and sending out information to other members prior to a meeting, a board member or trustee might come to a board or trustee meeting with the following information:

- This is the project that interests me.
- Here is why.
- This is what I've found out about it, and this is the information I have gathered for your review.
- Here is the organization that is doing the best job to address the problem, and why.
- I ask that our family foundation commit a certain amount of money to my project. That amount will be a meaningful contribution to the project.

Table 16-2 contains a more detailed list of questions you might use to evaluate requests. Once you have the information you want, the family may discuss the matter and then table it until other members of the family can present and discuss their causes. Each member must educate, negotiate with, convince, or defer to others in the family to decide how the funds should be allocated.

Awarding Grants

What information should my foundation obtain from the charitable organizations that request grants?

As the granting foundation, you should inquire and obtain the following items to assess the reliability of the charitable recipient:

- name, address, and phone number of potential recipient;
- name and title of person submitting the request;
- tax-exempt status of the recipient (obtain a copy of the organization's determination letter);
- list of board members or trustees;
- financial statements;

- explanation of the project that the grant money is to be used for;
- names of others funding the project, if any;
- source of other funds for the project, if any;
- name and prior experience of person accountable for the project;
- name of requesting organization's auditor;
- permission to contact requesting organization's accountant; and
- written agreement in which the requesting organization agrees that it will
  - use grant money for the purpose requested,
  - not make taxable expenditures,
  - keep accurate records and receipts,
  - allow your foundation to inspect the project or program,
  - provide follow-up reports to your foundation, and
  - provide your foundation its tax returns.

Can a private nonoperating foundation grant scholarships to individuals?

Yes. A private nonoperating foundation can grant scholarships to individuals for travel, study, or similar purposes, subject to receiving advance approval of the scholarship grant-making plan from the IRS. If scholarships are made without obtaining advance approval, the grant will not be a qualifying distribution for purposes of the 5 percent minimum payout. The grant will also constitute a taxable expenditure by the private foundation, subject to excise tax.

Can a private foundation make a grant to an overseas charity?

Yes. United States foundations can make grants to foreign charities subject to the qualifying distribution requirements of the Internal Revenue Code.

Federal tax law requires a private nonoperating foundation to make qualifying distributions equal to the 5 percent minimum payout each year. A private nonoperating foundation that chooses to make a grant to a foreign charity will ordinarily make the grant in one of two ways to satisfy the 5 percent minimum payout requirement:

1. First, if the foreign organization has applied for and received an Internal Revenue Service determination letter that it is a public

charity, the grant to the foreign public charity will automatically be a qualifying distribution for purposes of the 5 percent minimum payout requirement.

2. Alternatively, if the foreign organization has not received such an IRS determination letter, the private foundation's grant to the foreign organization will not be a qualifying distribution unless the foundation has made a good-faith determination that the foreign organization meets the qualifications of an organization that could receive such a letter from the IRS.

The IRS has published guidelines regarding when a United States grant-making foundation will be considered to have made a good-faith determination that the foreign organization is the equivalent of a United States public charity, and any private foundation that desires to make such a grant should carefully follow these guidelines.

Termination

CR *I understand that a private foundation is designed to be perpetual, but what if the foundation has outlived its usefulness or the family's bloodline ends?*

Most families provide that the board or trustee may allow the foundation to expire if it no longer can serve its purpose. In most cases, the money in the foundation is distributed to the charities the foundation supported in the past.

ASSISTANCE IN FORMING PRIVATE FOUNDATIONS

Sources of Information

CR *What are some good resources for information about private foundations?*

The Council on Foundations is an excellent resource for foundations. It publishes books and papers on topics of interest, hosts the "Philanthropic Advisors Network" and offers the "Community Foundation Locator" to help individuals find foundations in their areas.

The Association of Small Foundations (ASF) is a professional organization for people who run their own foundations with few or no professional staff. It has about 2,400 member foundations whose assets range from under $100,000 to more than $250 million (size of the foundation is not the defining aspect of their membership). Members receive a newsletter disseminating information of interest. ASF also holds meetings nationally and regionally at which members learn the details of operating a small foundation. In addition to the quarterly newsletters, ASF conducts an annual survey of its members to answer such questions as, what salary levels and administrative costs are appropriate for foundations of various sizes? You can find the contact information for these organizations in Appendix B, Resources for Charitable Giving.

Professional Assistance

What role should an attorney play in regard to a private foundation?

Normally, attorneys see their role as one of helping their clients determine whether it is appropriate for the client to establish a foundation. The attorney should help the client consider other options such as outright gifts, scholarship funds at universities, donor-advised funds at local community foundations, and supporting organizations. In addition, an attorney can and should provide guidance in governing a foundation, managing grant making, and avoiding the prohibited transactions.

Do I need an attorney to set up and maintain a private foundation?

Sometimes individuals form and operate their foundations by themselves. When they do have professional advisors review their books and records, it is sometimes because the foundations are under IRS audit. Although some individuals have done a reasonably good job threading their way through state and federal regulations, more often than not some items must be addressed and cleaned up to bring the foundations into compliance.

Based on our professional experience, it is not so much a matter of how much money an individual has as a matter of whether he or she has found the right advisors to file the forms and keep the entity in compliance. Advisors with experience who routinely advise charitable entities may charge more per hour than general practitioners do, but the former tend to be more efficient than the generalists; they know what they are doing.

The cost of operation, then, will depend in part on the expertise of your advisor. Before determining whether to establish a private foundation, check out your other options: the donor-advised fund at the community foundation or the supporting organization. You may find that one of the alternatives is better suited to your needs.

Alternatives to Private Foundations

CR *What are some of the more attractive alternatives to private foundations?*

Two common alternatives to private foundations are:

1. Donor-advised funds through community foundations
2. Supporting organizations

Both of these charitable giving vehicles provide some or all of the advantages of a private foundation. They can be used to control the timing of tax benefits and provide name identification to the donor. These alternatives also avoid many of the restrictions and limitations to which private foundations are subject.

You should explore all of your charitable alternatives with professional advisors who have the experience and knowledge to guide you through the intricacies of each alternative, including a private foundation. If you share your dreams, feelings, objectives, financial resources, and level of commitment with your advisors, you will be able to make an informed decision as to how you can reach your specific goals.

CR *Why would I prefer a private foundation to a supporting organization or donor-advised fund?*

The primary advantage of a private foundation over a supporting organization or donor-advised fund is control. A donor who establishes a private foundation can manage the contributed funds for public benefit and achieve his or her charitable objectives by way of making grants to other charitable organizations. A supporting organization, community foundation, or donor-advised fund must not be controlled, directly or indirectly, by the donor or the donor's family, or by other disqualified persons.

chapter 17

Supporting Organizations

OVERVIEW OF SUPPORTING ORGANIZATIONS

What is a supporting organization?

A *supporting organization (SO)* is a special type of public charity created under the Internal Revenue Code (IRC). It is set up exclusively to support the activities of one or more traditional public charities. An SO can support the charities financially by running programs that expand or complement those of the supported charities.

Is a supporting organization a corporation or a trust?

An SO is either a charitable trust or a nonprofit corporation. In either form, the SO's organizational documents must be drafted in compliance with state and federal laws governing charitable organizations. It is treated as a public charity under the IRC, and the deduction limitations are the same as for contributions to public charities.

A supporting organization must be

- operated, supervised, or controlled by the supported organization; or
- supervised or controlled in connection with the supported organization; or
- operated in connection with one or more publicly supported organizations.

◌ঽ *How does a supporting organization differ from other public charities?*

With the exception of supporting organizations, all public charitable organizations must receive broad-based public support; otherwise, they will be classified as private foundations. While a supporting organization may have broad-based financial support, broad-based financial support is not required to sustain its status as a public charity.

Also, the traditional public charity may engage in a wide and changing range of activities as long as the activities are authorized by the charity's organizational documents and fall within the limits of activities permitted by a charity under the IRC. An SO does not have this flexibility or freedom. A supporting organization must either be controlled by the supported charity or be operated in connection with the supported charity. It does not have complete freedom to go off and "do its own thing."

◌ঽ *What is the income tax treatment of gifts made to an SO?*

Gifts of cash to an SO are deductible up to 50 percent of the donor's contribution base in the year of contribution. Unused deductions can be carried forward for a period of 5 years. Gifts of appreciated property, such as real estate, investment assets, or business interests (if held long enough to qualify for long-term capital gain treatment), are deductible at full market value up to 30 percent of the donor's contribution base. A 5-year carryover is also available for any deductions that cannot be used in the current tax year.

*Ο*ℜ *What types of charitable activities can be undertaken with a supporting organization?*

SOs have been adapted to undertake many different types of charitable endeavors. Some SOs provide direct financial support to one or more publicly supported charities on an annual basis. Other SOs undertake an activity for a publicly supported charity that the charity itself would not undertake but for the involvement of the supporting organization. For example, the SO may own property that a public charity developed and uses as the charity's primary training facility for youth counselors and volunteers.

*Ο*ℜ *Some friends of mine have called supporting organizations "designer charities." What do they mean by that?*

An SO is sometimes described as a "designer charity" because the person who sets it up decides who the potential charitable beneficiaries will be and also retains the right to recommend how the SO's funds are to be distributed among those charities. The charitable recipients may vary from year to year, depending on the SO's grant-making decisions. As long as the supported charities were originally listed in its governing instrument, the SO is free to support those charities in whichever way it pleases.

*Ο*ℜ *I like the idea of having a donor-advised fund at my local community foundation, but I don't want my gift to be added to its common endowment. I would rather not use the foundation's investment manager either. Is there an alternative that would give me more control?*

Instead of setting up a donor-advised fund at the community foundation, you might want to investigate setting up a supporting organization at the community foundation. That way you can take advantage of the administrative support the foundation's staff provides, but you can have the board or trustees of your SO control the investments.

CR *Would it not make more sense for us just to leave a bequest to the charities of our choice rather than go through the expense and hassle of creating a supporting organization?*

Only you can answer that question. Many people have problems giving large sums to a charity with little or no control over how those dollars are going to be used now and in the future. By funneling charitable dollars through a supporting organization, individuals and families who are concerned with retaining some control over their charitable gifts can pretty much determine how those dollars will be used.

Also, by funneling charitable dollars through an SO, donors effectively create a "charitable gift that keeps on giving." A donor-founder receives the same tax deduction regardless of whether his or her gift is to a supporting organization or to a more conventional public charity. Yet, with an SO, the founder and the founder's family can forever help decide how to use the SO's assets.

CR *Why would I want to set up a Type III supporting organization?*

A Type III supporting organization is most commonly established by individuals or families who are interested in philanthropy with a certain level of control but without a lot of complexity. The SO's board members or trustees can consist of the founder, the founder's spouse, and a controlling majority of disinterested individuals. One of the most attractive features of a Type III SO is the founder's (or the family's) right to select these disinterested board members or disinterested trustees.

CR *For whom is a supporting organization most appropriate?*

A supporting organization is generally appropriate for people who want their families to remain involved in the philanthropic focus of the organization without becoming immersed in the red tape typically associated with a private foundation. An SO is superior in this way because of its affiliation with other, larger charities that, in essence, provide the administrative and legal oversights with which family foundations generally have to comply. Although the supported public charity to which a supporting organization is linked exercises significant control over the SO, the person who wants to maintain some influence yet avoid the management responsibilities of other types of charities may want to consider a supporting organization.

COMPARISON OF SUPPORTING ORGANIZATIONS AND PRIVATE FOUNDATIONS

CR *What is the difference between a supporting organization and a private foundation?*

A supporting organization, like a private foundation, is often established and funded by a single individual or family. Unlike private foundations, however, SOs are afforded many of the benefits of being a public charity while avoiding the taxes and regulations imposed on private foundations.

CR *What are the advantages of a supporting organization over a private nonoperating foundation?*

For tax purposes, a supporting organization is characterized as a public charity rather than a private foundation. As a result of this characterization, many of the tax laws applicable to private foundations do not apply to SOs. For example:

■ Contributions of cash to supporting organizations are deductible up to 50 percent of the donor's contribution base, while cash contributions to private foundations cannot exceed 30 percent of the donor's contribution base.

■ Contributions of long-term capital gain property to a supporting organization are generally deductible at full fair market value. Contributions of long-term capital gain property to a private nonoperating foundation, with some exceptions, are limited to the donor's basis.

■ Private foundations are subject to excise taxes, including the excise taxes on investment income, and the penalty taxes on self-dealing, failure to distribute income, excess business holdings, investments that jeopardize charitable purpose, and taxable expenditures.

■ SOs are subject to taxes on excess benefit transactions, but are not subject to the rules governing excess business holdings, so can own business enterprises.

See table 18-1 in chapter 18 for a more detailed comparison.

TYPES OF SUPPORTING ORGANIZATIONS

CR *Are there different types of supporting organizations?*

Yes. A supporting organization must be organized and operated exclusively for the benefit of, to perform the functions of, or to carry out the purposes of one or more public charities. There are three types of SOs, commonly referred to as Type I, Type II, and Type III, because that is how they are categorized in the Internal Revenue Code.

- *Type I supporting organization:* is controlled by the supported charitable organization—like a subsidiary of the supported charity.
- *Type II supporting organization:* is controlled by the people who control the supported charity.
- *Type III supporting organization:* is controlled by individuals named by the founder of the SO and operated in conjunction with the supported charity.

A Type III SO is less well known than the other two types, but is the type used most often in connection with family philanthropy and estate planning. Because the Type III supporting organization is the one suited for private donors, we are discussing only Type III SOs in this book.

CR *What is a Type III supporting organization?*

A Type III supporting organization is typically set up by an individual or a family that agrees to operate the SO in such close association with at least one charity that it essentially becomes an extension of that charity. This supported charity does not control the Type III SO, nor does the founder or the founder's family. Instead, the SO is controlled by "disinterested" persons chosen by the founder. These people are disinterested because they cannot have any family ties to the founder or the founder's family. In addition, these people cannot be under the control of the founder or the founder's family, such as an employee of the founder. The founder may, but is not required to, name one or more of the supported charities (or their representatives) as members of the group that controls the SO.

ORGANIZATION AND OPERATION REQUIREMENTS

Organizational Structure

How do you set up a supporting organization?

The founder must decide on which organizational structure better serves his or her purpose—a nonprofit corporation or a charitable trust. When making this decision, the focus generally will be on the amount of flexibility that the founder wishes to retain and the personal liability protection the founder wants to afford the board members or the trustees.

After the founder selects the type of legal entity, the governing instruments must be drafted and signed. Thereafter, the organization applies to the Internal Revenue Service for tax-exempt status, by demonstrating how it meets the supporting organization requirements under the Internal Revenue Code, and files any other state-specific documents.

Do the organizational documents of a Type III supporting organization have to refer to a public charity?

Yes, the organizing documents must identify at least one public charity as a recipient of the new organization's support.

If I create a Type III supporting organization, will I have any control?

A Type III SO gives the founder and the founder's family the greatest flexibility; and, frequently, the founder and his or her family serve as trustees or directors of the supporting organization, along with representatives of the charities named. But the founder and his or her family are not permitted to control the supporting organization. Regardless of whether a Type III SO is created as a charitable trust or as a nonprofit corporation, disinterested board members or trustees must be given a majority of the votes. Under either structure, however, the founder, or his or her family, names the disinterested trustees or board members, who may be persons who are likely to have the same goals as the family. The key here, however, is that they are not legally obligated to do so.

Qℛ I thought that a supporting organization was controlled by the supported charity. Are you telling me that this is not correct?

Because there are three types of supporting organizations—two of which, Type I and Type II, are controlled by the supported charity—there is a common misconception that all supporting organizations must be controlled by the supported charity. The Type III SO is operated in such close association with at least one supported charity that Congress believed that control by the supported charity or charities was not necessary. This exception is what makes a Type III supporting organization so attractive to individuals and families as a viable alternative to private foundations.

General Requirements of a Type III Supporting Organization

Qℛ What are the requirements for a Type III supporting organization?

The Type III SO must

- *Name the charities it intends to support in its governing instrument.* The documents forming a Type III SO must name at least one supported charity. Typically, the founder names several charities as supported organizations in the documents.
- *Name at least one charity that will be attentive to the SO.* Supporting organizations are less regulated than foundations because the government anticipates that the supported charities will watch over the SO. To give the charity incentive to pay close enough attention to the SO, the level of support the SO provides one or more charities must be sufficient to assure the "attentiveness" of the charities. This attentiveness requirement can be met if the SO carries out an activity or function that the charity would not be able to do except for the support of the organization. For instance, if a local hospital lacks the funds to construct and operate a day-care center for its employees, an SO could supply and operate the facility, because without the SO's support, there would be no day-care facility at the hospital. Alternatively, the

SO must provide to charity sufficient financial support to ensure the attentiveness of the supported charity. This requirement for support and attentiveness is generally met if the support is given to a certain program or activity and the support is meaningful with respect to that program or activity.

- *Be controlled by disinterested individuals.* The founder's family cannot have control of the organization. The majority of an SO's directors or trustees must be disinterested outsiders. Actual control must rest with the disinterested persons. The founder or the founder's family, or persons they control, cannot have veto power and cannot require unanimous decisions of the directors or trustees. But the founder and his or her family may select the disinterested individuals who serve as either board members or trustees of the organization.

Organizational Tests

What specific provisions must be included in the organizational documents of a Type III supporting organization?

An SO must satisfy an organizational test in order to document that it is organized and operated exclusively for the benefit of, or to perform the functions of, or to carry out the purposes of, one or more public charities. The organizational test requires that the supporting organization's governing document

- limit the organization's purposes to the charitable purposes described in the Internal Revenue Code;
- not expressly empower the organization to engage in activities that do not further its purposes;
- designate the public charity or charities that it will support; and
- prohibit the support of organizations other than the specified public charity or charities.

Operational Tests

Are other compliance tests required?

A Type III SO must also satisfy an operational test that consists of two separate parts: the responsiveness test and the integral part test.

- *Responsiveness test:* To satisfy this test, the SO must either allow the supported charity a significant voice in the supporting organization's activities and investment and distribution policies, or be organized as a charitable trust under state law, and the supported charities have the right (enforceable in court) to enforce the trust and compel an accounting of the trust's expenditures.
- *Integral part test:* To satisfy this test, the SO must either perform or carry out the functions and purposes of the supported charity, or pay 85 percent or more of its income to or for use by the supported charity or charities.

Because the rules that govern the organization and operational activities of supporting organizations are quite technical, any individual or family that is contemplating establishing a Type III SO should use the services of expert professional advisors who have experience with SOs. Even a seemingly small mistake can have devastating consequences for a family and its charitable endeavors.

❧ *If our family establishes a Type III SO, how much will we have to contribute to qualify as a supporting organization?*

A Type III SO must support at least one of the designated charities each year sufficiently to motivate that charity to watch over the supporting organization. Two factors in particular generate such interest by the supported charity:

1. Support from your supporting organization is so great in comparison to the supported charity's other financial support that it will pay close attention to your SO and its activities.
2. Your SO is funding an activity that is important to the charity but that the charity cannot afford to engage in itself.

So, you see, the answer depends on the supported charity you name and the activity you fund. One way to ensure that your SO meets this requirement is to name at least one charity that has relatively low income. If the income of that charity is only $10,000 per year, a contribution of even $5,000 is so huge that the charity will certainly be interested in watching the activities of your SO.

Another alternative is to fund an important project of a large charity. For example, a family wanted to base its application to the IRS for SO status on support for not one, but two large charitable organizations—the School of Veterinary Medicine at Tufts University and the University of New England—with an annual contribution of only $35,000. In this case, these two institutions joined in and supported the family's application to support two activities of importance to these two schools. By working together, the SO and the two charities were able to establish, to the satisfaction of the IRS, that these two supported charities would continue to pay close attention to the operations of that supporting organization. In this case, the IRS likely was impressed that the supporting organization was providing benefits that two major nonprofit institutions deemed significant.

Payout Requirements

Does our Type III SO have to support, every year, all of the charities that I named in its organizational documents?

No. You are required to support only one named charity. That support must be of such a nature or of such importance to that supported charity that the supported charity will be motivated to make sure that the SO is being operated in accordance with its organizational documents and the law as it relates to supporting organizations.

Is a Type III SO restricted to merely making financial gifts to the supported charity?

No. The SO can also run programs that complement or extend the programs of the supported charity or are programs within the supported charity's area of interest but that require financial or human resources the supported charity lacks.

What are the payout requirements for a Type III supporting organization?

A Type III SO must make payments of substantially all of its income to, or for the use of, one or more supported charities. The amount of that support must be sufficient to ensure the "attentiveness" of the supported charity or charities. The IRS has ruled that "substantially all income" means that at least 85 percent of the SO's income must be paid out. For purposes of the 85 percent payout, income is defined as investment income, short-term capital gain income, and other income. Long-term capital gain income is excluded from the definition of income for purposes of the 85 percent payout requirement. Direct and indirect investment expenses are deductible against investment income and other income of the Type III supporting organization.

Does every Type III supporting organization have to satisfy the 85 percent payout requirement?

No. The 85 percent payout requirement is part of the integral part test. A Type III SO may also satisfy the integral part test by engaging in activities that benefit the supported charity or charities. This prong of the integral part test is known as the "but for" prong. Under this prong, a supporting organization can perform a specific function for one or more supported charities. For purposes of this test, the SO's activities should be limited to those activities that, but for the supporting organization's involvement, would not be conducted by the supported charity.

Obtaining Tax-Exempt Status

What is involved in the process of getting a supporting organization approved as a legitimate charity?

An application for recognition as a tax-exempt organization is filed with the Internal Revenue Service on Form 1023. This is the same form used by all types of charities seeking exemption from taxation on the basis of operating exclusively for specified charitable purposes.

In the case of a supporting organization, the portions of Form 1023 that must be completed depend on which type of SO is being applied for. In general, however, Form 1023 has to satisfy the IRS that the supporting organization will operate exclusively for permitted charitable purposes and that its structure fits properly within one of the three types of supporting organizations permitted under the Internal Revenue Code. There is also a filing fee, the amount of which depends upon the amount of funding of the supporting organization in its early years.

Funding the Supporting Organization

ભ *Can others contribute to our supporting organization as well?*

Absolutely. There is no limitation as to who and how many can make tax-deductible contributions to an SO. A primary difference between a supporting organization and the charitable organization that it supports is that the supported charity *must* receive its financial support from broad-based public sources, whereas a supporting organization may receive its support from a single source. As long as the SO qualifies under the Internal Revenue Code and the IRS regulations as a supporting organization, anyone contributing to an SO will get the same tax deduction, and be subject to the same rules for deductibility, as someone making a contribution to a traditional public charity.

ભ *What is the minimum amount of money a community foundation would accept to form a relationship with a supporting organization?*

Most community foundations are flexible in what they will do to accommodate SOs. This is especially true if the SO intends to develop a systematic or planned approach to charitable giving. Many community foundations spend the time getting involved with a supporting organization for as little as a $10,000 initial gift. You will have to contact your local community foundations and interview them with regard to their exact requirements.

ભ *If I name a community foundation as the primary charity of my Type III supporting organization, have I lost control?*

If a community foundation is one of the named charitable beneficiaries of a Type III supporting organization, the SO's directors or trustees can decide how the SO's funds are to be used and who the charitable recipient should be, so there is not much loss of control. The directors or trustees of the SO can retain grant-making power with regard to any charitable beneficiary of the organization, but the community foundation does have certain rights as a beneficiary and oversight entity of the SO.

Alternatively, if the gift is made to an "advise and consent" fund at a community foundation, the supporting organization offers its recommendation as to potential charitable recipients but control in this instance ultimately must be with the community foundation. Pragmatically, it would make sense that the community foundation would at least want to be responsive to the recommendations made by the directors or trustees within the specific dictates of the law so it will continue to receive the support from the SO.

A supporting organization, of course, has its own separate, legal, nonprofit status with the IRS. A community foundation, in this instance, is generally serving in a supervisory role and likely as a board member or trustee of the SO, with actual grant-making decisions left to the SO's collective directors or trustees.

CR *Can I fund my supporting organization from my charitable remainder trust?*

Yes, you can name a supporting organization as the charitable beneficiary of your charitable remainder trust.

THE SUPPORTED CHARITIES

CR *Can a Type III supporting organization give to charities other than those designated in its organizational documents?*

The Type III supporting organization is limited to supporting the charities identified in the organizational documents. The purpose of a supporting organization is to support those charities so identified.

CR *Is there a limit to how many charities I can name as supported charities?*

No. Neither the Internal Revenue Code nor its regulations currently limit the number of charities that can be named in the organizational documents of a Type III supporting organization.

CR *If our family establishes a supporting organization and names several public charities as supported organizations, can we substitute other public charities as supported organizations at a later date?*

No. As a general rule, substitution of the supported public charities is not permitted for Type III supporting organizations. Limited substitution of public charities is permitted if the substitution is conditioned upon an event that is beyond the control of the SO, such as dissolution of the public charity or the charity's loss of tax-exempt status.

MANAGEMENT OF THE SUPPORTING ORGANIZATION

‿ *How is a supporting organization managed?*

An SO will have a board of trustees (trust) or a board of directors (nonprofit corporation), and these individuals will manage the organization. The governing documents for the SO should state the objectives of the organization, and the trustees or directors have a fiduciary duty to carry out these objectives.

The SO's board of trustees or board of directors typically consists of the founder, one or more members of the founder's family, and several disinterested persons. The founder and his or her family members cannot control the board of trustees or board of directors but are involved with the SO on an ongoing basis. In general, a supporting organization is considered to be controlled by the founder if the founder and his or her family members have 50 percent or more of the total voting power of the board.

For example, the Smith Family Supporting Organization has a seven-person board of trustees. John and Jane Smith, the founders, are two of the seven trustees. The five independent trustees do not work for John Smith in any capacity or for a Smith-family business. The Smith Family Supporting Organization will not be considered to be directly or indirectly controlled by the Smith family under these facts. The IRS will, however, review all of the facts and circumstances of each case to determine whether disqualified persons do in fact control the board of trustees or board of directors.

‿ *Can I retain the right to reappoint board members annually?*

Yes. You may retain the right to reappoint board members annually.

ℭ *Can our family members be paid for their services to our supporting organization?*

With a supporting organization, there are no distinctions between family and disinterested individuals as far as compensation for services is concerned. The compensation must be reasonable for the type and degree of services provided. As a practical matter, the supported charity or the IRS might look more closely and question compensation paid to a member of the founder's family, especially if the family exercises a lot of influence over management of the SO, but there is no restriction on such compensation that would not also be applicable to anyone the SO compensates.

LIABILITY ISSUES

ℭ *Do the trustees or board members of the supporting organization have any personal liability relative to the business of the supporting organization?*

As long as the SO is properly created and registered as either a non-profit corporation or a trust, the board members do not incur personal liability for the acts of the SO. Notwithstanding, the SO can acquire insurance that protects the trustees or the directors from liability. Payment for the insurance is accepted as a reasonable expense and can be made from the operations of the supporting organization's assets. The types of insurance listed for private foundations in table 16-1, chapter 16, would also be appropriate for the trustees or directors of the supporting organization.

TERMINATION

ℭ *Can a supporting organization be terminated?*

Yes. The board of trustees or board of directors of a supporting organization can dissolve the organization. The organization's assets must be transferred to the named charitable beneficiaries, and the SO must notify the IRS of its termination.

chapter 18

Endowment Funds and Donor-Advised Funds

ENDOWMENT FUNDS

❧ What is an endowment?

An endowment is a permanent fund of donor contributions that helps to ensure the continuous mission of a charity. In essence, endowments are gifts that keep growing and giving. In an endowment fund, assets are permanently set aside and only the income or growth in the fund is made available to further the charity's mission and goals. An endowment fund allows the charity to do long-range planning and to determine the needs of the community and how the organization will meet those needs. Maintenance of an endowment requires good stewardship by the organization, maximizes its opportunities to support its mission, and increases its permanency and presence in the community.

ᚦ *Could we have the endowment fund bear our name and restrict use of the funds to our favorite projects?*

Yes. Although you can create an unnamed and unrestricted endowment fund, many donors have endowment funds that bear their names and/or restrict them to benefit specific areas of interest.

ᚦ *I was assisted through college with a memorial scholarship. Can I use an endowment fund to establish a perpetual memorial scholarship for worthy students?*

Yes, you could establish a memorial scholarship endowment at your alma mater to give annual scholarships to worthy young students who meet the qualifications that you establish. These annual scholarships could bear your name and become a permanent symbol of your belief in and support of the school or of a particular program of study.

DONOR-ADVISED FUNDS

Definition of Donor-Advised Funds

ᚦ *I've never heard of a donor-advised fund. Can you tell me what it is and what it does?*

Donor-advised funds (DAFs) are charitable "sub-accounts" that donors establish within a larger community foundation or other public charity. A DAF allows a donor to make contributions now and to take a charitable income tax deduction in the year of the contribution even though the actual distribution to the charities may be made in future years.

DAFs have been around for a long time. They are offered by local community foundations and some larger public charities that act as administrators for the funds and as intermediaries for giving. DAFs enable donors and their families or other designees to be actively involved by recommending when, how much of, and to what charities their funds' assets will be distributed. Legally, the funds' administrators can deny the advisors' recommendations, but as a practical matter, they honor the recommendations as long as they are not self-serving, they meet legal criteria, and they are being made to recipients that are U.S. charities.

In comparison to private foundations, donor-advised funds are easier and less expensive to create and are subject to fewer restrictions and regulations. Donors can start small—the initial contribution can be as low as $5,000—and build their funds along the way. Many estate planning and planned giving professionals consider the DAF a viable alternative to a private foundation for offering some control to donors. Table 18-1 compares donor-advised funds, foundations and supporting organizations.

ଔ *What are the advantages of a donor-advised fund?*

The donor-advised fund is another of the strategies that foster a culture of giving. DAFs offer families an opportunity to work together in setting their charitable priorities and talking through what matters most, and why. They give parents an opportunity to educate their children about the importance of charity. They promote long-term commitments to support worthwhile causes. Because they grow in value over time, DAFs let families play a role in grants that have a major positive impact on the grant recipients. Through DAFs, charitable giving becomes more than an isolated response to a fundraising drive or a December rush to the post office to "get a deduction this year."

A further advantage of donor-advised funds is that they enhance the prospect for larger grants because the funds can grow over time. Large grants are uniquely important to charitable organizations. They can help finance new medical equipment for a hospital, provide food and shelter for victims of natural disasters, fund a permanent scholarship or a new musical production, or rebuild a burned-out historic theater.

ଔ *Does the Internal Revenue Service approve of donor-advised funds?*

The Internal Revenue Code does not provide a formal definition of a DAF, because the DAF is a special fund within an existing charity, most often a community foundation. The IRS has acknowledged DAFs as legitimate planning tools and refers to them as "segregated funds" maintained for the specific purpose of allowing certain persons to provide ongoing advice regarding a charity's use of donated funds. Although the donors cannot have legal control over the segregated funds, they are, nonetheless, in a position to offer advice, and they

TABLE 18-1 Comparison of a Donor-Advised Fund, Private Foundation, and Supporting Organization

	Donor-advised fund	Private foundation	Supporting organization
Formation	▪ Generally funded by an individual or a family at a community foundation or a public charity ▪ Maintained by the administering organization ▪ Can be established within days by completing a simple application form provided by the administering organization ▪ Generally does not require the services of an attorney for drafting documents ▪ Administering organization usually handles all legal and administrative formation details	▪ Generally funded by an individual, a family, or a company ▪ Makes grants to public charities ▪ Is complex ▪ Start-up and administrative fees can be substantial ▪ Requires IRS approval	▪ Generally funded by an individual or a family ▪ Provides support to other charitable organizations ▪ Setup and administrative costs of Type III SO can be substantial ▪ Requires IRS approval
Annual distribution requirements	▪ None	▪ 5% annual distribution requirement	▪ Depending on structure, at least 85% of annual income
Excise taxes	▪ Not applicable	▪ 1%–2% of annual income	▪ Not applicable
Charitable income tax deductions	▪ Up to 50% of founders' contribution base for cash gifts and ordinary income property	▪ Up to 30% of founders' contribution base for cash and ordinary income property	▪ Up to 50% of founders' contribution base for cash gifts and ordinary income property

Charitable income tax deductions, *continued*	▪ Up to 30% for long-term capital gain property, deducted at fair market value	▪ Up to 20% for long-term capital gain property ▪ Only cost basis can be deducted for gifts of appreciated property, except for certain publicly traded securities, which can be deducted at fair market value	▪ Up to 30% for long-term capital gain property, deducted at fair market value
Control	▪ Founders have least degree of control over investments and distributions ▪ Founders give advice only ▪ Administering organization can accept or disregard founders' recommendations	▪ Founders control the disposition of the foundation assets ▪ Subject to rules that strictly regulate activities ▪ Rules require expert understanding and impose significant penalties for violations of those rules	▪ Founders of Type III SOs do not control the SO: instead appoint disinterested persons who control it ▪ Must satisfy "responsiveness" and "integral part" tests ▪ Failure to meet the tests causes the SO to be classified as a private foundation
Operation	▪ Founders benefit from investment and other professional expertise of administering organization ▪ Consolidated management of fund assets can yield higher quality and more efficient investment results	▪ No preexisting administrative organization ▪ Founders create as trust or corporation ▪ Founders typically handle administration and investments	▪ No preexisting administrative organization ▪ Founders create as trust or corporation ▪ Founders may benefit from investment and other professional expertise of the supported organization

exercise substantial influence over the amount, timing, or recipients of distributions from the funds.

◌ℛ *Why is a community foundation willing to create donor-advised funds?*

Community foundations generally maintain separate trusts or funds for donors' contributions to provide donors with many different options for planned giving. Frequently, community foundations have unrestricted funds as well as restricted funds. Unrestricted funds are used for the community as determined by the community foundation's board. Restricted funds are accounts that allow donors, when they originally establish the funds, to limit the use of the funds to designated charities, certain types of charities, certain designated purposes, or scholarships.

A donor-advised fund is a form of restricted donation in which the donor or members of the donor's family can make suggestions to the community foundation as to how the cash in the fund should be distributed. DAFs are important to most community foundations because some donors are much more willing to make contributions if they have a voice in how their contributions are used.

◌ℛ *We would like to establish a scholarship fund in memory of our deceased son for seniors graduating from our local high school. We would like to make an initial contribution of $40,000. What do you recommend?*

You have an excellent opportunity to create a donor-advised fund in conjunction with the local community foundation. Setting up a DAF will permit you, or persons you designate, to make recommendations to the community foundation's board as to likely recipients. You would establish scholarship criteria, review applications, conduct interviews, and then make your recommendations to the board. The board would oversee the entire process and have the final say. In the absence of unusual actions on your part, the board will likely adopt your recommendations.

An alternative method to meet your goals is to make your contributions to the community foundation's scholarship fund. This fund most likely has in place already the criteria, the application process, and a committee to review the applications and make the selections.

The choice between these alternatives depends on whether you want to stay involved in the process or whether you would like to delegate the matter to someone else. In either case, your gift will be used for its intended purpose and will benefit many young persons.

   I would like to make sure that my donor-advised fund will continue after my death so my children and grandchildren can participate. Will a community foundation establish my fund in perpetuity?

The standard agreement governing donor-advised funds at most community foundations allows you to be the fund advisor while you are living and often will extend the advisor role to your children. Usually, however, after that second generation passes away, any unexpended cash in your fund will fall into the foundation's general fund for its directors to distribute. Depending upon the size of your fund, you may be able to get the board to approve a permanent fund. Sometimes, all you have to do is ask for a modification of the standard agreement. Keep in mind, however, that many community foundations with experience know that, by the third generation, grandchildren have moved away and may have lost interest. This may make governance of the DAF problematic.

Establishing a Donor-Advised Fund

   How can my wife and I find an organization for our donor-advised fund and then go about setting it up?

First you should familiarize yourself with the various charities in your community, especially your community foundation, if there is one. Many of the major charities, such as United Way and the Salvation Army, will be able to help you set up a donor-advised fund or can tell you what charities offer them. Once your community knows that you wish to create a DAF, it should not take long for you to find out which organizations offer them.

    You should review the policies of the organizations that offer these funds, and perhaps visit each of them. Once you find an administering organization that appeals to you, you might enter into an agreement with the organization. As part of that agreement

- You establish the fund in your name or in the name of the family (such as the "Jane and John Johnson Fund").

- You and your wife make an irrevocable outright gift of money or property to the fund.

- You designate the specific charities or types of charities to receive distributions from your fund, or designate the purposes that the distributions are to support.

- You relinquish all legal control over how the organization invests or distributes your contribution.

- Although your contribution belongs to the charity in every sense of the word, you participate by making recommendations to the administering organization as to which charities should receive grants from your fund, as well as the amounts of those grants. The administering organization has the final say on making distributions, but it tries to honor your wishes, if possible.

- The organization usually will charge a modest administration fee, which it will deduct from the total value of the property that you contribute.

Do these organizations administer donor-advised funds essentially the same way?

No. Many DAFs are established with and administered by community foundations. Community foundations, as the name implies, often have a local, in contrast to a national, focus. Other organizations may have a bias in favor of their particular missions, such as funds sponsored by religious organizations. Still other organizations differ in permitting grants to be made from both principal and income, or only from income.

In addition, the past decade has seen the emergence and rising popularity of donor-advised funds established by commercial mutual fund companies. These commercial DAFs typically have a broad, often national, focus. Thus, by reason of their broader focus and substantial administrative and other resources, some donors find them preferable to community foundation funds.

Funding the Donor-Advised Fund

Are there requirements for the contributions that we make when we establish our donor-advised fund?

No. In general, you can make as many contributions as you want and can make them when you want; although any given administering organization may have rules that limit the number of contributions you may make during any 1 year. You are entitled to claim a charitable income tax deduction for each contribution to your fund, subject to the annual deductibility limits, which are 50 percent of your contribution base for cash and 30 percent of your contribution base for appreciated property.

Controlling the Distributions from Donor-Advised Funds

Do I have control over who gets the grants from my donor-advised fund?

Tax laws require that your charitable gifts be irrevocable and unconditional for you to receive the associated tax benefits. If you were to retain absolute control over the assets you transfer to a donor-advised fund, there would be no "gift" for purposes of a charitable deduction. Grants from the fund can be made only to domestic organizations that are tax-exempt public charities; or to federal, state, or local governmental organizations, such as state colleges or universities, qualified to receive tax-deductible charitable contributions.

While the administering organization will allow you to recommend how assets are disbursed, all recommendations are subject to the approval of the organization's trustees or directors. Chances are that the charities you choose to support to fulfill your philanthropic goals will be acceptable, but you should keep in mind that the organization has final decision-making authority regarding grant recipients.

Where can we get help in choosing the charities that should be recipients of distributions from our donor-advised fund?

Selecting charities is a major task that most families underestimate. Soliciting charities for grant requests and then evaluating the requests take a lot of time, knowledge, and experience. Without a trained staff, these tasks are difficult. One of the functions of a community foundation is to take on these tasks and screen the requests. The foundation's staff can then forward to your family the requests that they think would be of interest to you, based on your family's criteria. The family still gets to decide which charities to support and the amount of support.

Many people wish to set up a family foundation so their children can carry on the family's philanthropic values. The biggest impediment to the foundation is often the succeeding generation's lack of time for the project. With a donor-advised fund, this time commitment can be reduced to a manageable level while still keeping future generations involved in administering your gift.

Prohibited Material Restrictions

℞ *If we do not agree with the administering organization's choice of a recipient for a grant, can we direct the organization to revoke the gift?*

No. Your contributions to your DAF are irrevocable. If you retain the power to revoke your fund's gifts, the contributions to your fund will not qualify for the charitable income tax deduction.

℞ *How much control can my husband and I retain over our donor-advised fund?*

While donors typically have a great amount of influence over their donor-advised funds, they do not have control over the funds in a legal sense. For example, you cannot retain the power to

- name the persons to whom your fund must distribute, even if the distributions are made through a legitimate charity, or
- direct the timing of the distributions other than the restriction noted above that some or all of the principal not be distributed for a specified period.

℞ *Can we place any restrictions on the fund when we set it up?*

You can place four restrictions on your donor-advised fund. These are paraphrased as follows:

1. You can give your fund a name or designation that is the same as or similar to your name or otherwise memorializes you and your spouse or your family.
2. You can require the administering organization to use the income and assets of your fund for a designated purpose or for one or

more specific charitable organizations, as long as your designated use is consistent with the charitable, educational, or other bases for the exempt status of the administering organization.

3. If you are establishing a restricted DAF—one administered in an identifiable or separate fund—and the organization that holds your fund is, in fact, the legal and equitable owner of the fund and exercises ultimate and direct authority and control over the fund, you can require that some or all of the principal is not to be distributed for a specified period.

4. In the instrument of transfer, you can require that the ultimate charitable recipient retain the contributed property, if such retention is important to the achievement of charitable or other similar purposes in the community. An example is to transfer a woodland preserve that you required a public charity to maintain as an arboretum for the benefit of the community.

☞ *What steps does the community foundation take to ensure that I don't have too much control?*

A well-run community foundation or other charity that operates donor-advised funds will usually have the following processes in place for your protection and their own:

■ The staff of the community foundation conducts an independent investigation to evaluate your recommendation within the context of the needs of all charities most deserving of your fund's support.

■ The community foundation publicizes guidelines that enumerate specific charitable needs that are consistent with your fund's charitable purposes and your advice is consistent with such guidelines.

■ The community foundation has a program to publicize to donors, and other persons, the guidelines enumerating specific charitable needs that are consistent with your fund's charitable purposes.

■ The community foundation distributes monies in excess of amounts that it distributes from your fund to the same or similar types of charities or charitable needs as those you recommend.

■ The community foundation's written or oral solicitations for contributions specifically state that donor-advised funds will not be bound by advice offered by the funds' donors.

The bottom line is that a donor can offer advice only, and the charity that actually distributes the cash from the DAF has ultimate control.

Comparison to Private Foundations and Supporting Organizations

CR Can you please compare donor-advised funds, supporting organizations, and private foundations?

Table 18-1 earlier in this chapter compares these three types of charitable strategies that offer donors varying degrees of control over investment and distribution of charitable contributions.

chapter 19

Overview of Investing Charitable Donations

CR *Why do I need to know about investing charitable donations?*

If you are a trustee or a director of a charity, you have a special duty to make sure that the charitable funds donated to your charity are invested in a prudent manner. This duty extends to the charities and the individuals supported by your charity. You may be personally liable if you violate this duty.

If you have created your own charitable organization—whether it is a foundation, a supporting organization, a charitable remainder or lead trust, or any other charitable entity—and you remain involved as a trustee or director or officer, you also have a duty to the charities and individuals that your organization benefits.

FIDUCIARY DUTY

CR *What is meant by fiduciary duty, and how does it apply to charitable investing?*

A *fiduciary* is a person or entity that holds a trust relationship with another. Anyone who controls assets or exercises power or authority for the benefit of someone else (the beneficiary) is said to be a fiduciary, and the responsibilities the fiduciary has to the beneficiary are called *fiduciary duties*. The terms "trustee" and "fiduciary" are frequently used synonymously, primarily because the first and most common fiduciaries were trustees.

Directors and trustees of charitable organizations have a fiduciary duty to the recipients of the charities and the causes they support. Trustees of charitable remainder trusts and charitable lead trusts, or any other trust that benefits both charitable and noncharitable beneficiaries, are fiduciaries to all beneficiaries. Thus, none of the assets under the control of a charitable organization or trust actually belong to the entity itself or to the persons who are responsible for the entity but, rather, are held "in trust" for a specific purpose or for specific beneficiaries.

○R *Why is it important that I understand the fiduciary issue as it relates to investments?*

Charitable fiduciaries fall under rules similar to those for trustees of retirement and pension plans. These fiduciary responsibilities are a result of the Employee Retirement Income Security Act (ERISA) and the Third Restatement of Trusts. Both require a trustee (fiduciary) to adhere to the prudent investor rule. The Internal Revenue Service and the regulations under the private foundation rules have also adopted the prudent investor rule as the standard to be used in determining jeopardizing investments.

○R *What is the prudent investor rule?*

The *prudent investor rule* states that a fiduciary must exercise ordinary business care and prudence, under the facts and circumstances prevailing at the time of making the investment, in providing for the long-term and short-term financial needs of the organization or trust to carry out its exempt purposes. In exercising this standard of care and prudence, the fiduciary may take into account the expected return on an investment and the need for diversification within the investment portfolio. Some evidence indicates that this standard imposes the same level of skill as that of a professional money manager in making investment decisions. A fiduciary must diversify investments among many types of investments, taking into account the charitable purposes and beneficiaries of the organization or trust.

Fiduciaries can be held personally liable for breach of violation of their responsibilities, even to the extent of having to restore lost profits. While state law may protect board members or trustees of nonprofit organizations to some extent, there is always some potential liability. Charitable remainder trusts and charitable lead trusts pose even greater potential liability because these trusts are not subject to state statutes protecting charitable organizations.

○⃔ *Are guidelines available to use in determining if I am following the prudent investor rule?*

A "standard-of-care" investment approach offers some guidance. This approach holds that:

- Permitted investments include any imaginable financial instrument on either a direct or a pooled basis.
- Investments will be judged as part of an overall portfolio, not position by position.
- Prudence is judged at the time the portfolio is created, not on the basis of hindsight.
- Capital gain is treated the same as dividends and interest to allow a total return standard.
- Managers may take inflation into account to preserve the long-term value of investment assets.

PRINCIPLES OF INVESTING

○⃔ *I have been asked to serve on the investment committee of a local charity. I do understand a little about stocks and bonds, and I can read a financial statement. Do I need to know more than these basics to be effective?*

In general, the boards or trustees of charities have a weak understanding of their portfolios. They know the income that is generated by the charity's portfolio and the stocks or bonds that are in their portfolio, but, overall, the portfolio tends to be a loose collection of assets that are unrelated to the changing economic or investment scenarios.

Successful investment planning is like cooking a gourmet meal. Many ingredients go into making the meal, but the most important factor is to make the meal suitable to the people who eat it. Successful investing means having a unique set of goals that take into consideration finances, willingness to accept risk, length of the investment horizon, need for liquidity, and perhaps even tax considerations.

Institutional investors differ in one major way with charities: Institutional investors have a well-developed written investment policy statement. This investment policy statement is what drives the entire portfolio management process from construction to measurement of performance. Therefore, the single most important function of those in charge of investing the funds in a charity is to match an understanding of their specific requirements with the capital markets.

ᐃ *As a trustee of a charity, what would be a good process for me to recommend to the other trustees to create an investment policy statement for our charity?*

While you can take a number of roads to create an investment policy statement, a portfolio process that seems to work requires four steps:

1. Formulation of investment policy objectives.
2. Establishment of an investment strategy.
3. Selection of the securities or investment manager.
4. Review of performance periodically.

Investment policy objectives summarize the charity's goals and the investment options available to the investment advisor that are consistent with the charity's needs and risk tolerances. Investment strategy refers to the value-added decisions the investment advisor makes based on judgments about markets, interest rates, economic analysis, or securities. Selection of securities or an investment manager is based on which specific securities or managers will best implement the investment strategy. Performance measurement provides critical feedback to the investment advisor and charity with respect to absolute and relative returns.

ᐃ *Is an investment policy statement something that a board of trustees should tackle without professional advice?*

No, professional advice is almost always critical in establishing an investment policy statement for a charity. An investment policy statement is "owned" by the charity that created it. The board of trustees must buy into the policy guidelines, because these guidelines will affect any investment decisions. Because of the importance of an investment policy statement, it deserves all of the expertise the board can give it.

An investment advisor can be invaluable in the process. He or she can offer a great deal of input, experience, and wisdom in creating the investment policy statement. To do this, the investment advisor that you choose must spend sufficient time with the board of trustees to help define the charity's investment goals, tolerance for risk, any portfolio constraints, and unique preferences. The investment advisor must listen and interact closely with the board of trustees to ascertain the quantitative and qualitative considerations that affect the amount and types of risk appropriate for the charity. This analysis, coupled with the investment advisor's understanding of capital markets, is what creates the investment policy statement.

Investment Policy Statement

  We have been told to create an investment policy statement for our foundation. What is an investment policy statement?

An *investment policy statement (IPS)* is a "playbook" from which the trustees or officers of the foundation choose certain types of investments. The IPS is formulated after in-depth discussion by the foundation leaders and advisors of time horizon, spending policy, growth objectives, and risk. Once the IPS is formulated, investments are made according to the IPS asset allocation guidelines. In future meetings, investment performance can be compared to the goals of the foundation and the performance of the investment allocation benchmarks, which were followed when establishing the IPS.

  What are the components of an IPS?

The IPS incorporates three main components:

1. *The goal:* The expectations of the charitable entity are expressed in plain English, such as "The foundation wants to distribute 5 percent of its assets each year to charities that it supports,

while growing the assets so that the foundation will be financially sound in perpetuity."

2. *The objective:* Given its risk tolerance, this is the target return that
the investments have to earn to meet the charitable entity's goal.

3. *The time frame:* This is the investment horizon of the charitable
entity, setting up the framework for periodic review of the portfolio in relation to the goal of the charitable entity.

Specific items that should be included in the IPS include benchmarks from which to compare investment performance, risk tolerance,
asset allocation, liquidity requirements, procedures for selecting and
dismissing money managers, allowable investments, and methods to
minimize risk. The IPS does not have to be overly complex, as long
as the objectives are specific enough to define the plan's needs and goals.

ᏍᏅ *Creating an IPS seems like a lot of work. Is this really necessary?*

Creating an IPS leads to an increase in return on investment and a
decrease in liabilities for the charity. The primary role of an IPS is to
provide a stable base for a charity's assets, including the organizational structure, goals, objectives, time frames, resources, and limitations. Choosing a path of consistent and disciplined investing most
likely will increase revenues and decrease the pressure on fundraising, if fundraising is necessary. Even small returns lead to a huge difference in the charity's financial health in the future.

By adopting an IPS, a charity protects officers, directors, and
trustees from fiduciary pressures and liabilities. Legal developments
have recently given board members and trustees a choice: discharge
or delegate. It they delegate correctly, they can escape liability for the
actions of others, as well as for investment losses. If they do not, they
will retain full responsibility and liability. Adopting an IPS helps to
decrease liabilities and reduces the chance of falling victim to fraudulent schemes, inappropriate investments, and inadequate supervision.

Setting Investing Goals

ᏍᏅ *What kind of investing goals should charities have?*

Charitable organizations of all kinds, whether public or private,
should assess how their assets are allocated and how they want their

portfolio to perform. To do this, they must have objectives and set goals for themselves. But even when charities set goals, they usually lack specificity. The goals must be more detailed, as well as prioritized, and often must be compromised to determine what is realistically possible, given the charity's resources. Many charities, including some charitable remainder trusts and charitable lead trusts, require high rates of return to meet their goals, when in reality they often aren't possible, given market expectations. If these returns are possible, they should be sought after, but only if the charity can tolerate the fluctuating volatility. Also, charities frequently have competing objectives (e.g., high returns with no risk), meaning that if they pursue one objective, they sacrifice the other.

Factors That Affect Investment Performance

ℭ *What are the primary factors that affect the performance of an investment portfolio?*

This is a difficult question. Perhaps the best way to address it is to refer to a study titled "Determinants of Portfolio Performance," by three investment analysts, Gary Brinson, Randolph Hood, and Gilbert Beebower. The results were published in 1986 and updated in 1991.

The study examined the returns of 91 large pension funds to determine the primary factors that influenced the variability of investment performance. Even though these large pension plans were being directed by some of the best money managers in the world, the study is relevant for individual investors as they make their own investment decisions.

The study was able to identify three primary factors that could influence the overall performance of a portfolio: market timing, security selection, and portfolio design (asset allocation).

Market timing assumes that one can accurately forecast the ups and downs of the stock and bond markets. Market timers are making the assumption that they know when to exit and, more important, when to reenter the market.

Security selection is based on the assumption of knowing which stocks to buy and which to sell.

Portfolio design, or asset allocation, is based on which kinds of investments (as in asset classes) to use and how to mix them within the investment portfolio.

જ *Which factors had the most important effect on the performance of the investment portfolio?*

The results of the Brinson study surprised many when it found that more than 90 percent of the variability of the portfolios' performance was attributed to portfolio design and asset allocation. The study found that security selection accounted for less than 5 percent and market timing less than 2 percent of the variation of the portfolios' return. While one may question the conclusions reached by the Brinson study, the critical importance of portfolio design (asset allocation) relative to long-term performance should not be diminished.

જ *Why is it important to understand the differences between an investment's historical performance results and the actual results achieved by investors?*

Investors should note that there is a difference between statistical historical performance and actual behavioral historical performance. A study done by Dalbar Financial Services in 1993 and updated in 1996 was unique in that it tracked the actual inflow and outflow of investments made in stock and bond mutual funds. It showed statistically that, on a buy-and-hold basis over a 14-year period, an investor would have averaged a 16.0 percent rate of return in the S&P 500 and would have averaged 12 percent in government bonds over the investment years 1984 to 1996.

What's surprising about the study is that the investors' actual results were quite different. By tracking the actual inflows and outflows of money at the mutual fund companies, the study found that the actual investors' outcome, due to behavioral patterns, resulted in their return being only 6.0 percent for stocks and 6.4 percent for bonds.

This study shows that investors must recognize that behavior patterns can be an enormous challenge to overcome. By establishing an investment policy statement in advance, they are in a much better position to weather the course of time and stay with their original objectives.

Inflation

જ *How does inflation factor into a charity's investment decisions?*

Charities must consider the effects of inflation; it is part of the prudent investor standard. Inflation has had a devastating impact on fixed-income portfolios, so charities must be able to invest in stocks to deal with inflation. Investing to protect assets from decreasing because of inflation is important to charities because, for the most part, they are ongoing concerns, many times with an infinite life span. It is not unusual for inflation to double in 20 years, so the question is, "Did the portfolio double during this period?" Sadly, in most cases, this is not so.

Risk

CR *What are examples of risk in investing?*

A number of risks affect investments. They include:

- Market risk associated with the rise and fall of securities markets
- Interest rate risk associated with the rise and fall of interest rates
- Inflation risk associated with changes in the real value of assets and investment returns
- Reinvestment risk associated with the reinvestment of future cash flows
- Credit risk associated with the default risk of the underlying companies
- Currency risk associated with changes in the rate of foreign exchange relative to the U.S. dollar
- Common factor risk associated with risks inherent in securities of similar character, such as large cap stocks, stocks with low price-to-earnings ratios, and international stocks

A charity's IPS must state, through asset allocation, targets, boundaries, and diversification limits, which types of risk and in what amounts are appropriate for the charity. The portfolio should then be designed to maximize returns within the limits of risk set by the IPS.

CR *How does a charity decide its risk tolerance?*

Determination of risk tolerance is not an exact science, but it can be measured to a certain extent. Table 19-1 at the end of this chapter is a good example of a questionnaire that addresses risk.

Asset Allocation

CR *What does asset allocation mean as it relates to trust investments?*

Asset allocation decisions deal with the categories of investments (stocks, bonds, cash equivalents, real estate, etc.) to be included in a portfolio and the portions of the portfolio to be invested in each.

Asset allocation is critical to the success of a charity, as long as the charity understands its risk tolerance and sets goals within its risk limits. Focusing holdings on fewer, carefully selected stocks, along with assets in other classes that will balance market ups and downs, will provide a better opportunity for a charity's portfolio to outperform the market over time. Asset allocation has come a long way over the past century and will continue to be part of successful investing in the future.

CR *What key areas should we address when we formulate our asset allocation strategy for our private foundation?*

The key areas that you should address as you formulate your asset allocation are

- the time horizon for your investments;
- future charitable gifts from the founder, the founder's family, or others;
- the foundation's grant-making/spending policy;
- growth objectives relative to inflation;
- risk tolerance;
- anticipated fixed and variable costs; and
- anticipated duration of the foundation.

CR *What is the efficient market concept, and how does it apply to charitable investing?*

Economic evidence shows that, from a typical investment perspective, the major capital markets of the United States are highly efficient in the sense that available information is rapidly digested and reflected in the market price of securities. As a result, charitable trustees and other charitable fiduciaries are confronted with potent evidence that the application of expertise, research, and due diligence, in an effort to "beat the market" in publicly traded securities, ordinarily promises little or no payoff. In fact, at the given level of market risk, after taking into consideration investigative and transaction costs, there is a high likelihood of a negative payoff when trying to beat the market or succeed at market timing—that is, trying to outguess the market.

Asset allocation decisions are the most important factor affecting total portfolio volatility.

ℂ How does asset allocation affect volatility?

Using asset allocation will help to smooth overall portfolio volatility, as long as one combines assets that respond differently to a variety of economic conditions. Still, although volatility can be smoothed, common experience and instincts tell us that a portfolio with a heavier weight in stocks will be more volatile and will have a wider range of returns because stock prices fluctuate more wildly than bond prices do. However, adding stocks to portfolios potentially increases returns, as stocks historically have produced nearly twice the return of bonds. This further supports the asset allocation process and how important it is for successful investing.

Volatility is often associated with risk, although it is a mistake to interchangeably use the words "risk" and "volatility." This is because volatility is not necessarily the major risk confronting a charitable portfolio. In fact, the major risk of a long-term charity is inflation and not volatility. Still, charities should know their volatility tolerance, which is different with every organization and person.

ℂ How does asset allocation affect portfolio risk?

Asset allocation is not a difficult concept to grasp. It is basically a technique for controlling the amount of risk in a portfolio by combining different types of assets. For this to be effective, however, charities must be able to tell managers how much risk they are willing to take. This is no easy task, but to be successful, these institutions must be willing to answer the question, "How much are we willing to lose?" Optimal combinations of assets are intended to produce the lowest amount of risk for any level of anticipated return, or the highest return for any level of risk.

The two forms of risk are specific risk (that associated with any one stock or bond) and market risk (that associated with a broader market). Diversifying a portfolio with multiple securities greatly reduces specific risk, while asset allocation reduces market risk. In terms of reducing risk for a given level of return, the most important decision is how to mix equities, fixed-income investments, and cash.

Diversification

℣ *Should a charity diversify the assets in its portfolio?*

Yes. Directors and trustees of charitable organizations have always held the duty to diversify, as it is a fundamental component of portfolio theory.

℣ *What is diversification?*

Risk can be mitigated if you better understand and reduce the two broad categories of investment risk. Systematic risk includes risks within systems, such as markets, inflation, and interest rates. Unsystematic risk includes business and financial risk.

   Sir John Templeton said, "To diversify means that you do not put all of your assets in any one type of investment. Similarly, it is not wise to invest only in the shares of any one company, industry, or nation. If you search all the nations, you are likely to find more good bargains and perhaps better bargains. Clearly you will reduce risk because bear markets and business recessions occur at different times in different nations. By diversifying among different types of assets, the value of your portfolio will not fluctuate as much."

Choosing an Investment Advisor

℣ *Is being knowledgeable about investing important if you have a professional managing the charity's money?*

Yes, it is. While it is important to have a professional managing the charity's investments, knowledgeable leadership in a charity is critical to a successful portfolio. The best charities have boards or trustees that understand money management and alternative investments. As the ultimate decision-making body, the board or trustees must understand how the charitable portfolio is structured and how it will behave. Problems often arise in charities because their boards or trustees choose investments based on wrong or incomplete information, or they follow a comfortable path with familiar investments. A disciplined approach to investing based on a well-thought-out investment policy statement and implemented by a professional manager will result in a solid allocation of assets.

How would a charity choose an investment manager?

There are more than 12,000 different mutual funds and more than 2,000 money managers. It is not easy to choose an investment manager. No method of choosing an advisor is perfect, but in appendixes A and C, you will find some suggestions on how to choose one.

TABLE 19-1   Investment Management Questionnaire

Part I: Investment Philosophy and Objectives

(To be completed by the investment committee of the board, or by the full board if there is no committee. For organizations that maintain multiple funds, these questions should be answered with regard to the endowment or other perpetual or long-term funds.)

Goals and Objectives

1. How would you categorize your overall investment objectives? Choose one.
   - ____ Growth—maximum growth of capital with little or no income consideration
   - ____ Growth with income—primarily capital growth with some focus on income
   - ____ Balanced—equal emphasis on capital growth and income
   - ____ Income-oriented—primary emphasis on income
   - ____ Capital preservation—preservation of original value regardless of income or growth

2. What average annual "absolute" rate of return, if any (as opposed to a return "relative" to a market index), do you consider appropriate for long-term investment?
   - ____ % per year
   - ____ % per year above inflation (Consumer Price Index)
   - ____ Prefer a relative standard

3. Relative to popular stock market indexes (such as the S&P 500), rank your preferences for portfolio performance; 1 is your strongest preference and 5 is what you least prefer.
   - ____ Outperform the market in *up* market years
   - ____ Decline less than the market in *down* market years
   - ____ Outperform the market, on average, over an extended period
   - ____ Match market performance over an extended period
   - ____ Ignore relative performance and focus solely on the absolute return goal(s) identified in question 2 above.

4. Please rank from 1 to 5 your preference for the following investment performance reporting options, with 1 being your strongest preference.
   - ____ Measuring current return relative to required distributions
   - ____ Comparing account returns to an "absolute" percent return target
   - ____ "Relative" comparison (comparing the account returns to various market indexes)

TABLE 19-1   Investment Management Questionnaire,
continued

___ Comparing to a "real" return (i.e., exceeds the inflation factor by X%)

___ Using "absolute" and "relative" total return measures without regard to yield

5. Please describe any specific return requirements or performance-reporting concerns that have not been addressed by the preceding questions.

_____

_____

_____

Risk

6. Please rank the following risks in the order of greatest concern, with 1 being your highest concern.

___ The failure to generate enough current income to cover required distributions

___ The possibility of not achieving an intended rate of return

___ Decreasing purchasing power as a result of inflation

___ Wide swings in the value of our investments over 3 to 5 years

___ A large drop in the value of any one or more investments, wholly apart from overall portfolio performance

7. What is the maximum loss you could tolerate in your most aggressively invested portfolio over the following time frame?

___ % per quarter   ___ % in any 2-year period

___ % per year   ___ Other (please describe)

_____

8. Compared to a broad stock market index such as the S&P 500, how much fluctuation can you tolerate in the equity portion of your portfolio in any given year?

___ Much more fluctuation than the market

___ Slightly more fluctuation than the market

___ Approximately the same fluctuation as the market

___ Slightly less fluctuation than the market

___ Much less fluctuation than the market

9. Please describe any risk concerns that the preceding questions have not addressed.

_____

_____

_____

**TABLE 19-1   Investment Management Questionnaire,
*continued***

Questions for Selecting an Investment Manager

10. Which statement best reflects your opinion as to how a manager should implement your investment goals?

    ___ We should establish overall objectives for the plan and allow the manager complete discretion regarding implementation.

    ___ We should establish asset allocation parameters with the investment manager and then allow the manager discretion in selecting investments within those parameters.

    ___ We should establish asset allocation parameters with the investment manager and then actively participate in and/or supervise the day-to-day selection of investments.

11. How do you feel about giving investment discretion to a third-party investment management firm? Choose one.

    ___ Very comfortable   ___ Somewhat uncomfortable
    ___ Somewhat comfortable ___ Very uncomfortable

12. Select the statement that best describes how you currently make investment decisions.

    ___ We collect and analyze the facts and make decisions on our own.

    ___ Others advise us and we make decisions based on their advice.

    ___ Our advisors make the decisions.

13. Please briefly list or describe those aspects of your current investment management process that are working well and those that you believe have problems or could be improved. (Examples are performance, performance reporting, asset allocation, etc.)

    Working Well:

    _____

    _____

    _____

    _____

    Concerns—May Need Improvement:

    _____

    _____

    _____

Part II: General Information

(This portion to be completed by the Executive Director.)

1. Institution: _____

TABLE 19-1   Investment Management Questionnaire,
continued

2. Senior Staff: Name   Phone
   Executive Director _____   _____
   Senior Devel. Off. _____   _____
   CFO   _____   _____
   Board Chairman   _____   _____
   Invest. Comm. Ch._____   _____

3. Type of Institution:
   School or College   Retirement Home
   Hospital   Church
   Pension Plan   Other Religious Organization
   Public Foundation   Social Service Agency
   Private Foundation   Other Public Charity

4. Business Structure:
   ___ Unincorporated Nonprofit Association
   ___ Nonprofit Corporation (Type) _____
   ___ Limited Liability Company (Type) _____
   ___ Other _____

5. Mission Statement: (Attach copy or brief narrative description.)

6. Approximate Annual Budget: $_____
   (For reference purposes, please attach a copy of your most recent
   financial statements.)

7. Origins:
   Founded By:
   _____ Date: _____
   Founded in (City, State, & Country)
   _____

8. Incorporation: State: _____ Date: _____

9. Address of Institution Headquarters:
   _____
   _____

10. Geographic Service Area: (Describe and also list states in which you
    have at least one full-time employee and a physical location.)
    _____
    _____
    _____

TABLE 19-1   **Investment Management Questionnaire,** *continued*

Part III: Development (Fundraising) Information

(This portion to be completed by the Senior Development Officer.)

1. Current staffing of development program:

Full-time development staff	Position	
Other staff (names) who spend time in development	Regular position	% of time spent in development

2. What percentage of your organization's total income comes from donations (gifts as opposed to fees for services, sales of products, etc.)?

   _____

3. When did you start a full-time fundraising program?

   _____

4. When did you start soliciting and/or accepting planned gifts?

   _____

5. Please indicate the composition of gift income, by category, over the last 3 years.

	Average annual % in last 3 years	Highest annual % in last 3 years	Lowest annual % in last 3 years
Charitable institution contributions			
Corporate gifts			
Grants			
Bequests			
Lifetime planned gifts			
Special events			
Gifts in kind; sponsorships			
Other			

6. Of the categories listed above, which do you believe are most likely to increase or decrease as a percentage of total annual gift income over the next 3 years?

TABLE 19-1   Investment Management Questionnaire,
continued

Most likely to increase: _____

_____

_____

Most likely to decrease: _____

_____

_____

7. Please rank each of the following areas to indicate your fundraising priorities in terms of the allocation of development staff time for the coming year.

Fundraising categories	Rank (1–5)	Allocable % of staff time
Current annual giving		
Planned (deferred) giving		
Capital campaign		
Events; sponsorships		
Corporation/foundation grants		

8. What are the types, ages, and minimum dollar amounts of the deferred gifts and trusts that your organization accepts?

	Accepted (Y/N)	Minimum age	Minimum $ amount
Gift annuities			
Charitable remainder trusts			
Pooled income funds			
Donor-advised funds			
Life interest agreements in real property			
Life insurance			
Other			

9. Please briefly describe the additional staff support, funding, administrative support, or other assistance, if any, that you believe would permit you to raise funds for your organization more effectively over the next 3 years.

_____

_____

_____

_____

_____

appendix A

Working with Advisors and Charities

ROLE OF ADVISORS

C3 What is the role of professional advisors in charitable planning?

In charitable planning, as in all types of planning, having capable advisors is the best way to accomplish your goals and keep control of your affairs. By selecting professionals from different disciplines, you gain access to various areas of expertise. No single advisor knows everything, has experienced every type of situation, or is capable of being all things to all persons. A team of professional advisors will give your matters appropriate attention and will provide value to your planning efforts.

C3 Who should be on my charitable planning team?

Your team should include you as the client, your tax advisor, your legal advisor, and your financial advisor. One advisor should take the lead to ensure that there are clear communications among the parties. The best way to ensure good communication is to include all team members in all meetings.

Each team member plays a critical part in your planning, but may do so at different times. For example, during the design stage, each professional team member should be given an opportunity to have input on the various elements of the plan, with each advisor giving his or her own perspective based on your goals and objectives. Your attorney may well take the lead. In the implementation stage, the accountant and the financial advisor will take center stage to file income tax and gift tax returns, to apply for federal identification numbers, to transfer assets, and to acquire financial products if necessary, coordinating these functions with your attorney.

CR *What should I expect from my professional advisors after we implement the plan?*

Once you and your advisors implement the plan, the advisors should help you monitor the plan to make sure that your goals are being met at all times and that your plan is performing as anticipated.

A major benefit of working with independent professionals is that they can provide an impartial perspective as to the validity and achievement of a planning goal. Even when you achieve your goals, life events occur, perhaps giving a different perspective to past goals and creating new ones. Once you have reached a goal, it makes a great deal of sense to review what has occurred since you set the goal and since you achieved the goal. Your advisors serve as guides to tell you what is possible based on your new thoughts or experiences. Good advisors encourage you to broaden your goals and then help you revise and implement the plan for you to achieve them.

CR *Currently, my key advisors do not seem to work well together. When my attorney comes up with a new idea, my accountant always seems to find a problem with it. Often my accountant is correct, but he can dampen the creativity I am looking for with my advisory team. How can I get all of my advisors to work well together as a team?*

Often, the problem of conflicted advisors stems from a client not truly understanding what it is he or she wishes to accomplish. This confusion sends mixed messages to advisors and creates tension as different advisors attempt to discern the best course of action given incomplete information. This leads to further confusion and often conflict.

First and foremost, a client needs to go through a process of thinking and organizing. This process must include key family members, such as a spouse, to help clarify goals, objectives, values, and mission. Some family wealth planners suggest developing a written letter of intent as a method to create a blueprint to facilitate meetings and discussions with advisors.

ଔ *Planning with charitable remainder trusts seems complicated to me. Can I avoid being overwhelmed by complexity?*

Yes. The important thing to do is to surround yourself with a team of trusted advisors who are familiar with the use of these trusts. Your team should consist of an attorney, a financial advisor, and an accountant. These advisors should thoroughly understand your charitable goals and objectives. Their job is to make sure that you understand the proposed charitable trust so that you are able to make informed choices. Understanding leads to peace of mind because you know that your plan will work as intended.

Creating a charitable trust is not simply about a document that, once signed, sits on a shelf or in a lock box. It is an integral part of your overall estate plan and, as is true of your full estate plan, should be periodically monitored and reviewed with your team.

ଔ *I want to choose a financial advisor to help me implement my charitable planning, especially in investing the contributions that I am making to my private foundation. What recommendations can you make in finding a top-notch financial advisor?*

Research is critical in identifying a financial advisor. You will, undoubtedly, be familiar with a number of financial advisors in your community, so you can begin with those. Ask friends who you respect and who have estates similar in size to yours for the names of their advisors. Contact your attorney and accountant, even your bank trust officer, to find out who they would recommend.

Once you have prospects, ask each of them for the following information:

- ownership of the company each works for or has founded;
- number of investment professionals in the company;

- length of time key personnel have been there and their qualifications;
- value of the assets that each of your prospects has under management;
- number of accounts that each prospect has;
- a copy of a sample portfolio;
- minimum account size;
- names of charities that each represents;
- type of investment style that each favors (e.g., income, balanced, growth, value, large cap, small cap, international, equity, or fixed income);
- typical number of holdings that each has;
- average turnover of the portfolio (the higher the turnover, generally, the higher your taxes will be, as gains will count as current income).

In addition, ask the following questions:

- What type of investment approach do you use; is it bottom up or top down?
- Do you pick stocks based upon fundamental or technical analysis?
- What sectors do you invest in?
- How does the market cap of your portfolio compare to the S&P 500; is it higher or lower?
- How does its price/earnings (P/E) ratio compare to the S&P 500?
- Is your earnings growth higher or lower than the S&P 500?
- What is your dividend yield compared to the S&P 500; is it higher or lower?
- What investment process do you use to pick stocks—quantitative or qualitative?
- Do you have in-house research or do you rely on the street?
- When you select stocks, do you look for companies trading at a sharp discount to private market value, companies trading at a discount to their growth rate, or companies trading at the lower end of their fundamental benchmark?
- What is your investment approach to sell stocks: when price objectives are not met within a specified time period, when more

attractive alternatives are found, or when there is a change in fundamentals?

- What are your trailing and calendar period returns, including cumulative time weighted returns over the last quarter; year-to-date; and 1, 3, 5, 10, and 15 years, if available? (The longer, the better, so you can see how the manager has fared in market corrections. Since 1994, most good managers should have excellent returns; one wants to see how the manager fared in adverse situations. Calendar returns focus on shorter time periods and gauge the consistency of performance over time. High index returns suggest bull markets, while low or negative returns suggest bear markets.)

℺ *Once I obtain all of this information and ask the questions, how will I know if the advisor is good?*

While you may not fully understand all of the information that you get, you will get a feel for the competency of the firm you are interviewing. As you meet with several firms, a picture of comparison will begin to form; you will see which firms did better or worse over the same periods of time. You will also be able to recognize each firm's investment philosophy and approach.

If you do not understand an answer, ask for clarification. Good advisors will take the time to give you answers that you understand. Questions are a great way to find out if you have rapport with an advisor. For example, if you are a bottom-line person and the advisor wants to give you long explanations, you may want to find someone more in tune with your personality. In contrast, if you enjoy the interchange and you feel comfortable, you may have found the right advisor.

In any event, get references and check them out. There are a lot of good talkers out there, but performance counts. The more you can find out about an investment advisor, the better off you are. If you have any problem in getting good references or information, you should avoid working with an investment advisor. And, don't worry about asking questions and gathering information. Investment advisors are highly regulated by the state and federal governments. Investment advisors are used to full disclosure—and the law requires it. (See appendix C for additional resources.)

USING THE CHARITY'S ADVISORS

ଓ *One of my favorite charities has offered to pay for the costs associated with creating a charitable remainder trust for me. Do I need to hire my own attorney?*

Many charities accommodate their donors by assisting them with the creation of CRTs. Often, charities provide skilled advice. However, a charity is probably ill-equipped to advise you regarding your overall estate plan. You should consult your estate planning attorney to ensure that your CRT coordinates with the rest of your estate plan.

ଓ *A local charity I support has offered to provide me with a lot of estate planning help in exchange for my contribution to a charitable trust, in which I name it as a beneficiary. In addition, it will do all the trust administration work for free, provided I make it my irrevocable charitable beneficiary. Is this a common practice? Are there any concerns I should have about this approach?*

A number of larger nonprofit organizations have developed internal resources to assist in the development of planned gifts. These resources often include individuals with legal and tax expertise. Many of the larger organizations have attorneys on staff available to help a potential donor through the often-complex maze of options available in the charitable giving area. The sole purpose of a planned giving or development professional is to raise funds for his or her cause. As a result, he or she may not be as objective as one would like.

In return for an irrevocable commitment, some organizations will offer other services, including charitable remainder trust administration services. The donor should be wary of anything that sounds too good to be true. For example, we know of a married couple who were creating CRTs and were influenced by the offer of the charity to have their attorneys draft the CRTs and pay the couple's legal fees. In our experience, charities do not pay for the legal work unless they are being named *irrevocably* as the charitable remaindermen in the

CRT. The charity never mentioned to the couple that they had the option under the law to reserve the right to change the charitable beneficiaries at any time up until death.

Many planners and legal advisors advocate having independent representation and advise and caution their clients to err on the side of retaining control while alive, since no one can know what might happen in the future. If you want to keep the option open to be able to change your mind as to the beneficiary, you should avoid making any irrevocable commitments.

Independent advice is paramount in good planning. While using the staff of a charity may be helpful, having a solid team of advisors to review recommendations is essential in creating a plan that truly meets your needs and allows you to maintain control during your life.

appendix B

Resources for Charitable Giving

TABLE B-1 Charitable Giving Resources

Government resources	General information
Internal Revenue Service 800-829-3676 www.irs.ustreas.gov	Provides IRS Publication 78, *Charitable Contributions: A Cumulative List of Organizations,* which lists many of the qualified charities.

Private resources	General information
The African American Women's Fund 100 East 85th St. New York, NY 10028 212-249-3612 www.dogonvillage.com/aawf	A national philanthropic initiative to support education & empowerment of African-American women; organized as a donor fund under the Twenty-First Century Foundation.
American Institute of Philanthropy 4905 Del Ray Ave., Ste. 300W Bethesda, MD 20814 301-913-5200 www.charitywatch.org	Grades charities based on the amount of money spent on charitable programs & the cost of fundraising; produces a *Charity Rating Guide.*

TABLE B-1 Charitable Giving Resources, *continued*

Private resources	General information
Asian Pacific Fund 225 Bush St., Ste. 590 San Francisco, CA 94104 415-433-6859 www.asianpacificfund.org	A San Francisco/Bay Area organization focusing on issues & research relative to Asian donors & the needs of the Asian community.
Association for Healthcare Philanthropy 313 Park Ave., Ste. 400 Falls Church, VA 22046 703-532-6243 www.go-ahp.org	Established in 1967 to advance philanthropy & manage resource development; published the *1999 Guide to Giving Opportunities at Health Care Institutions.*
Association of Small Foundations 4905 Del Ray Ave., Ste. 308 Bethesda, MD 20814 888-212-9922 www.smallfoundations.org	A professional association for people who run their own foundations with few or no professional staff. The size of the foundation is not a determinant for membership. ASF holds national & regional meetings where members can learn about operating a small foundation. Conducts an annual survey of its members to answer such questions as, What salary levels & administrative costs are appropriate for foundations of various sizes?
BBB Wise Giving Alliance 4200 Wilson Blvd., Ste. 800 Arlington, VA 22203 703-276-0100 www.give.org	Result of merger of National Charities Information Bureau & the BBB's Philanthropic Advisory Service. Provides information on charities, including their stated purpose, kinds of programs sponsored, management & fundraising methods, tax status, financial status, & administrative & fundraising expenses as they relate to program expenditures & total assets. Provides the charity's IRS Form 990.
CASE—Council for Advancement and Support of Education 1307 New York Ave., Ste. 1000 Washington, DC 20005-4701 202-328-2273 www.case.org	Provides an annual publication for charitable planning—*CASE Guide to Advancing Education: Giving Opportunities at Colleges, Universities, and Independent Schools.*

TABLE B-1   Charitable Giving Resources, *continued*

Private resources	General information
Center for the Study of Philanthropy 365 Fifth Ave., Rm. 5116 New York, N.Y. 10016-4309 212-817-2010 www.philanthropy.org	Has research & surveys available on African-American, international, Jewish, Latino, Middle Eastern–American, & women's philanthropic issues & related charitable giving concerns.
Center on Nonprofits and Philanthropy 2100 M St. NW Washington, DC 20037 202-833-7200 www.urban.org/centers/cnp.html	Hosts the Urban Institute National Center for Charitable Statistics. Provides statistics on charities, including their IRS Forms 990, which states who runs them, where & how they spend money, major expense categories, management/operation, & fundraising.
The Center on Philanthropy at Indiana University 550 W. North St., #301 Indianapolis, IN 46202-3272 317-274-4200 The Fund Raising School 317-684-8933 800-962-6692 www.philanthropy.iupui.edu	An organization devoted to improving the practice of philanthropy through research, teaching, & public service; also sponsors The Fund Raising School, which offers training sessions around the country.
CharityAmerica.com 264 N. Main St. Natick, MA 01760 877-KIN-DACT 508-903-4100 www.charityamerica.com	Dedicated to uniting donors, volunteers, businesses, & qualified charities.
Chronical of Philanthropy 33 West 42nd St., 1525GB New York, NY 10036 212-642-2130 www.philanthropy.com	Online publication that brings together research, donors, & charities.
Consortium of Foundation Libraries www.foundationlibraries.org	A site for sharing resources & coordinating information for philanthropy.

TABLE B-1   Charitable Giving Resources, *continued*

Private resources	General information
Council on Foundations 1828 L St., NW Washington, DC 20036 202-466-6512 www.cof.org www.communityfoundationlocator.com	Provides resources for grant-making foundations & corporations, including both family & community foundations; hosts the "Philanthropic Advisors Network" and the "Community Foundation Locator," which helps individuals locate foundations in their areas.
Forum of Regional Associations of Grantmakers 1828 L St., NW, Ste. 300 Washington, DC 20036-5168 202-467-0383 www.rag.org	A national group of regional associations of grant makers.
The Foundation Center 79 Fifth Ave. New York, NY 10003 212-620-4230 www.fdncenter.org	Publishes the *National Directory of Corporate Giving* & produces several training programs; tracks how charitable donations are distributed; has an "Electronic Reference Desk" that is a free service & allows people to send questions to the Foundation Center's librarians who will answer e-mail questions within 2 days. Site also contains research on giving in African-American populations at www.fdncenter.org/learn/topical/african.html.
Foundations On-Line www.foundations.org	Provides a searchable database of charitable grant makers; a service of the Northern California Community Foundation, Inc.
GiveVoice.org www.givevoice.org	A joint venture of the National Council of Nonprofit Associations & Independent Sector; dedicated to advocacy for nonprofits; provides policy updates & links to regional & state groups for nonprofit advocacy.

TABLE B-1   **Charitable Giving Resources,** *continued*

Private resources	General information
Giving Capital: Wealth Management Solutions 400 Lexington Ave., Ste. 1609 New York, NY 10170 212-557-4820 www.givingcapital.com	Provides resources for nonprofits & donors, including online donations; "Powering New Ways to Give" is this organization's motto.
GuideStar Philanthropic Research, Inc. Attn: GuideStar Customer Service 427 Scotland St. Williamsburg, VA 23185 757-229-4631 www.guidestar.org www.guidestar.com	A "watchdog" group with searchable database of information on 850,000 IRS-recognized charities.
Hispanics in Philanthropy 5950 Doyle St., Ste. 7 Emeryville, CA 94608 510-420-1011 www.hiponline.org	An association of more than 450 U.S. & Latin American grant makers & nonprofit leaders whose goal is to promote more Hispanic participation in all areas of philanthropy.
Independent Sector 1200 18th St., NW, Ste. 200 Washington, DC 20036 202-467-6100 www.indepsec.org	A society that promotes the general welfare of all citizens & fosters collaborative efforts between people, government, business, & the independent sector.
Internet Nonprofit Center The Evergreen State Society P.O. Box 20682 Seattle, WA 98102-0682 206-329-5640 www.nonprofits.org	For smaller charities, provides a searchable database of entities that have filed for tax-exempt status with the IRS; provides information on work that nonprofits perform, fundraising, & filings.
LEAVE A LEGACY™ www.leavealegacy.org	The National Committee on Planned Giving's national program that also has regional subdivisions.
National Black United Fund, Inc. 40 Clinton St., 5th Fl. Newark, NJ 07102 973-643-5122 www.nbuf.org	Dedicated to enhancing African-American institutions through philanthropy; acts as a coordinating & planning body for local black funds & organizations.

TABLE B-1 Charitable Giving Resources, *continued*

Private resources	General information
National Center for Family Philanthropy 1818 North St., NW, Ste. 300 Washington, DC 20036 202-293-3424 www.ncfp.org	Established in 1997 as a focus group on family giving; provides support for developing & creating a family legacy.
National Committee on Planned Giving 233 McCrea St., Ste. 400 Indianapolis, IN 317-269-6274 www.ncpg.org	The National Committee on Planned Giving is the professional association for people whose work includes developing, marketing, and administering charitable planned gifts. Those people include fundraisers for nonprofit institutions, and consultants and donor advisors working in a variety of for-profit settings. Publishes an annual report, *Giving USA*.
National Council of Nonprofit Associations 1030 15th St., NW, Ste. 380 Washington, DC 20005 202-962-0322 www.ncna.org	A network of 38 state & regional associations representing more than 17,000 nonprofits.
National Network of Grantmakers 1717 Kettner Blvd., Ste. 110 San Diego, CA 92101 619-231-1348 www.nng.org	A membership association of funders committed to progressive change.
The NonProfit Times 120 Littleton Rd., Ste. 120 Parsippany, NJ 07054-1803 973-394-1800 www.nptimes.com	Provides a newsletter devoted to issues regarding management of nonprofits.
The Philanthropic Initiative, Inc. 77 Franklin St. Boston, MA 02110 617-338-2590 www.tpi.org	Founded in 1989, this organization helps donors develop strategies for increasing the impact of their donations.

TABLE B-1   Charitable Giving Resources, *continued*

Private resources	General information
Philanthropy Journal P.O. Box 12800 Raleigh, NC 27605 919-890-6240 800-853-0801 www.philanthropyjournal.org	A publication of the A.J. Fletcher Foundation, provides media & news resources for philanthropy.
The Philanthropy Roundtable 1150 17th St., NW, Ste. 503 Washington, DC 20036 202-822-8333 www.philanthropyroundtable.org	A national association of donors, corporate giving representatives, foundation directors & trustees.
Social Welfare Research Institute McGuinn Hall 515 Boston College 140 Commonwealth Ave. Chestnut Hill, MA 02467 617-552-4070 www.bc.edu/swri	Promotes academic research into philanthropy as it is undertaken today. Several different statistical analyses of donors & donations are available at this site.
Urban Institute National Center for Charitable Statistics	*See* Center on Nonprofits and Philanthropy.
Women's Philanthropy Institute 134 W. University, Ste. 105 Rochester, MI 48307 248-651-3552 www.women-philanthropy.org	An organization that provides educational resources to women donors & those who want to encourage donations from women.

appendix C

Resources for Professional Advisors

TABLE C-1   Referral Organizations

Organization	Services
American Academy of Estate Planning Attorneys 9360 Towne Centre Dr., Ste. 300 San Diego, CA 92121 800-846-1555 www.estateplanforyou.com	Provides member referrals.
American Institute of Certified Public Accountants (AICPA) 1211 Avenue of the Americas New York, NY 10036-8775 888-862-4272 www.aicpa.org	Provides member referrals, including CPAs, PFSs (personal financial specialists), & CPA/ABVs (CPAs accredited in business valuation).
Appraisal Institute 550 W. Van Buren St., Ste. 1000 Chicago, IL 60607 312-335-4100 www.appraisalinstitute.org	Provides training & certification to real estate appraisers (MAI, SRA, & SRPA) & makes member referrals.

TABLE C-1   Referral Organizations, *continued*

Organization	Services
Certified Financial Planner Board of Standards (CFP Board) 1700 Broadway, Ste. 2100 Denver, CO 80290-2101 303-830-7500 www.cfp-board.org	Makes referrals of CFP™ practitioners to the public.
Esperti Peterson Institute (EPI) 1605 Main St., Ste. 700 Sarasota, FL 34236 941-365-4819 www.epinstitute.org	Maintains registry of masters & fellows in estate & wealth strategies planning.
Financial Planning Association (FPA) 3801 E. Florida Ave., Ste. 708 Denver, CO 80210 800-322-4237 www.fpanet.org	Provides referrals of CFP™ practitioners to the public. Provides free information about financial planning & choosing a financial planner.
Institute of Business & Finance (IBF) 7911 Herschel Ave., Ste. 201 La Jolla, CA 92037-4413 800-848-2029 www.icfs.com	Makes CFS referrals to the public (formerly Institute of Certified Fund Specialists).
International Association of Registered Financial Consultants (IARFC) P.O. Box 42506 Middletown, OH 45042 800-532-9060 www.iarfc.org	Provides referrals of registered financial consultants to the public.
National Association of Estate Planners and Councils (NAEPC) 270 S. Bryn Mawr Ave., P.O. Box 46 Bryn Mawr, PA 19010-2196 610-526-1389 www.naepc.org	Provides member directory that can be searched by state & specialty.
National Association of Family Wealth Counselors (NAFWC) P.O. Box 308 Franklin, IN 46131 888-597-6575 www.nafwc.org	Provides directory of members by name, state, & status.

TABLE C-1 Referral Organizations, *continued*

Organization	Services
National Network of Estate Planning Attorneys (NNEPA) 1 Valmont Plaza, Fourth Fl. Omaha, NE 68154-5203 800-638-8681 www.netplanning.com	Provides member referrals; provides continuing education & tools for estate planning attorneys.
Society of Financial Service Professionals (SFSP) 270 S. Bryn Mawr Ave. Bryn Mawr, PA 19010-1295 888-243-2258 www.financialpro.org	Provides member referrals to the public (formerly American Society of CLU & ChFC).

TABLE C-2 Licensing and Regulatory Agencies

Agency	Functions	Area regulated
Internal Revenue Service (IRS) 1111 Constitution Ave., NW Washington, DC 20224 800-829-1040 www.irs.gov	"Enrolled" means licensed by the federal government; "agent" means authorized to appear in place of the taxpayer at the IRS. (Only EAs, attorneys, & CPAs may represent taxpayers before the IRS.)	Enrolled agents (EAs)
National Association of Securities Dealers (NASD) Regulators 1735 K St., NW Washington, DC 20006 800-289-9999 www.nasd.com www.nasdr.com	Self-regulates the securities industry & the NASDAQ stock market through registration, education, & examination of member firms & their employees; creation & enforcement of rules designed for the protection of investors; surveillance of markets operated by NASDAQ; & cooperative programs with government agencies & industry organizations.	Registered broker/dealers, investment advisors/advisory firms, representatives; various series licenses

TABLE C-2   Licensing and Regulatory Agencies, *continued*

Agency	Functions	Area regulated
National Association of State Boards of Accountancy (NASBA) 150 Fourth Ave. North, Ste. 700 Nashville, TN 37219 615-880-4200 www.nasba.org	Serves as a forum for the nation's state boards of accountancy, which administer the Uniform CPA examination, license CPAs, & regulate the practice of public accountancy in the U.S.; sponsors committee meetings, conferences, programs, & services to enhance the effectiveness of its member boards.	CPAs
Securities Investor Protection Corporation (SIPC) 605 15th St., NW, Ste. 800 Washington, DC 20005-2215 202-371-8300 www.sipc.org	Protects customers of SEC-registered broker/dealers against losses caused by the financial failure of a broker/dealer (but not against a change in the market value of securities); funded by its member securities broker/dealers.	Broker/dealers
State insurance commissions	Administer & enforce the state's insurance laws.	Insurance sales
U.S. Securities and Exchange Commission (SEC) 450 Fifth St. Washington, DC 20549 800-732-0330 www.sec.gov	An independent, quasijudicial regulatory agency that helps establish & administer federal securities laws; regulates firms engaged in the purchase or sale of securities, people who provide investment advice, & investment companies.	Registered investment advisors/advisory firms, broker/dealers, representatives

TABLE C-3 Professional Licenses and Designations

Designation	Accrediting institution & requirements
ABV: Accreditation in Business Valuation (available to CPAs)	AICPA: meet experience requirements, pass exam, be member of AICPA, hold CPA license; maintain substantial involvement in business valuation & take classes to maintain certification.
AEP: Accredited Estate Planner (available to estate planning practitioners who have completed certain graduate estate planning courses)	NAEPC & American College: pass exam in trust banking, insurance, accounting, law; meet NAEPC's continuing education requirements.
ASA: Accredited Senior Appraiser	ASA: pass exams, submit appraisals for peer review, meet ethical standards.
Broker/dealer (one that is licensed to buy & sell investment products for or to clients; "dealers" sell securities they own, "brokers" buy & sell securities on behalf of investors)	SEC
CBA: Certified Business Appraiser	IBA: complete exam (or hold similar certification from another organization), submit two formal/comprehensive business appraisal reports.
CDP: Certified Divorce Planner	ICDP: take class, pass exam.
CEBS: Certified Employee Benefit Specialist	International Foundation of Employee Benefit Plans: complete study program, pass exams, abide by principles of conduct.
CEP: Certified Estate Planner	Liberty Institute: complete course, pass exams.
CFA: Certified Financial Analyst (available to experienced financial analysts—securities analyst, money manager, & investment advisor focusing on analysis of investments & securities of company or industry groups)	Association for Investment Management & Research: complete course, pass 3 annual exams, fulfill AIMR ethics requirements, submit to regulatory authority of AIMR.

TABLE C-3   Professional Licenses and Designations, *continued*

Designation	Accrediting institution & requirements
CFP: Certified Financial Planner (available to those with a bachelor's degree who have completed a financial planning curriculum at a U.S.-accredited college or university & have 3 years of financial planning experience or 5 years without a degree)	CFP Board of Standards: pass exam, adhere to CFP Board code of ethics, periodically disclose investigations or legal proceedings related to professional or business conduct, take 30 hours of continuing education every 2 years, complete biennial licensing requirement with CFP Board, submit to regulatory authority of the CFP Board.
CFS: Certified Fund Specialist (available to financial services professionals)	IBF: complete course, pass exam, adhere to IBF code of ethics, take 15 hours of continuing education per year, register annually.
ChFC: Chartered Financial Consultant (for accountants, attorneys, bankers, insurance agents, brokers, & securities representatives with 3 years of business experience)	American College: complete 10-course curriculum, pass exams, adhere to code of ethics, take 60 hours of continuing education every 2 years.
CIC: Chartered Investment Counselor (available to those employed by an ICAA member firm who have 5 years of experience in an eligible occupation)	ICAA: complete the CFA exam, provide work & character references, endorse ICAA Standards of Practice, complete an ethical conduct questionnaire.
CIMA: Certified Investment Management Analyst (the only advanced designation specifically for investment consultants; must have 3 years of experience in investment management consulting)	IMCA: complete program, pass exam, adhere to code of ethics, recertify every 2 years by taking 40 hours of continuing education.
CIMC: Certified Investment Management Consultant (for financial consultants)	Institute for Investment Management Consultants: meet ethical, experience, & continuing education requirements, pass 2 levels of NASD-administered exams.

TABLE C-3 Professional Licenses and Designations, *continued*

Designation	Accrediting institution & requirements
CLU: Chartered Life Underwriter (for insurance & financial services professionals with 3 years of business experience)	American College: pass 10 college-level courses, abide by the college's code of ethics.
CMA: Certified Management Accountant	IMA: have experience, take classes, abide by ethics standards; continuing education required to maintain designation.
CPA: Certified Public Accountant	Licensed by states: pass Uniform CPA exam, satisfy work experience & statutory & licensing requirements of the state(s) in which one practices.
CPCU: Chartered Property Casualty Underwriter	American Institute for CPCU: take classes, pass exams, have experience, abide by code of ethics.
CPMA: Certified Professional Management Advisor	Quantum Institute for Management Advisors: hold a CPA license, take classes, pass exam; continuing education required to maintain certification.
CSA: Certified Senior Advisor	Society of CSAs: attend 3-day program or complete correspondence course & testing, take home-study exams to maintain certification.
CTFA: Certified Trust & Financial Advisor	ICB: have experience, take self-study course, pass exam.
CVA: Certified Valuation Analyst	NACVA: have a CPA license, be a member of NACVA, take classes, submit references, complete exam.
Fellow of the Esperti Peterson Institute (EPI) (for financial advisors & accountants who have technical knowledge of financial, estate, insurance, & investment tools)	EPI: complete program, attend classes annually, participate in monthly conference calls, prepare a case design book for a hypothetical client.
J.D.: Juris Doctor, or Doctor of Jurisprudence (the basic law degree; replaced the LL.B. in the late 1960s)	Accredited law schools: complete required studies, pass exam.

TABLE C-3 Professional Licenses and Designations,
continued

Designation	Accrediting institution & requirements
LL.M.: Master of Laws (an advanced law degree)	Accredited colleges and university: complete required studies, pass exams, usually in a specialized area of law, e.g., taxation. Prerequisite: Juris Doctor.
LUTCF: Life Underwriters Training Council Fellow	LUTC: complete classes, pass ethics exam, belong to a local life underwriters association.
M.B.A.: Master of Business Administration	Certain colleges & universities: complete required studies, pass exam.
MS: Master of Science (in taxation) (graduate-level study in financial planning, wealth management, tax planning, retirement planning, & estate planning)	College for Financial Planning: complete 12 courses with 3.0 (B) grade-point average.
MSFS: Master of Science in Financial Services	American College: complete 36 course credits, including 2 residency sessions.
M.S.T.: Master of Science in Taxation	Accredited colleges & universities: complete required studies, pass exam.
PFS: Personal Financial Specialist (available to CPAs)	AICPA: meet experience requirements, pass exam, be a member of AICPA; experience & course work required to maintain accreditation.
RFC: Registered Financial Consultant (for those with a securities/insurance license or one of the following: CPA, CFA, CFP, CLU, ChFC, J.D., EA, or RHU)	IARFC: meet education, examination, experience, & licensing requirements, take 40 hours per year of continuing education, abide by IARFC code of ethics.
RFP: Registered Financial Planner (for members of RFPI)	RFPI: complete study course, have experience in field.
RHU: Registered Health Underwriter (available to those involved in the sale & service of disability income & health insurance)	American College: complete 3-course curriculum; meet experience, ethics, & continuing education requirements.

TABLE C-3 Professional Licenses and Designations, *continued*

Designation	Accrediting institution & requirements
RIA: Registered Investment Advisor (one who recommends stocks, bonds, mutual funds, partnerships, or other SEC-registered investments for clients)	SEC and/or state securities agencies: file an ADV (Advisor) form detailing educational & professional experience, file a U-4 form disclosing any disciplinary action.
SRA: Society of Real Estate Appraisers	The Appraisal Institute: must be experienced in the analysis & valuation of residential real estate with 4,500 hours of appraisal experience, 181 hours of appraisal instruction, & have passed an appraiser exam, have a BA/BS, & pass a demonstration report (a sample appraisal) exam.

TABLE C-4 Professional Organizations

Organization	Functions
American Bar Association (ABA) 750 N. Lake Shore Dr. Chicago, IL 60611 312-988-5522 www.abanet.org	Ensures the continuation of programs promoting quality legal services, equal access to justice, better understanding of the law, & improvements in our justice system; provides members with information & tools; sponsors workshops, seminars, CLE sessions, & publications.
The American College Life Underwriters Training Council (LUTC) Program 270 S. Bryn Mawr Ave. Bryn Mawr, PA 19010 610-526-1458 www.amercoll.edu/lutc	Provides educational programs & certification for insurance professionals.
American Institute of Certified Public Accountants (AICPA) 1211 Avenue of the Americas New York, NY 10036-8775 888-862-4272 www.aicpa.org	Provides resources, information, & leadership focusing on advocacy, certification & licensing, communications, recruiting & education, & standards & performance.

TABLE C-4   Professional Organizations, *continued*

Organization	Functions
Association for Advanced Life Underwriting (AALU) 2901 Telestar Ct. Falls Church, VA 22042-1205 703-641-9400 www.aalu.org	Proposes & monitors legislation & regulation regarding advanced life underwriting; provides education & leadership in improving the business environment for advanced life insurance professionals.
Esperti Peterson Institute (EPI) 1605 Main St., Ste. 700 Sarasota, FL 34236 941-365-4819 www.epinstitute.org	Provides scholarship, research, instruction, publications, & speakers' bureau for estate planning professionals.
Estate planning councils	For those who specialize in tax, estate, & business planning, provides opportunity to interact, exchange ideas, & pool knowledge; organized at local level.
Financial Planning Association (FPA) 3801 E. Florida Ave., Ste. 708 Denver, CO 80210 800-322-4237 www.fpanet.org	Embraces the principles of International Association for Financial Planning (IAFP) & Institute of Certified Financial Planners (ICFP); open to everyone affiliated with the financial planning profession. (Formerly the IAFP & ICFP.)
International Association of Registered Financial Consultants (IARFC) P.O. Box 42506 Middletown, OH 45042 800-532-9060 www.iarfc.org	Fosters professional development through education; provides a clearinghouse of industry information; distributes information on legislation affecting financial planning, including taxes.
Investment Counsel Association of America (ICAA) 1050 17th St., NW, Ste. 725 Washington, DC 20036-5503 202-293-4222 www.icaa.org	Represents the interests of federally registered investment advisor firms, lobbies Congress & government agencies, promotes standards among investment advisors.

TABLE C-4 Professional Organizations, *continued*

Organization	Functions
Investment Management Consultants Association (IMCA) 9101 E. Kenyon Ave., Ste. 3000 Denver, CO 80237 303-770-3377 www.imca.org	Develops & encourages standards for investment consultants, promotes & protects the interests of the profession, provides education & information-sharing among members.
Million Dollar Round Table (MDRT) 325 W. Touhy Ave. Park Ridge, IL 60068-4265 847-692-6378 www.mdrt.org	Provides members with resources for improving technical knowledge, sales skills, & client service while adopting high ethical standards; comprises top 6% of life insurance producers worldwide.
National Association of Enrolled Agents (NAEA) 200 Orchard Ridge Dr., Ste. 302 Gaithersburg, MD 20878 301-212-9608 www.naea.org	Promotes professionalism & interests of its members; acts as advocate of tax-payer rights.
National Association of Estate Planners and Councils (NAEPC) 270 S. Bryn Mawr Ave., P.O. Box 46 Bryn Mawr, PA 19010-2196 610-526-1389 www.naepc.org	Provides professional education & designations for estate planners & estate planning attorneys.
National Association of Family Wealth Counselors (NAFWC) PO Box 308 Franklin, IN 46131 317-736-8750 www.nafwc.org	Provides opportunities for education & networking.
National Association of Insurance and Financial Advisors (NAIFA) 2901 Telestar Ct. Falls Church, VA 22042-1205 877-866-2432 www.naifa.org	Serves as advocate for insurance agents & consumers; encourages legislation to protect policyholders, develops policy, advances its position with lawmakers & regulators; enhances professional skills of members, promotes ethical conduct, & offers education; organized at state & local levels (formerly National Association of Life Underwriters).

TABLE C-4   Professional Organizations, *continued*

Organization	Functions
National Association of Personal Financial Advisors (NAPFA) 355 W. Dundee Rd., Ste. 200 Buffalo Grove, IL 60089 888-FEE-ONLY www.napfa.org	Helps fee-only professionals enhance skills, market services, & gain a voice with government & consumers; publishes monthly *NAPFA Advisor* & offers educational opportunities to members.
National Association of Tax Professionals (NATP) 720 Association Dr. Appleton, WI 54914-1483 800-558-3402 www.natptax.com	Serves professionals working in all areas of tax practice, provides assistance with federal & state tax questions, & presents workshops.
Planned giving councils & roundtables	Promote the concept of planned giving; organized at local level, but many are associated with the National Committee on Planned Giving.
Registered Financial Planners Institute (RFP) 2001 Cooper Foster Park Rd. Amherst, OH 440-282-7176 www.rfpi.com	Provides training & certification.
Risk and Insurance Management Society (RIMS), Inc. 655 Third Ave. New York, NY 10017 212-286-9292 www.rims.org	Provides products, services, & information for managing all forms of business risk; offers member publications, education for the ARM designation, & other services.
Societies of CPAs	Promote the accounting profession within government & to the public; provide members with education, information, & opportunities to interact with colleagues & participate in community service projects; organized at local level.
Society of Financial Service Professionals (SFSP) 270 S. Bryn Mawr Ave. Bryn Mawr, PA 19010-1295 888-243-2258 www.financialpro.org	Sets & promotes standards of excellence for professionals in financial services; supports members' commitment to advanced education & high ethical standards. (Formerly Society of CLU & ChFC.)

appendix D

The Contributory Book Series and Protocol for *Giving*

Eileen Sacco, Publisher

History of the Contributory Book Series

With the publication of the first edition of *Wealth Enhancement and Preservation* in 1995, the Institute formally established its Contributory Book Series, in which 52 highly regarded professionals from across the United States participated to create a comprehensive book on financial planning. Since 1995, the Institute established research projects that culminated in the following texts:

- a second edition of *Wealth Enhancement and Preservation* (1996), with research from 10 additional contributing authors;
- *Legacy: Plan, Protect and Preserve Your Estate* (1996), with a select contributor group of 87 members from the National Network of Estate Planning Attorneys, which focused on the most commonly asked questions about estate, business, and tax planning;
- *Generations: Planning Your Legacy* (1999), a reconceptualization of *Legacy*, with 49 new contributors adding completely up-to-date

information after passage of the 1997 and 1998 tax laws and more comprehensive questions and answers;

- *Ways and Means: Maximize the Value of Your Retirement Savings* (1999), the Institute's first cross-discipline text, merged the expertise and experience of both the legal and financial planning professionals to assist the public in understanding how to plan properly for retirement and how to coordinate the results of that effort with their estate planning.

- *21st Century Wealth: Essential Financial Planning Principles* (2000), which incorporated research from 51 expert financial planning professionals, presents to the planning public the most up-to-date, and simple and sophisticated financial planning strategies made available by the Taxpayer Relief Act of 1997 and the IRS Restructuring Act of 1998, new rulings issued by the Department of the Treasury and the Internal Revenue Service, and the excitement surrounding the new millennium. This book also launched the Institute's relationship with its new publisher, Quantum Press.

- *Strictly Business: Planning Strategies for Privately Owned Businesses* (2002) was developed to help business owners understand and plan for their unique situations. Ninety-one professional authorities contributed their experience, knowledge, and skills to this text. The Economic Growth and Tax Relief Reconciliation Act of 2001 was passed just as *Strictly Business* went to press, which required a massive rewrite and reconciliation of the text with the act. As a result, it was the first book published for business owners that included details of the new law.

- And Quantum Press now presents *Giving: Philanthropy for Everyone,* an essential reference on charitable giving for people at all economic levels. The contributions of 80 of the country's expert estate, tax, and charitable planning attorneys, accountants, and financial advisors made this book possible.

The objectives of each book in the series are to

- be the most professional research project of its kind that will be recognized as unique in both its focus and scope;

- ascertain the critical planning questions that clients are asking their professional advisors nationwide and the precise answers of those advisors;

- publish meaningful text that will ensure the readers that they can get immediate assistance from professionals on the basis of the planning concepts and strategies learned from the book;

- heighten the public's understanding of the knowledge and contributions that highly experienced financial advisors, attorneys, and accountants bring into the lives of their clients;

- improve the quality of financial, estate, and business planning services offered by professionals to clients by sharing the ideas and techniques of a number of authorities in a highly condensed, user-friendly form; and

- be recognized as a major contribution to the financial, estate, and business planning literature.

The Institute staff invested many hundreds of hours in establishing protocols for the first *Wealth Enhancement and Preservation* research project. The Institute and, now, the Quantum Press staff have added elements to the protocols and have diligently adhered to these protocols in all subsequent contributory book projects.

Protocol

Definition of "Authority" or "Expert"

The Institute defines an "authority" or "expert" as an outstanding professional who is technically competent, is an effective communicator, and has a proven record of a minimum of 5 years meeting his or her clients' needs.

Research Protocol

As with all previous contributory books, the first step in following the protocol was to create the "Research Questionnaire" for *Giving*, which is an outline of potential topics for the final book, organized in a cohesive chapter format. However, every contributing author is encouraged to provide his or her own input outside the parameters of the "Research Questionnaire." Time, demanding schedules, and the difficulty for the contributors to explain very complex technical laws and regulations in clear and concise English led the Institute and Quantum Press to establish a protocol of a minimum of 30 questions and answers from each contributing author.

Qualifying Professionals: The Application Process

When originally developing the protocol for the first research project, the Institute submitted its definition of *expert* and the objectives of the research project to trusted financial planning colleagues and asked them to design the criteria that would help the Institute not only identify potential contributors but also judge the level of their expertise and credentials. On the basis of the input of these colleagues, the Institute established criteria for an authority and an expert and developed an extensive "Application and Profile" for the financial planning professionals and the criteria for evaluating each applicant, which are weighted according to the input received from our colleagues and established by Bob Esperti, Renno Peterson, and the Institute staff prior to the first research project. Before contacting prospective contributors for every book project, Quantum Press staff asks several of the fellows of the Esperti Peterson Institute in Wealth Strategies Planning to review and update the criteria, application, and requirements for attorneys, financial advisors, and accountants.

Applicants must provide a completed "Application and Profile," along with "ADV Part II" if they are registered investment advisors with the Securities and Exchange Commission and U-4 forms if they are registered with the National Association of Securities Dealers (NASD). Quantum Press staff carefully reviewed and graded each professional under the established evaluation procedures. Depending on the discipline in which each applicant is licensed, Quantum Press checked the NASD website, state securities division, state insurance commission, state board of accountancy, or state bar association for disclosures (arbitrations, claims, lawsuits, etc.). Before Quantum Press finally accepted an applicant for *Giving*, editors Robert A. Esperti and Renno L. Peterson reviewed the "Application and Profile" and conducted telephone interviews of every applicant they did not know personally.

The telephone interviews allow the editors to determine the level of each applicant's knowledge of estate, tax, and charitable planning and to satisfy themselves that the applicant was committed to the project and understood all its parameters. The interviews also allowed the applicants to ask any additional questions about the individuals who would be editing their research.

Quantum Press then mailed to each applicant a letter of either nonacceptance or acceptance. With an acceptance letter, Quantum Press also mailed a "Contributing Expert and Authority Agreement," a "Research Questionnaire," and specifications for submitting a photograph, a personalized introduction, and biographical information.

The applicants who were ultimately accepted into the *Giving* project submitted a total of 2,310 questions and answers, amounting to more than 700 manuscript pages.

Research Editing Protocol

The Quantum Press staff combined and organized the research from all the contributing authors by "Research Questionnaire" category. The managing editor reorganized and outlined the research, based on its content, into a standard book structure and delivered the manuscript to the senior legal editor, who eliminated those questions and answers that were *not* common to a majority of the contributors. The remaining research *and* the eliminated questions and answers were delivered to Bob and Renno. They read the research questions (and confirmed whether the eliminated research was not applicable), combined similar material, and edited the remaining questions and answers into the cohesive and understandable questions and answers that appear in this text.

The managing editor and senior legal editor reviewed the resulting working manuscript for clarity and technical accuracy. Quantum Press provided a working manuscript to each contributing author for review. In this way, Quantum Press ascertained the validity of the responses and added to the quality of the final text, and contributors were able to increase the level of their participation in the research project. A number of contributing authors supplied additions to the working manuscript.

The logistics of a Contributory Book Series project is daunting, to say the least. The process of initiating the project; creating the materials for the invitees, applicants, and contributing authors; following up on all of the invitations; checking the applications and credentials; collecting all the necessary information and paperwork, including the questions and answers; and turning the material into a book calls for extraordinary organization and commitment from the contributors, editors, and Quantum Press and its staff. In fact, this brief overview of the process does not do justice to the 20 months of work simply because the volume of information and protocol developed for these projects consists of hundreds of pages of material and thousands of hours of effort. The Institute and Quantum Press are proud of the degree of professionalism displayed by all participants in the creation and completion of *Giving*.

appendix E

Contributing Authors

Karl W. Adler, J.D.
Adler, Tolar & Adler
1700 N.E. 26th Street, Suite 4
Ft. Lauderdale, FL 33305-1413
954-566-3237
fax 954-566-3239
kwadler@bellsouth.net

David B. Auer, J.D., LL.M.(tax), CPA
Family Wealth Counsel®
7030 South Yale, Suite 300
Tulsa, OK 74137
918-493-2584
fax 918-493-1667

Joel R. Baker, CPhD
The Private Consulting Group
P.O. Box 66
Buellton, CA 93427
805-688-8562
fax 805-688-2985
jbaker@privateconsulting.com

Lemuel M. Bargeron, CLU, CFP
First Financial Resources
Estate & Financial Services, Inc.
P.O. Box 758
Cartersville, GA 30120
800-879-1641
fax 770-386-4486
lem@ffrga.com

Suzann L. Beckett, J.D.
Estate Planning Law Group, LLC
543 Prospect Avenue
Hartford, CT 06105
860-236-1111
fax 860-236-0050
suzann@eplg.ws

Daniel M. Betzel, J.D.
Betzel & Kauffman Co., L.P.A.
11299 Stonecreek Drive, Suite B
Pickerington, OH 43147
614-864-1200
fax 614-864-1284
dbetzel@betkauf.com

James T. Blazek, J.D.
James T. Blazek & Associates, P.C.,
    L.L.O.
11580 West Dodge Road
Omaha, NE 68154
402-496-3432
fax 402-496-4519
blazek@radiks.net

Richard A. Bockoff, J.D.
Law Office of Richard A. Bockoff
512 Wallace
Birmingham, MI 48009
248-644-2427
fax 248-594-2083
1010 Klish Way
Del Mar, CA 92014
858-481-4327
fax 858-481-0655
bockoffr@aol.com

Robert E. Bourne, J.D.
Robert E. Bourne, P.C.
412 Ashman
Midland, MI 48640
989-835-6511
fax 989-835-6521
rbourne@voyager.net

Eden Rose Brown, J.D.
Law Office of Eden Rose Brown
310 Pioneer Trust Building
117 Commercial Street NE
Salem, OR 97301
503-581-1800
fax 503-581-1818
eden@brownlaw.net

Charles C. Case Jr., J.D.
Wealth Strategies
49 Beldan Lane
Centerville, MA 02632
508-790-3050
fax 508-790-3049
charliecasejr@yahoo.com

Teresa H. Cherry, CPA, CFP
Wealth Design Network
111 East Wacker Drive, Suite 990
Chicago, IL 60601
312-540-9840
fax 312-540-9844
wealthdesign@aol.com

Neil R. Covert, J.D.
Covert & Black, LLC
311 Park Place Boulevard, Suite 360
Clearwater, FL 33759
727-449-8200
fax 727-450-2190
ncovert@covertlaw.com

**Louis U.G. Crenshaw, M.B.A., CLU,
    J.D.**
Louis U.G. Crenshaw & Associates,
    P.C.
2157 Commons Parkway
Okemos, MI 48864
517-347-2100
fax 517-347-2152
adlca@tcimet.net

Barbara A. Culver, CFP, CLU, ChFC
Resonate, Inc.
4750 Ashwood Drive
Cincinnati, OH 45241
513-605-2500
fax 513-605-2505
bculver@resonatecompanies.com

Nancy L. Dilley, J.D.
Dilley & Rominger, PLC
330 East Fulton
Grand Rapids, MI 49503
616-454-9200
fax 616-458-6446
dillrom@aol.com

John M. Donaldson, J.D., LL.M.
Prism Design Group, L.L.C.
1204 Harvard Road
Grosse Pointe Park, MI 48230
313-881-5700
fax 313-881-2664
jmd4@earthlink.net

Keith R. Dorson, M.B.A.
Win Win Investment Planning
616 East Southern Avenue, Suite 102
Mesa, AZ 85204
480-890-0100
fax 480-890-7826
kdorson@wwinvestment.com

Jeffrey R. Dundon, J.D., LL.M.(tax)
Law Offices of Jeffrey R. Dundon,
   Co., LPA
156 East Spring Valley Road
Centerville, OH 45458
937-438-3122
fax 937-291-5491
jeff@dundon.com

Marie Mirro Edmonds, J.D.
Marie Mirro Edmonds Co., LPA
807 East Washington Street,
   Suite 200
Medina, OH 44256
330-725-5297
fax 330-722-5932
marie@marieedmonds.com

Robert A. Esperti, J.D.
Esperti Peterson & Cahoone
3561 East Sunrise Drive, Suite 135
Tucson, AZ 85718
520-529-9060
fax 520-529-9360

Douglas K. Fadel, J.D.
Marquardt & Fadel, Attorneys at Law
500 North Marketplace Drive,
   Suite 201
P.O. Box 159
Centerville, UT 84014
801-294-7777
fax 801-294-7787
douglaskf@aol.com

Randy A. Fox, CFP
Prism Design Group, LLC
1770 Park Street, Suite 204
Naperville, IL 60563
630-369-0916
fax 630-369-0956
rfox@prismdesigngroup.com

Douglas G. Goldberg, J.D.
Goldberg Law Center, P.C.
2500 North Circle Drive, Suite 100
Colorado Springs, CO 80909-1161
719-444-0300
fax 719-444-0342
dgoldberg@deathcheaters.com

Robert A. Goldman, J.D., CPA
Goldman & Associates
100 Larkspur Landing Circle,
   Suite 112
Larkspur, CA 94939
415-461-1490
fax 415-461-1497
rgoldman@goldmanattorneys.com

Paul A. Gydosh Jr., CFP
Kensington Wealth Partners Ltd.
7650 Rivers Edge Drive
Columbus, OH 43235
614-431-4336
fax 614-431-4305
pagydosh@Lnc.com

Rodney J. Hatley, J.D., LL.M. (tax)
Attorney & Counsellor at Law
3655 Nobel Drive, Suite 330
San Diego, CA 92122-1050
858-200-1900
fax 858-200-1920
rjhesq@earthlink.net

David F. Hokanson, MSFS, ChFC
Family Wealth Counselors LLC
5340 College Boulevard
Overland Park, KS 66211-1621
913-338-3383
fax 913-338-4507
hokanson@thinkingbeyond.com

Edward F. Hooper, J.D., CLU, ChFC
Hooper Law Office
4650 West Spencer Street
Appleton, WI 54914
920-993-0990
fax 920-968-4650
hooperef@execpc.com

Russell K. Jalbert, CFP
Quadrant Group, Inc.
40 Oak Hollow, Suite 340
Southfield, MI 48034
248-350-3400
fax 248-350-3336
rkjalbert@aol.com

Patrick A. Jeffers
Wealth Strategies Collaborative
1605 Main Street, Suite 700
Sarasota, FL 34236
941-954-4241
fax 877-272-0325
patj@epinstitute.org

Reid S. Johnson, MSFS, CIMC, CFP, ChFC
The Planning Group of Scottsdale, LLC
8777 N. Gainey Center Drive, Suite 265
Scottsdale, AZ 85258-2133
480-596-1580
fax 480-596-2165
reid@theplanninggroup.com

David E. Kauffman, J.D.
Betzel & Kauffman Co., L.P.A.
11299 Stonecreek Drive, Suite B
Pickerington, OH 43147
614-864-1200
fax 614-864-1284
dkauffman@betkauf.com

Scott Keffer
Wealth Transfer Solutions, Inc.
2535 Washington Road, Suite 1120
Pittsburgh, PA 15241
412-854-7860
fax 412-854-7864
wealth@icubed.com

Bruce D. Ketron, J.D., LL.M.
Ketron & Associates
703 Second Street, 4th Floor
Santa Rosa, CA 95404
707-542-1700
fax 707-542-1727

Russell W. Ketron, CFP
Ketron Financial, LLC
1701 Novato Boulevard, Suite 204
Novato, CA 94947
415-892-0928
fax 415-898-2441
russ@rketron.com

E. Michael Kilbourn, CLU, ChFC, AEP
Kilbourn Associates
3033 Riviera Drive, Suite 202
Naples, FL 34103-2750
239-261-1888
fax 239-643-7017
mike@kilbournassociates.com

Jeffrey L. Knapp, J.D.
The Knapp Law Firm LLC at The Wealth Strategies Center
11 South Finley Avenue
Basking Ridge, NJ 07920
908-696-0011
fax 908-696-0030
knapplaw@eclipse.net

Alan T. Kondo, CFP, CLU
918 East Green Street
Pasadena, CA 91106
626-449-7783
fax 626-449-7785
alan@alankondo.com

W. Vito Lanuti, J.D.
323 Main Street
Seal Beach, CA 90740
562-596-7550
fax 562-596-3661

Jeffrey M. Levine, J.D., LL.M.(tax), CFP
Jeffrey M. Levine Financial Consultant, Inc.
4 Executive Park Drive
Albany, NY 12203
518-489-8538
fax 518-489-8677
jeffrey.levine@lpl.com

Raymond E. Makowski, J.D.
Raymond E. Makowski, P.A.
4651 Salisbury Road, Suite 160
Jacksonville, FL 32256-6190
904-296-4777
fax 904-296-4779
rempa1@myexcel.com

Stephen J. Mancini, J.D.
The Law Firm of Strazzeri Mancini
LLP
3655 Nobel Drive, Suite 330
San Diego, CA 92122
858-200-1900
fax 858-200-1920
sjm@strazzerimancini.com

Jane A. Marquardt, J.D., LL.M.
Marquardt & Fadel, Attorneys at Law
500 North Marketplace Drive,
Suite 201
P.O. Box 159
Centerville, UT 84014
801-294-7777
fax 801-294-7787
janeam@aol.com

W. Aubrey Morrow, CFP
Financial Designs, Ltd.
5075 Shoreham Place, Suite 230
San Diego, CA 92122-5964
858-597-1980
fax 858-546-1106
aubrey@financialdesignsltd.com

Richard E. Mundinger, CFA
RBC Dain Rauscher
Vice President - Financial
Consultant
Consulting Group
3430 East Sunrise Drive, Suite 250
Tucson, AZ 85718
520-299-4444 or 800-497-1377
fax 520-299-3671
richard.mundinger@rbcdain.com

Greg Noll, J.D.
Telthorst & Noll, LLC
3620 S.W. Fairlawn Road, Suite 201
Topeka, KS 66614
785-272-8794
fax 785-273-0924
greg@telnol.org

John J. Peck, J.D.
Legacy Law Center
825 Gum Branch Road, Suite 127
Jacksonville, NC 28540
910-347-7782
fax 910-347-8893
jpeck@gibralter.net

**Arlin L. Penner, CLU, ChFC, CIMA,
SIMC**
SalomonSmithBarney - Member
Citigroup
15141 E. Whittier Boulevard,
Suite 400
Whittier, CA 90603
800-356-1333
fax 562-693-1841
arlin.l.penner@rssmb.com

Renno L. Peterson, J.D.
Esperti Peterson & Cahoone
1605 Main Street, Suite 700
Sarasota, FL 34236
941-365-4819
fax 941-366-5347

John S. Pfarr, J.D.
Pfarr & Wallin, LLP
37 Sunset Terrace
Essex, CT 06426
860-767-8382
pfarrlaw@aol.com

Lawrence K.Y. Pon, CPA/PFS, CFP
Pon & Associates
240F Twin Dolphin Drive
Redwood City, CA 94065
650-508-1268
fax 650-508-1233
lkypon@aol.com

Kevin D. Quinn, J.D.
Kevin D. Quinn, Attorney at Law
30 Hannum Brook Drive
Easthampton, MA 01027
413-527-0517
fax 413-529-8027
kdqplan@worldnet.att.net

Bernard M. Rethore, J.D.
Graves & Rethore, P.C.
2400 East Arizona Biltmore Circle
Building 1, Suite 1135
Phoenix, AZ 85016
602-381-6253
fax 602-381-6260
bmr@gravesandrethore.com

Thomas Rogers, J.D., CPA
Wealth Strategies Collaborative, Inc.
Sweetwater Square, Suite 102
900 Fox Valley Drive
Longwood (Orlando), FL 32779-
   2551
407-869-4163
fax 407-862-0185
thomrogers@attoney-cpa.com

Charles S. Rominger, J.D.
Dilley & Rominger, PLC
330 East Fulton
Grand Rapids, MI 49503
616-454-9200
fax 616-458-6446
dillrom@aol.com

Robert A. Ross, J.D.
Ross Law Office
216 South 4th Avenue
Sturgeon Bay, WI 54235
920-743-9117
fax 920-743-9180
raross@dcwis.com

Marvin J. Rudnitsky, J.D.
Rudnitsky & Hackman, LLP
9 Courtyard Offices, Suite 130
Selinsgrove, PA 17870
570-743-2333
fax 570-743-2347
mrudnit@ptd.net

Richard A. Sarner, J.D.
Law Offices of Richard A. Sarner
184 Atlantic Street
Stamford, CT 06901
203-967-8899
fax 203-967-8886
465 Park Avenue, Suite 10C
New York, NY 10022
800-392-8550
rsarner@aol.com

**Carol Peskoe Schaner, J.D., LL.M.,
   CPA**
Quinlivan & Kaniewski LLP
6 Hutton Centre, Suite 1150
South Coast Metro, CA 92707
714-241-1919
fax 714-241-1199
c.schaner@quikanlaw.com

Scott C. Schultz, J.D.
Schultz & Associates Law Center,
   P.C.
969 Willagillespie Road
Eugene, OR 97401
541-485-5515
fax 541-485-5518
scott@schultz-law.com

Cecil D. Smith, J.D.
Cecil Smith & Associates, PC
6799 Great Oaks Road, Suite 110
Memphis, TN 38138
901-754-7540
fax 901-754-3010
2900 Vanderbilt Place, Suite 102
Nashville, TN 37212-2518
615-320-5313
cecil@smithlawusa.com

Chris E. Steiner, J.D.
Bayer, Papay & Steiner Co., LPA
4540 Heatherdowns Boulevard
Toledo, OH 43614
419-381-8884
fax 419-381-7684
steiner@plansthatwork.net

Joseph J. Strazzeri, J.D.
The Law Firm of Strazzeri Mancini
 LLP
3655 Nobel Drive, Suite 330
San Diego, CA 92122
858-200-1900
fax 858-200-1920
jjs@strazzerimancini.com

Richard D. Tanner, President
Ownership Advisors Inc.
9150 South Hills Boulevard,
 Suite 300
Cleveland, OH 44147
440-526-2525
fax 440-576-4328
rtanner@koptis.com

Eric A. Tashlein, CFP
Connecticut Capital Management
 Group, L.L.C.
63 Cherry Street
Milford, CT 06460
203-877-1520
fax 203-877-2729

Matthew A. Tavrides, J.D.
Matthew A. Tavrides, P.A.
390 North Orange Avenue,
 Suite 2700
Orlando, FL 32801
407-843-8441
fax 407-422-8556
matpa@gdi.net

Robert M. Telthorst, J.D.
Telthorst & Noll, LLC
3620 S.W. Fairlawn Road, Suite 201
Topeka, KS 66614
785-272-8794
fax 785-273-0924
rob@telnol.org

W. Michael Todd, J.D., CPA
10 Pine Street
Manchester, MA 01944
978-526-4402
fax 978-526-1843
legacy@gis.net

William G. Touret, J.D., CFP
William G. Touret, P.C.
One Washington Mall, Fifth Floor
Boston, MA 02108-2603
800-345-0080
fax 617-523-7614
wgtouret@bostonplanning.com

Edward L. Weidenfeld, J.D.
The Weidenfeld Law Firm, P.C.
1828 L Street, N.W., Suite 500
Washington, DC 20036
202-785-2143
fax 202-452-8938
edward@weidenfeldlaw.com

Brent J. Welch, CFP, ChFC, CLU
Family Wealth Counselors, LLC
9538 State Road 16
Onalaska, WI 54650
608-783-0003
fax 608-782-0002
bjwelch@charter.net

**William T. Whittenberg Jr., J.D.,
 LL. M.**
Whittenberg, Knudsen & McLellan,
 LLP
200 Broadway, Suite 306
Lynnfield, MA 01940
781-599-4000
fax 781-581-2650
wtw@wealthdesign.com

Arnold Fitger Williams, J.D.
Arnold Fitger Williams, Counselor
 at Law
3617 Thousand Oaks Boulevard,
 Suite 303
Thousand Oaks, CA 91362-6690
888-523-2358
fax 888-523-2358
afwilliams@counsellor.com

David A. Williams, CSA, RFC
Williams Financial Group, LLC
4400 Coldwater Canyon Avenue,
  Suite 100
Studio City, CA 91604
818-761-7100
fax 818-761-7140
davidwms@pacbell.net

Eric H. Witlin, J.D.
USA Retirement Network
1177 High Ridge Road
Stamford, CT 06905
203-321-2172
fax 203-321-2188
ehwitlin@irastrategies.net

Benjamin W. Wong, CFP
5776 Stoneridge Mall Road,
  Suite 396
Pleasanton, CA 94588
925-227-8858
fax 925-227-8859
benwong@foothillsecurities.com

Rodney C. Zeeb, J.D.
Rodney C. Zeeb, Attorney at Law
1800 Blankenship Road, Suite 150
West Linn, OR 97068
503-655-2785
fax 503-655-2795
rodz@rodzeeb.com

Drake Zimmerman, J.D., CFA, CFP
Zimmerman and Armstrong
  Investment Advisors, Inc.
1100 North Beech, Building 9
Normal, IL 61761
309-454-7040
fax 309-454-6914
drake.zimmerman@gte.net

David J. Zumpano, J.D., CPA
Estate Planning Law Center
555 French Road
New Hartford, NY 13413
315-793-3622
fax 315-793-0076
djzesq@aol.com

appendix F

Geographic Listing of Contributing Authors

Arizona
Keith R. Dorson
Robert A. Esperti
Reid S. Johnson
Richard E. Mundinger
Bernard M. Rethore

California
Joel R. Baker
Richard A. Bockoff
Robert A. Goldman
Rodney J. Hatley
Bruce D. Ketron
Russell W. Ketron
Alan T. Kondo
W. Vito Lanuti
Stephen J. Mancini
W. Aubrey Morrow
Arlin L. Penner
Lawrence K.Y. Pon
Carol Peskoe Schaner
Joseph J. Strazzeri
Arnold Fitger Williams

California, *cont'd.*
David A. Williams
Benjamin W. Wong

Colorado
Douglas G. Goldberg

Connecticut
Suzann L. Beckett
John S. Pfarr
Richard A. Sarner
Eric A. Tashlein
Eric H. Witlin

District of Columbia
Edward L. Weidenfeld

Florida
Karl W. Adler
Neil R. Covert
Patrick A. Jeffers
E. Michael Kilbourn
Raymond E. Makowski
Renno L. Peterson

Florida, *cont'd.*
Thomas Rogers
Matthew A. Tavrides

Georgia
Lemuel M. Bargeron

Illinois
Teresa H. Cherry
Randy A. Fox
Drake Zimmerman

Kansas
David F. Hokanson
Greg Noll
Robert M. Telthorst

Massachusetts
Charles C. Case Jr.
Kevin D. Quinn
W. Michael Todd
William G. Touret
William T. Whittenberg Jr.

Michigan
Richard A. Bockoff
Robert E. Bourne
Louis U.G. Crenshaw
Nancy L. Dilley
John M. Donaldson
Russell K. Jalbert
Charles S. Rominger

Nebraska
James T. Blazek

New Jersey
Jeffrey L. Knapp

New York
Jeffrey M. Levine
Richard A. Sarner
David J. Zumpano

North Carolina
John J. Peck

Ohio
Daniel M. Betzel
Barbara A. Culver
Jeffrey R. Dundon
Marie Mirro Edmonds
Paul A. Gydosh Jr.
David E. Kauffman
Chris E. Steiner
Richard D. Tanner

Oklahoma
David B. Auer

Oregon
Eden Rose Brown
Scott C. Schultz
Rodney C. Zeeb

Pennsylvania
Scott Keffer
Marvin J. Rudnitsky

Tennessee
Cecil D. Smith

Utah
Douglas K. Fadel
Jane A. Marquardt

Wisconsin
Edward F. Hooper
Robert A. Ross
Brent J. Welch

index